Chinese Religious Life

Chinese Religious Life

Edited by

David A. Palmer, Glenn Shive, and Philip L. Wickeri

OXFORD
UNIVERSITY PRESS

Oxford University Press, Inc., publishes works that further
Oxford University's objective of excellence
in research, scholarship, and education.

Oxford   New York
Auckland   Cape Town   Dar es Salaam   Hong Kong   Karachi
Kuala Lumpur   Madrid   Melbourne   Mexico City   Nairobi
New Delhi   Shanghai   Taipei   Toronto
With offices in
Argentina   Austria   Brazil   Chile   Czech Republic   France   Greece
Guatemala   Hungary   Italy   Japan   Poland   Portugal   Singapore
South Korea   Switzerland   Thailand   Turkey   Ukraine   Vietnam

Published by Oxford University Press, Inc.
198 Madison Avenue, New York, New York 10016

www.oup.com

Oxford is a registered trademark of Oxford University Press.

Library of Congress Cataloging-in-Publication Data
Chinese religious life / edited by David A. Palmer, Glenn Shive, and Philip L. Wickeri.
p.   cm.
Includes index.
ISBN 978-0-19-973139-8; 978-0-19-973138-1 (pbk)
1. China—Religion—21st century.   2. China—Religious life and customs.
3. Religion and politics—China.   I. Palmer, David A., 1969–   II. Shive, Glenn Landes.
III. Wickeri, Philip L. (Philip Lauri), 1947–
BL1803.C45 2011

200.951—dc22   2010031639

Printed in the United States of America
on acid-free paper

For Anne, Janice, and Leila who continue to sustain us on our journeys

{ ACKNOWLEDGMENTS }

The editors of this book wish to express their deep appreciation to the Henry Luce Foundation for its generous grant to the Hong Kong America Center in support of this publication project. We especially recognize Mr. Terrill Lautz and Ms. Helena Kolenda of the Luce Foundation staff for their belief in the value of this effort from its beginning. Without their support, this project would not have been possible.

We would also like to thank the Ecole française d'Extrême-Orient and the French Centre for Research on Contemporary China for its support of David's field research in China and Taiwan.

Many of the chapter authors participated in an international conference held at the Chinese University of Hong Kong, June 29–30, 2007, on the theme of "Religion and Social Integration in Chinese Societies: Exploring Sociological Approaches to the Study of Religion in the Chinese World," co-organized by the Chung Chi College Centre for Religion and Chinese Society, the Ecole française d'Extrême-Orient, and the Societies-Religions-Secularisms Institute (CNRS, France), which was generously funded by the Chiang Ching-kuo Foundation, the UGC-Procore Fund, the Department of Cultural and Religious Studies of CUHK, and the Institute of Chinese Studies of CUHK. The discussions at this conference, which was attended by leading international scholars of Chinese religion, contributed greatly to the conceptual framework of this book.

We thank Ms. Janice Wickeri for her dedicated work in copyediting the manuscript and preparing it for publication and Ms. Pauline Lau of the Hong Kong America Center for administrative support throughout the project. We are also grateful to Mr. Charles Nolley of the Governors State University in Chicago and Ms. Yang Ling of Guangzhou for their assistance in visual aspects of the project.

We appreciate the efforts of our authors to write their respective chapters in the spirit and framework of the book. In addition to those who contributed their writing, we benefited from the following advisors to the project, especially in the early stages as we conceived the scope and nature of the book: Prasenjit Duara, Liu Chengyou, Lo Ping-cheung, Bernard Luk, Steven K. Luk, Dennis McCann, Peter Ng, David Suh, Wong Wai-ching, Wu Xiaoxin, and Zhuo Xinping.

We all appreciate the hospitality of Chung Chi College of the Chinese University of Hong Kong in graciously hosting our meetings. Finally, we thank the staff and reviewers at Oxford University Press for publishing this volume in the spirit of promoting a wider understanding of Chinese religious life.

David A. Palmer, Glenn Shive, and Philip L. Wickeri

{ CONTENTS }

{ CONTRIBUTORS }

Adam Yuet Chau is University Lecturer in the Anthropology of Modern China in the Department of East Asian Studies at the University of Cambridge.

Lizhu Fan is Associate Dean of the School of Social Development and Public Policy and Professor in the Department of Sociology at Fudan University, Shanghai.

Vincent Goossaert is a Senior Research Fellow in the History of Chinese Religion at the Centre National de la Recherche Scientifique (CNRS) and Deputy Director of the Societies-Religions-Secularisms Institute (GSRL), Paris.

C. Julia Huang is Associate Professor in the Institute of Anthropology, National Tsing Hua University, Taiwan.

André Laliberté is Associate Professor at the School of Political Studies, University of Ottawa.

Richard Madsen is Distinguished Professor and Chair of the Department of Sociology at the University of California, San Diego.

David A. Palmer is Assistant Professor in the Department of Sociology and Fellow of the Centre for Anthropological Research at the University of Hong Kong.

Glenn Shive is Executive Director of the Hong Kong-America Center, located at the Chinese University of Hong Kong.

Elijah Siegler is Associate Professor in the Department of Religious Studies at the College of Charleston.

Wai Lun Tam is Professor in the Department of Cultural and Religious Studies at the Chinese University of Hong Kong.

Yik-fai Tam is Lecturer in the Religious Studies Program, Department of History, Pennsylvania State University.

Francesca Tarocco is a Leverhulme Trust Research Fellow in the School of Arts, Histories and Cultures at the University of Manchester.

Elena Valussi teaches Eastern Humanities in the History, Humanities and Social Sciences Department of Columbia College, Chicago.

Robert P. Weller is Professor and Chair of Anthropology and Research Associate at the Institute on Culture, Religion and World Affairs at Boston University.

James D. Whitehead is Distinguished Fellow, EDS-Stewart Chair at the Ricci Institute for Chinese-Western Cultural History, University of San Francisco.

Philip L. Wickeri is Adjunct Professor of Interdisciplinary Studies at the Graduate Theological Union, Berkeley and Advisor to the Archbishop on Historical and Theological Studies, Hong Kong Sheng Kung Hui (Anglican Church).

Keping Wu is Assistant Professor in the Department of Anthropology at the Chinese University of Hong Kong.

Fenggang Yang is Professor of Sociology and Director of the Center on Religion and Chinese Society (CRCS) at Purdue University.

Chinese Religious Life

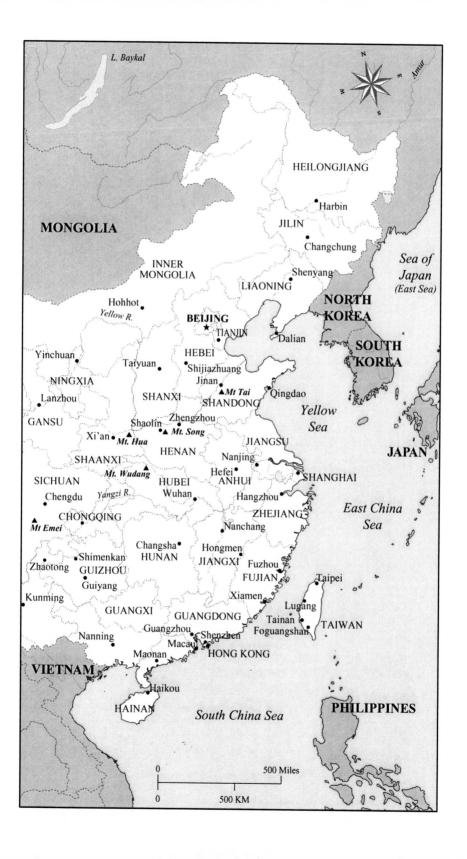

Introduction
Philip L. Wickeri

Religious life is flourishing in China, and on many different levels. The growth of religion is evident not only on the mainland, but in Taiwan, Hong Kong, and Macau, and in overseas Chinese communities as well. On the mainland, in the People's Republic of China, religious life has reemerged over the last thirty years. Despite official sanctions in some areas, there is a new openness in a society in the midst of rapid social, political, and economic change. Buddhists visit a popular temple in east China to burn incense or ask the monks to conduct special services for their families. Villagers gather at festival time to usher in the lunar New Year and perform a communal sacrifice to the local gods. Muslims in far Western China proceed to their neighborhood mosque five times a day for prayers. Buddhists in Taiwan discover a renewed interest in service to society. An elderly woman consults a fortune-teller to find out about the future prospects of her son and his family who are about to go overseas. Christians go to a newly opened or reopened church in the early morning to prepare for Sunday services. A cook places fruit, specially prepared food, and incense before a small altar at the back of his restaurant. A small group of women and men meet in a park to practice *taijiquan,* an exercise for the body as well as the spirit.

These are some of the popular images of Chinese religious life that have become increasingly familiar in the period of openness and reform that began in the late 1970s. On the mainland, Chinese people, as well as visitors or residents from overseas, can observe or participate in any number of public religious gatherings. But there are also less familiar expressions of belief, as well as aspects of religious life that are not as easily visible, and often far from open. A group of people gather in a restaurant to learn about new spiritual practices from a young monk. Tibetan monks demonstrate for religious freedom in a small city outside Lhasa. A local healer advises elderly pensioners about efficacious forms of meditation and Chinese medicine. A wealthy temple opens a factory that produces a variety of religious articles for private and public devotion. A Catholic church is forcibly closed by the police for meeting in an "unregistered" place of worship. University-based academics hold a conference about the revival of religion in rural China and its implications for contemporary society.

This book is an introduction to Chinese religious life in its great diversity. It is a book for the general reader written by an international team of well-known scholars who approach their subject from a variety of different disciplines. The emphasis throughout is on religion in contemporary Chinese public life—culture, society, and politics—and the ways in which religion is practiced in communities where it shapes the lives of individuals and families. Religious life has been closely intertwined with its public expression in Chinese society, from ancient times until today. As such, religion provides a lens through which to observe many of the complex issues that challenge China and the world at large, issues related to the economy, gender and sexuality, the environment, human rights, ethnicity, and globalization. There is no single "model" of religion and public life in China, and a wide range of imaginable possibilities can be found. This book aims to enable the general reader to relate to the themes being discussed in each chapter, by treating them as universally relevant and open-ended areas of religious life, but with aspects that are particular to Chinese history and culture. Religion in China must be understood on its own terms, but it is interpreted in this volume in ways that can make it more widely accessible for readers without a specialized knowledge of China.

There are different interpretations of "religion" and "the religious" in China that are presented by the authors of this book. What is consistent is an emphasis on *religious practice*. This represents a different starting point from understandings of religion that begin with faith, doctrine, or systems of belief. In chapter 4, Adam Chau introduces five modalities for "doing religion" in China. These are relatively well defined forms that people can adapt and combine to deal with different concerns in their lives, and the contents within these forms can vary widely. According to Chau, the "five modalities of doing religion" are (1) the *discursive* or *scriptural*, based on the composition and use of religious texts; (2) the *personal-cultivational*, involving a long-term interest in cultivating and transforming oneself; (3) the *liturgical*, which makes use of procedures conducted by priests, monks, or other ritual specialists; (4) the *immediate-practical*, aiming at quick results making use of using religious or magical techniques; and (5) the *relational*, emphasizing the relationship among humans, deities, ghosts, and ancestors as well as among people in families, villages, and religious communities. These five modalities cut across different religious traditions and may be applied to the study of Buddhism, Daoism, folk religion, Islam, Christianity, or Confucianism, whether understood as a religion or a philosophy. They are not forms that are exclusive of one another, although some traditions may emphasize one modality more than the other. An individual or a community may "do religion" in one way or in all five. In this book, our emphasis is on the ways in which religion is lived out in China, and Chau's typology is a helpful way of understanding religious practice.

The scope of religion and religious practice in China is very broad, as it is with religion all over the world. It embraces individuals' hopes for security, health, prosperity, meaning, identity, sense of purpose, and transcendence. It also includes public needs for enforcing norms of morality and social behavior, as well as occasions and spaces for social interaction. Politically, religious practice is related to the search for legitimacy, loyalty, and adherence, unifying collective (or ethnic) identity, as well as to faith, ideals, and rituals. Religion may also provide a means to generate social resistance, oppose the state, or foment rebellion. From the standpoint of religious communities themselves, religion includes forms of worship, techniques, and rituals; cosmologies, ideologies, and theologies; moral norms as well as self-cultivation regimens; origin myths and utopian or apocalyptic visions. Individual religious figures are also very diverse, and often idealized: charismatic leaders, saints, awakened ones, immortals, prophets; also gods, ghosts, and ancestors. A variety of organizational forms combine some or all of these elements to meet individual, social, and political demands or community needs. In China, different organizational forms may or may not fit into an accepted framework of public life. The traditional Confucian elite, troupes of ritual specialists, local temple organizations, the Buddhist *sangha*, the Roman Catholic hierarchy, a millenarian movement, the modern Chinese intelligentsia, and a predominantly Muslim ethnic group are all examples of organized forms of religious life or public religious practice.

To speak of *public* religious life in China is not to downplay the importance of individual or community religious practice. Rather, religious practice, which includes individual and community dimensions as well, is interpreted in this book in relationship to the public realms of culture, society, and politics. In traditional China, public life was formally framed in terms of specialized rites and ritual practice (*li* in Chinese). This established status distinctions in public life and governed the proper or accepted conduct of relationships between fathers and sons, husbands and wives, rulers and subjects. In traditional China, temples, rituals, and traditional festivals became spheres for the public negotiation of relations within communities and among social groups. Religion was interwoven into the very fabric of society.

In modern and contemporary China, traditional notions of religion and society could no longer be assumed. Public life involves the activity of autonomous subjects and society is understood as the sphere within which subjects form a collectivity. The debates over culture, social responsibility, and "public morality" in China, mediated and at times orchestrated by the Chinese Communist Party, have shaped both the scope and extent of individual participation in social and cultural life, which includes religion. Public life is a contested space in China today, and religion has a growing importance within that space. Many questions involving religion are being discussed and debated in China. What does "civil society" mean in contemporary society? What is the role of intermediate organizations and social movements? How do individuals and groups shape the evolution of society and culture through their conscious public actions? What is the role of the state and the

Communist Party in public life? These are among the questions that are addressed in this volume insofar as they relate to religious practice and religious life.

Unlike many books on Chinese religions, we do not discuss Chinese folk religion, or particular religious traditions—Daoism, Buddhism, Christianity, or Islam—in separate chapters. In several chapters of this book, we introduce particular religious communities and communities of religious practice. Chapter 9 provides a historical overview of the development or religion in China, and chapter 10 treats the social organization of specific religious communities in the twentieth century. But our general perspective is on religious practices and cultural expressions, as well as social and political issues that cut across different traditions or affect all religious communities. We speak of the life of religious communities in relationship to culture, society, and politics. This allows us to speak of the diversity of Chinese religions in ways that can be more readily understood by the general reader.

In this book, *China* refers to what is sometimes called "Greater China," including the People's Republic of China on the mainland, Taiwan, Hong Kong, and Macau, as well as overseas Chinese communities in Southeast Asia and beyond. Several chapters deal mainly, but not exclusively, with religious life in mainland China. Our interest throughout the book is to introduce and present religious life in contemporary Chinese societies so that implicit or explicit connections can be made with religious life elsewhere.

The chapters of the book have been arranged topically, and begin with a journey through Chinese religious life. The chapters have been ordered with a view to draw the reader into a deeper understanding of the layers and nuances of religious life in China. The movement of the book from part I through part IV is a progression from descriptive and analytical treatments of religious life; to considerations of social and cultural issues as they relate to religion; to chapters on historical, organizational, political, and economic aspects of the subject, ending with a section on globalization and a conclusion on the religious future. Each chapter includes illustrative stories, vignettes, and descriptions of places and events, as well as highlighted inserts dealing with important subjects, religious terminology, and other aspects of general religious interest. The book also includes a wide range of photographs, charts, illustrations, and maps.

Part I begins with descriptive analyses of different ways of being religious in the Chinese world. Chapter 1, "Spirituality in a Modern Chinese Metropolis," by Lizhu Fan and James Whitehead, introduces readers to a situation that may be at once familiar and different. The authors' focus is on Shenzhen, a new city just across the border from Hong Kong, and the spirituality of its urban residents. They find that the people's moral capital and spiritual heritage is flourishing in a rapidly modernizing context. The scene shifts in chapter 2 to "Communal Worship and Festivals in Chinese Villages." Here, Wai Lun Tam reflects on the diversity of village religious life in rural southern China and its two main aspects: seasonal sacrifices to ancestors and religious festivals in local temples. The seasonal changes find expression in the rhythms of religious life for villages and families all over southern China. Chapter 3 surveys "The Religious Life of Ethnic Minorities." Philip L. Wickeri and Yik-fai Tam introduce the wide range of religious beliefs and practices among the minority communities found all around China, with brief case studies of the indigenous Dongba religion, Tibetan Buddhism, Islam among the Uyghur, and the Christianity of the Miao. In chapter 4, Adam Chau presents a model for understanding the "Modalities of Doing Religion" in Chinese culture. His five forms, or "modalities" (which have briefly introduced above), represent an important new model for understanding Chinese religious practices.

The four chapters in Part II are concerned with religious perspectives on cultural and social subjects. In chapter 5, David A. Palmer reflects on "The Body: Health, Nation, and Transcendence." All religious communities have their own interpretations of illness and health, and the author shows the cosmological underpinnings of the subject in traditional Chinese religions. The religious understanding of the "body" and associated healing practices continues to be influential in Chinese societies despite the pressures of secularization. Chapter 6 addresses issues of "Gender and Sexuality" as they relate to Chinese religious life. C. Julia Huang, Elena Valussi, and David A. Palmer discuss religiously grounded gender constructs, sexuality and religious life, women's roles in the revival of religion, and conceptions of masculinity in their wide-ranging treatment of the subject. Robert P. Weller introduces "Chinese Cosmology and the Environment" in chapter 7, where he addresses questions about nature and the environment in light of current interests in ecology and globalization. Although official environmental policy does not at present draw on older Chinese religious traditions, he remains hopeful that the alternative views of nature in Chinese cosmologies can contribute to the global ecological movement today. Chapter 8 deals with "Religious Philanthropy and Civil Society" in modern and contemporary China. André Laliberté, David A. Palmer, and Keping Wu offer an overview of philanthropy, charity, and social service in Chinese religions, and discuss their relevance for civil society on the mainland and in greater China.

Part III is concerned with issues of religious life in relationship to politics and the economy. The first two chapters are broad historical treatments of religion and society in traditional China and the twentieth century. In chapter 9, entitled "Religion in Chinese Social and Political History," David A. Palmer shows how religious ideas, practices, and communities discussed in parts I and II can be understood in China's evolving sociopolitical system, from the second millennium BCE to the end of the nineteenth century. Vincent Goossaert picks up the narrative in chapter 10 on "The Social Organization of Religious Communities in the Twentieth Century." He traces the development of modern and contemporary religious institutions in China in order to understand modes of belonging in religious communities and ways of quantifying religious participation. In chapter 11, André Laliberté introduces "Contemporary Issues in State-Religious Relations." He discusses the evolution of the religious policy of the Chinese Communist Party and the contentious political issues facing religions on the mainland. The focus shifts to the economy in chapter 12, "Market Economy and Religious Revival." Here, Fenggang Yang contrasts the difference between religious life in a centrally planned economy with the economic reforms that have introduced capitalism on the mainland over the last three decades. Despite continuing economic restrictions, the market reforms have contributed to the revival of religious life in mainland China in ways that both confirm and challenge existing sociological theories.

The final section of the book (part IV) consists of one chapter and our conclusion. In chapter 13, Richard Madsen and Elijah Siegler introduce "The Globalization of Chinese Religions and Traditions." Immigration, the growth of transnational religious associations, the influence of overseas Chinese religious communities on mainland China, and the growing popularization of Chinese religions in the West are all aspects of the globalization of Chinese religious life. In our conclusion, Glenn Shive identifies areas for further study, including the growing importance of all religions in global politics and the relevance of Chinese religious life for enhancing international relationships as well as intercultural exchange and understanding.

Chinese *pinyin* Romanization is used throughout this book, except in the case of proper names where another Romanization is widely known or preferable. A number of websites are available that introduce the pronunciation of *pinyin*, for example, *Nciku* (http://www.nciku.com/). Every effort has been made to avoid specialized terminology or Chinese terms, but the use of some such terms has been necessary in some places. A glossary has been included for important terms mentioned in the text as well as selected Chinese terms in *pinyin* Romanization. The bibliography is designed for the general reader, and lists, according to subject, only books currently available in the English language.

This book began in 2005 as a project of the Hong Kong America Center on Chinese religion and public life. The project was made possible by generous support from the Henry Luce III Foundation. After several preliminary meetings, the editors and other advisors identified a wide range of scholars whom they thought could contribute to the volume. From these, the selection of chapter authors and contributors was made. Their names and affiliations appear at the beginning of this volume. Most authors met together twice in Hong Kong, in the summers of 2007 and 2008. At these meetings, the authors introduced their chapter subjects, responded to questions and suggestions from other authors, and discussed the project as a whole. The finalized chapters were subsequently reviewed by two of the editors. Suggestions for substantial changes (if any) were discussed with and approved by the authors. The final arrangement and text of the chapters was made by decision of the editors, and we are responsible for any errors in content and interpretation that remain.

Not all the authors would agree with one another either on the interpretation of Chinese religious life that is presented in each chapter, or on some specific points that are contested or controversial in nature. This is as it should be because there is diversity of viewpoints on almost all aspects of religious life in China. As such, this book does not represent a consensus opinion on Chinese religion. Rather, it is an expression of the diversity of interpretations of Chinese religious life by well-known scholars. It is, in effect, an invitation to readers to discuss and explore the subject at a deeper level and from different perspectives.

It has been more than thirty years since the reemergence of religious life in the People's Republic of China and the renewal of the academic study of religion. Since then, many departments of religious studies and social scientific research have been opened, and they have produced a rich harvest of books and essays on religious life in China. In addition, theological seminaries, training centers, and other institutions have been opened that have contributed to the development of religion and religious studies in China by Chinese scholars and religious believers themselves. This book is an attempt by a variety of authors writing in English to make their own contribution to that dialogue, as we introduce religion and religious life in China to general readers in other parts of the world.

PART I

Ways of Being Religious in the Chinese World

Spirituality in a Modern Chinese Metropolis
Lizhu Fan and James D. Whitehead

The Scene: A Vegetarian Restaurant

It is Saturday in Shenzhen, the bustling free economic zone an hour's train ride from Hong Kong. At noon one of the city's largest vegetarian restaurants is crowded: families gather for a leisurely meal together, and shoppers stop in for a quick snack before returning to their weekend errands.

But there is something different about this restaurant. While waiting for a table, many people browse through the impressive array of books that line the lobby's long bookshelf. Here they find titles on a range of practical, moral, and religious themes—achieving peace of mind in today's complex world, honesty in personal and business relationships, understanding problems in marriage and family life, and life strategies to improve physical and emotional health. Others glance through the posters and notices listing upcoming lectures and workshops offered by Chinese and international figures, many with Buddhist or other religious affiliations.

The steady traffic to and from the buffet area is not the only movement among the gathered diners. People regularly leave their tables and make their way through the kitchen area to another room on the same floor. At the front of the room, a small religious altar has been set up for this occasion; the room holds no other furnishings. The visitors watch as five traditionally robed young Buddhist monks engage in a series of ritual activities while paying homage to several Buddhist images—bowing and burning incense, chanting aloud, and reading the sutras. Restaurant patrons come and go during this time, some joining the monks in ritual gestures, but most simply sitting attentively for a while before returning to the restaurant area and continuing their day's activities.

At one point, a middle-aged monk enters the room, to be greeted respectfully by some members of the seated crowd and by the younger monks. Quickly the room fills to capacity, leaving many disappointed people in the hall outside. Quiet falls as the older monk begins to speak. After his lengthy lecture the crowd disperses, the ritual objects are packed, and the monks depart.

What is going on here? A religious ritual, to be sure; but of what kind? This location is a restaurant—part of the regular economic life of Shenzhen, not a sacred site registered with the local religious affairs bureau. The ritual forms here are Buddhist, and monks have played important roles in the event. But our interviews reveal that the monks are not the initiators of this gathering, and few of those in attendance identify themselves as Buddhists. The session's host is Mr. Yang, the restaurant's owner. Mr. Yang understands this commercial setting, with its appealing vegetarian menu, its array of morally uplifting books, its up-to-date information about local spiritual resources, and its frequent opportunity for simple ritual participation, as part of his own spiritual practice.

In Shenzhen, on the border between mainland China and Hong Kong, the dynamics of modernization interact with the search for spiritual meaning. To better understand this phenomenon it will help to familiarize ourselves with the city itself.

The City: Shenzhen

Not long ago, the city of Shenzhen was a sleepy fishing village. In 1979 as part of the program of Opening and Reform program, Deng Xiaoping declared this city and a vast track of surrounding territory a special economic zone, a laboratory for free-market reforms that would later be extended to the rest of socialist China. During the 1980s, a first wave of immigrants, predominantly unskilled laborers and recruits from the People's Liberation Army, arrived to supply needed construction and factory workers as many Western companies rushed to begin production at this inexpensive site.

In the 1990s a second wave of immigrants, including many middle-class Chinese, came to fill the demand for management personnel or to start their own businesses. With generous tax incentives in place for foreign investment, the city exploded from a town of 80,000 into a rough-edged metropolis of twelve million, of whom six million are temporary workers or "floating residents," who labor in various jobs without the benefits of legal residency.

Western observers are often appalled by what they find in Shenzhen: dangerous factory conditions, environmental damage, widespread graft and corruption. In fact, an Industrial Revolution and an Information Revolution are taking place simultaneously in this extraordinary city. What appears to many foreigners as disorder appeals to workers here as opportunity. China watcher Ian Buruma captures these contrasts: "The atmosphere is young and brash. A raw, even primitive, vitality—life reduced to food, sex and money—flows through these new streets like a muddy river." Buruma continues, "But for many young Chinese that is precisely its attraction. To be relieved of the burdens of home, history, and tradition is a form of liberation. Opportunities await at the frontiers of the wild south—opportunities to make money, but also to carve out a modicum of personal freedom."[1] In many ways, the city of Shenzhen is unique in China: more than 90% of its inhabitants were born elsewhere; the average age of current residents is less than thirty. Social and psychological forces here differ dramatically from those that still prevail in the interior regions where most Chinese live. The speed of change in Shenzhen has outpaced even the rapidly modernizing urban metropolises along China's eastern coast.

But while this free economic zone is not typical of China today, it may hold significant clues to this country's future. With the dynamics of globalization cast here in such sharp relief, Shenzhen presents a compelling site for examining the impact of social change on religious consciousness.[2]

The Spiritual Search in Shenzhen

The metropolis of Shenzhen boasts new and refurbished worship sites of each of the five religious communities officially recognized by law in the People's Republic of China—Daoism, Buddhism, Islam, and Protestant and Catholic Christianity. And although accurate numbers are difficult to determine, membership in these registered religious groups is on the rise here as well as elsewhere throughout mainland China. But evidence from Shenzhen reveals another, often overlooked, dynamic of Chinese modernization. One of the most significant—and surprising—developments has been the extent to which the urbanized Chinese in Shenzhen adopt and adapt elements of their common spiritual heritage as part of an intentional spiritual search.

Today, urbanized Chinese in Shenzhen, most of them children of the revolutionary generation, are reclaiming elements of traditional belief and practice as part of a personal spiritual awakening. Confronted by new questions of meaning and purpose, many of these residents did not turn to the now-approved religious institutions of Buddhism or Christianity. Instead they gave very personal expression to their spiritual search in the age-old idiom of China's common spiritual heritage. Despite determined opposition over the past hundred years—from state Confucianism, from Christian missionary efforts, from the Westernizing efforts of Chinese intellectuals, and from Maoist-Marxist political philosophy—this spiritual sensitivity survives in the mainland today.

The continuing vitality of this common religious heritage in rural areas of mainland China has been convincingly documented in contemporary field studies.[3] To date, the influence of traditional beliefs in city settings has received less attention. A look at Shenzhen suggests that the values and practices of China's common spiritual heritage continue to energize contemporary Chinese caught up in the cultural dynamics of urbanization.

BOX 1.1 Common Spiritual Heritage

By *common*, we refer to the moral and spiritual convictions widely embraced by Chinese across history and still today. Central elements include Heaven (*Tian*) as transcendent source of moral meaning; the energy that animates the universe (*qi*); ancestor veneration; and cosmic recompense (*baoying*). Despite the intensely local character of Chinese religiousness, these beliefs are core values and symbols for most Chinese.

The term *spiritual* moves the conversation away from thorny questions provoked by the term *religion*—with its many Western (institutional, monotheistic) nuances—in the direction of a moral orientation and spiritual worldview that is diffused throughout this culture. This enduring orientation is more than cultural, though it has never been organized into an institutional structure such as Buddhism or Christianity.

The term *heritage* points to the long tradition of belief and practice (which many scholars have designated China's "indigenous religion") that endures today as a resource or moral capital for China's future. Viewed through an anthropological lens, this heritage is often identified as *popular religion.*

Fateful Coincidences

The middle-class Shenzhen residents who participated in this study had all moved to this burgeoning metropolis in the previous decade. Leaving settled lives in other provinces, they were intent on making a new life in a new China. Their relocation brought with it many dislocations.

Ms. Wang, for example, reflected on the disappointments that marked her path to Shenzhen. Her earlier plans—to study abroad, to marry after a long engagement, to find a steady job—had all been dashed. But after these many reversals of fortune, she found herself in Shenzhen with an excellent job that offered quick promotion. In a brief time her life had turned around dramatically; now she was financially comfortable and at peace.

But Ms. Wang wondered how those earlier crises and reversals contributed to her life today. Apparent coincidences marked the winding path of her life's journey. Despite the pain they had caused at the time, many of the misfortunes suffered along the way seemed to have led to this new and much better life. How to explain this? To help fathom her contemporary mystery, Ms. Wang recruited a theme from China's past: fateful coincidence (*yuanfen*). The meaning of the term is close to what we might call in English "a lucky break," but in Chinese tradition a fateful coincidence covers both "good" luck and "bad" luck. And Chinese sensitivity recognizes that apparent coincidences are not luck at all, but part of one's fortune. This deeply embedded aspect of Chinese culture became fused many centuries ago with the Buddhist notion of karma: in a universe that is thoroughly moral, there are no mere coincidences. The events of our lives, for better or for worse, are related to past behavior, virtuous or otherwise.

There are psychological advantages to this traditional belief. By assigning causality of negative events to fateful coincidences that are beyond personal control, groups are able to "soothe relationships, reduce conflict, and promote social harmony."[4] Similarly, when positive events are seen to result primarily from fateful coincidences, personal credit is not directly assigned, thus reducing pride on one side of the relationship and envy and resentment on the other.

During her years in Shenzhen, Ms. Wang reported, her interpretation of these fateful coincidences had undergone a transformation. Earlier, she had understood the concept as a simple coincidence or a casual chance event. Today she sees fateful coincidences as having shaped her fortune in a favorable way. This insight has made her grateful. Her new appreciation of fateful coincidences also has moral consequences: Ms. Wang reports a heightened sensitivity now to the ethical dimensions of her professional life. She is determined to conduct her life according to high moral principles, so that her favorable fateful coincidences will continue. For Ms. Wang, the term *fateful coincidence* has shifted from cultural cliché to become a meaningful marker of a moral life.

Fathoming Our Destiny

Chinese have always believed that a person's life is somehow related to the influence of a transcendent force named Heaven. What had once been seen as the ruler's "divine right" to rule (his "mandate of heaven") was interpreted by the philosopher Mencius as part of every person's destiny. The ancient belief in destiny links the givenness of personal fate and the changing circumstances and individual choices that keep life open-ended. For the Chinese, as for other cultures, a person's destiny was seen as both fixed and flexible.

For many centuries, the "fixed" or fated side of life seemed to dominate. One had to accept one's lot in life, as peasant, as farmer, as wife. Imagining an alternate destiny was all but impossible. Profound changes in its recent history have attuned China's younger generation to more choices and new possibilities. In place of state-sponsored guarantees of lifetime employment—the socialist "iron rice bowl"—young people today can and must choose their careers. If this provokes anxiety, it also brings freedom, with a sense that one's destiny is not only fixed but flexible. In contemporary Shenzhen, residents frequently speak of taking their destinies into their own hands.

Mr. Zhou, for instance, was surprised by the changes that had taken place in his own life. His small printing business, producing mailing envelopes, deposit slips, and receipt books, had grown rapidly, in pace with Shenzhen's expanding economy. After several early years of struggle, Zhou was suddenly quite successful; he now owned a house and even a private automobile. This financial success triggered deeper questions about his life. Previously, Mr. Zhou reported, he had never reflected on the direction of his life or its long-term purpose. But his sudden good fortune led him to question: why is this success mine? While others he knew who were equally hardworking were still struggling, his life and career had quite suddenly begun to flourish. To make sense of this turn of events, Mr. Zhou found himself unexpectedly returning to traditional convictions in his culture about personal destiny. But, as Mr. Zhou well knew, to say, "my fate is good," is not to brag, but to express surprise and even gratitude for the good fortune that has come to a life. While the ancient idea of destiny did not fully explain Mr. Zhou's recent successes, it did make him more mindful of the good fortune that had been given him, and the responsibility that he now recognized came with it. As with Ms. Wang, this recovery of an ancient theme made Mr. Zhou more attentive to his life. This attentiveness reinserted Mr. Zhou into a conversation that has gone on for millennia in his culture.

Living in a Moral Universe

For other respondents in this fast-changing city, questions of morality were of greatest concern. For people who work in the largely unregulated businesses in Shenzhen, bribery and other forms of corruption are rampant temptations. Ms. Shen recalled her early experience in the city, when she was ready to cheat clients in pursuit of greater profits. As she became wealthier, she also experienced an increasing sense of guilt. During this period of regret, Ms. Shen accompanied a friend to a public lecture offered by a visiting Buddhist monk. One of his statements struck home: "If you are meant to have something, it will be yours." Puzzling over this cryptic statement, she began to question her own acquisitiveness and greed. Gradually she came to see her business pursuits as part of a larger life design. She determined to end her deceitful practices and adopt a pattern of strict honesty in her dealings with others.

Ms. Shen's moral musings took her back to the traditional Chinese belief in cosmic recompense.[5] In *The Ledgers of Merit and Demerit*, Cynthia Brokaw describes this notion as a "belief in a supernatural or cosmic retribution, a belief that has been a fundamental, at times *the* fundamental, belief of Chinese religion since the beginning of recorded history."[6] This belief, woven deep into the fabric of Chinese culture, is rooted in the conviction that the universe is moral. No action, good or bad, goes unrecompensed. To live a life of dishonesty will lead eventually to troubles that are one's due, just as virtuous behavior bears its own good fruit. Ms. Shen now recognized that living according to higher moral standards would affect her own future: good would come from this moral discipline. She began to believe that, even financially, she would have "what she was meant to have." Ms. Shen reported that this belief, alive again for her, motivated a new sense of purpose in her career and brought comfort to her life.

These moral themes—fateful coincidence, personal destiny, and cosmic recompense—are closely related. Apparent chance events, small and great, influence the shape and fortune of each person's destiny. Recognizing this connection has the moral result of making a person more responsible for his or her actions. Belief that the universe is itself moral links the concepts of destiny and cosmic recompense. Virtuous actions bring their own reward, but this reward, often registered in (apparently) chance events, gives shape to a person's destiny. This is how human fate is both fixed and flexible.

Moral and Social Capital in Shenzhen

Every culture possesses a patrimony of moral goodness and spiritual achievements. This storehouse of moral values, accumulated over many centuries, functions as an endowment to be cherished and conserved, as well as a moral asset to be invested in the future. We may see the spiritual resources to which residents of Shenzhen turned in times of change and crisis as a kind of "moral capital" made available to them from their own religious heritage.

China scholar Judith Berling introduced the term *moral capital* in her analysis of a seventeenth-century Chinese novel.[7] The novel argues that a virtuous life results in the accumulation of moral resources. Through meritorious actions of honesty and compassion, a person accrues virtue much as money (capital) might be saved. These accrued virtues become the spiritual inheritance that funds the next generation. A person who squanders the spiritual resources he has inherited from his family has nothing to hand down to his children. In a typically Chinese fashion, the novel insists that "moral capital (accumulated merit) is just as important a legacy for one's descendents as land or money." Berling concludes, "Religion as the management of moral capital thus involves taking responsibility: Learning to manage one's life and human relationships so as not to exhaust moral collateral."[8]

Moral capital—as a spiritual resource imbedded in a culture's past—funds those contemporary interactions of trust that have been named *social capital*. Sociologist John Coleman defines this term: "Social capital ... points to features of social life, such as networks of mutuality and norms of trust that enable participants to act together more effectively to pursue shared objectives."[9]

If social capital describes the human resources currently available in a particular society such as mainland China, the question arises: Where do these resources originate? What is their origin or wellspring? Francis Fukuyama has suggested that these valuable resources spring from "certain pre-modern cultural habits."[10] He then attempts to be more precise: the trust at the core of social capital has "its origins in ... phenomena like religion and traditional ethics."[11]

Trustworthiness, generally identified as a personal virtue or moral dynamic, can also be understood as an inherited reserve of social cohesion. At the core of social cohesion is the shared recognition of promises made and kept, of reliability that has

BOX 1.2 Civil Society, Social Capital, and Moral Capital

Civil society names the public sphere that has appeared between government (with its many controls) and the market (with its many demands) where organizations form to act in the public interest. In today's world of "multiple modernities," civil society will display different characteristics in various cultures.

Social capital names the resource of mutual trust and generosity that allows people to act together, over time, to contribute to a society's well-being. This is an observable dynamic and a necessary asset for the flourishing of civil society.

Moral capital names the moral values and spiritual motivations that fuel social capital, giving people reason to cooperate for the common good. This term points to "the moods and motivations" (Clifford Geertz, "Religion as a Cultural System," in *Anthropological Approaches to the Study of Religion*," ed. M. Banton [London: Tavistock, 1985], 176) that energize people to work with other citizens, often unlike themselves, in this new public sphere to build up their society.

Francis Fukuyama (*Trust: The Social Virtues and the Creation of Prosperity*) and Alan Wolfe (*Religion and Ritual in Chinese Society*) both point to the less observable but essential resource of moral capital, locating it in premodern reservoirs of religion and traditional ethics. A lesson of late modernity is that critical reason cannot successfully substitute for the motivating energies of religious symbols and rituals.

---

been established over many transactions. This communal confidence becomes a moral resource that accrues like other capital: it can be both accumulated and invested in the future; but it can also be squandered until moral bankruptcy looms. The contemporary resource of social capital in any society rests on a cultural inheritance of social virtues that give coherence to a society. The wellsprings of such social capital and the civil society it serves lie in the stories, symbols, and rituals— the moral capital—that provide a culture its identity and motivate its higher purposes.

In the preceding three stories from Shenzhen we have seen Chinese in a thriving urban environment returning to moral memories and religious images that had been considered by many scholars to be premodern, rural, and perhaps bankrupt in today's world. But in the late modern, urban China of Shenzhen these resources of a common spiritual heritage remain motivating resources for Chinese lives.

Adopting and Adapting China's Common Spiritual Heritage

While many of these urban middle-class residents in Shenzhen now enthusiastically embrace elements of China's traditional heritage, their experience of these beliefs and practices does not simply repeat the patterns of China's rural past. Both continuities with China's common spiritual heritage and differences are evident.

Continuities include (a) the practical nature of spiritual concerns; (b) an open or "non-sectarian"[12] attitude, which draws freely from plural sources of spiritual nourishment; and (c) the predominance of lay initiative over formal religious leadership. Differences include (d) the broader range of spiritual options currently available; (e) new settings for communal support and spiritual formation; and (f) the heightened awareness of personal decision in spiritual belief and practice.

Religious Continuities in Shenzhen

PRACTICAL NATURE OF SPIRITUAL CONCERNS

As is characteristic of traditional Chinese spirituality, the beliefs and practices of today's Shenzhen respondents are located in the midst of everyday life and focused on life's daily problems: health and healing, hope for good fortune, smoothing troubled relations. Ms. Shi, for example, is a news commentator at a local television station. Growing up during the Cultural Revolution, she had little direct experience of religious practice. Now, in her apartment in one of the modern housing complexes that surround the city of Shenzhen, she has set up a small altar. A statue of Guanyin, the Buddhist figure widely venerated among Chinese, plays a prominent role here. Ms. Shi places fresh fruit on the altar for a time, and then offers this fruit as a gift to friends who are suffering from bad health or family problems. Her sense is that this fruit now carries special power that will bring healing and consolation to these friends. In the midst of her busy professional life, she tries to spend time daily in meditation and in reading morally uplifting books. Although Ms. Shi insists that she is not a Buddhist, she finds the prayerful reading of Buddhist texts to be especially consoling. Ms. Shi acknowledges that her daily practices are part of a search for a calm life and peaceful heart, in the midst of a complex and confusing world. She embraces these activities as significant in her life and necessary for her spiritual well-being.

SPIRITUAL PRACTICES DRAWN FROM PLURAL TRADITIONS

Outsiders might also be struck by the eclectic range of Ms. Shi's devotions; her home altar displays items of ritual significance in Daoism and in Buddhism, as well as some with uniquely personal meanings. On the one hand, this creative assembly of images, with its commitment to personal relevance and individual choice, may be seen as a reflection of modern consciousness. But the openness and selectivity we see here also resonate with deeper cultural dynamics.

Historically, Chinese religiousness has drawn upon plural sources of spiritual nourishment. Resources separately identified with China's three great traditions— Confucianism, Daoism, and Buddhism—have been combined freely in local religious practice, without troubling considerations of denominational distinction or ritual orthodoxy. This characteristic openness, too, reflects the practical bias of China's common spiritual heritage.

For centuries the common ritual activities of China's peoples have existed symbiotically with the more formalized traditions of Confucianism, Daoism, and Buddhism. Chinese popular religion developed with no need to create its own distinct rituals, elaborate doctrines, or full-time professional leaders such as monks or priests. Chinese have traditionally borrowed beliefs and ceremonies originally developed within the "great traditions" of Daoism, Confucianism, and Buddhism, adapting these to suit local conditions. Yet the underlying worldview remains that of the common spiritual heritage.

LAY LEADERSHIP PREDOMINATES

China's local religious traditions, as Daniel Overmyer reminds us, "are characterized by their location in the midst of everyday life and their focus on practical aid and results.... Though clergy may be involved, for the most part these traditions are led, organized, and continued by the people themselves."[13] Because the ritual activities were so intimately woven into the patterns of daily life, it was natural that those who carried out ordinary village responsibilities would play the significant roles in village rituals.

In Shenzhen, lay leadership continues to characterize the informal gatherings and larger communal activities. Laypeople call on monks to conduct rituals, but they themselves are in charge. For example, a loose network associated with one of the vegetarian restaurants has adopted a Buddhist ritual as part of a larger social concern. Annually they undertake a symbolic "freeing of animals" to cultivate mercy and compassion in the world.

Notice of the time and place of the freeing of animals ceremony is distributed by flyers, e-mail, and word of mouth. Individuals, many of them previously unknown to the planners, bring cages of small birds and turtles purchased at the local market. A monk from the nearby registered monastery is hired to read the appropriate sutras and to guide the ritual activities releasing the animals from their cages. But the ordinary people are clearly the initiators and the hosts of this gathering.

This discussion of continuities between the rural spiritual heritage and its urban reappropriation has already hinted at some emerging differences. Here we will examine more explicitly three of these differences.

Religious Adaptations in Shenzhen

BROADER RANGE OF SPIRITUAL OPTIONS AVAILABLE

In Shenzhen, some people's religious practice involves simply the regular repetition of prayer formulas. But most respondents reported seeking deeper understanding by reading texts or commentaries on religious classics (Daoist stories, Buddhist sutras, works of Confucius and Mencius), or morally uplifting contemporary books. An extraordinary range of authors and titles is now available, resulting from both the loosening of editorial restrictions on mainland Chinese publishing houses and the burgeoning interest in new ideas and foreign views that has accompanied this city's globalization. As a result, more sources of spiritual nourishment are available in Shenzhen, and more personal choice is required.

Expanded media sources have played a crucial role in the spiritual revival in Shenzhen. Local bookstores abound with titles providing alternative life perspectives and moral advice. A steady stream of Buddhist and Christian television and Internet programming arrives from Taiwan and North America. Local and international religious entrepreneurs promote programs for health and healing and peace of mind, even as state propaganda urges a return to now largely discredited Communist ideals and values. And images and icons of Western popular culture flood the local media. Confronted by this vast array of possibilities, Shenzhen residents need to, and want to, find for themselves the sources of spiritual nourishment that suit their own situations and temperaments.

BOX 1.3 Buddhist Pop Music

Francesca Tarocco

The contemporary Chinese Buddhist world is inextricably linked with the popularization of a novel type of voice-based compositions pioneered in the 1930s and 1940s by the eminent monk Hongyi (born Li Shutong 1880–1942) and his disciples. Embracing Chinese musical modernity, a heady mixture of Western piano and brass band music, newly composed patriotic songs, Christian hymns, Japanese school songs, jazz and film music, Hongyi and other Buddhist activists incorporated some elements of this new soundscape in their own musical idiom. While marking a departure from traditional liturgical music, the songs are deliberately inscribed in Buddhist language and imagery. The most famous of these songs is *The Song of the Three Jewels* (*Sanbaoge*) written together with the prominent activist monk Taixu (1890–1947), author of the lyrics (Tarocco, *The Cultural Practices of Modern Chinese Buddhism: Attuning the Dharma*, London: Routledge, 2008). The soundscape of the contemporary Chinese-speaking Buddhist world, and of Taiwan in particular, would not be what it is without them. In today's China, Hongyi's songs are available in digital format through a number of retailers immediately associable with Buddhism, including shops attached to monastic compounds, but are also found in mainstream music and audiovisual stores. Both official and Buddhist China have found a niche market for the songs, and, in time, have variously appropriated them and adapted them to contemporary needs and tastes. In 1990, the Shanghai Music Publishing House produced an elegantly packaged critical anthology entitled *The Collected Songs by Li Shutong-Dharma Master Hongyi*, a work that ushered in several other Hongyi-related cultural products. In his writings and in personal communications, the recordist and editor of one collection has described the clerics involved as audience conscious and aimed to "rival [...] the ever-increasing influence of popular music and *karaoke*." Buddhist clerics seemed to him "insistent on the importance of not letting

continued

BOX 1.3 (continued)

Buddhist chant be reduced to some vestige of bygone days or to a means of expression reserved to specialist monks."

The long tradition of Buddhist adaptability and innovation carries on. European-style symphonic music, karaoke-style chanting, and CDs of pop Buddhist-inspired tunes are only a few of the many faces of the contemporary world of audiovisual Buddhism. Interestingly, the influence of Western musical idioms and theories, and of modern, mass-mediated songs, has determined a number of shifts in the perception of the past musical heritage and in the performance of traditional ritual repertoires. As retailers have invented various labels to identify "ethnic" and "world" music for listeners who seek a more varied, exotic musical fare, a new market is emerging today for "Buddhist music." Have the shifts in Buddhist discourses on music influenced religious behavior? Is modern technology affecting the way in which monastic chanting is learned, produced, and transmitted? Certainly, the examination of the web of interconnected global and local ideas and practices that contributed to their creation illustrates how new Buddhist songs are both radically new and remarkably traditional. Regardless of the fact that they are the product of Chinese musical modernity, they continue to be meaningful in ways that are unrelated to modernity, as a sort of spiritual emanation of powerful holy men like Hongyi. As in medieval China when the possession of the portrait of an eminent master was proof of a social and/or karmic connection between him and the owner of the portrait, the owners of a CD that displays Hongyi's portrait and the tunes and lyrics he wrote may feel similarly connected with the master.

NEW COMMUNAL SETTINGS: THE ROLE OF VEGETARIAN RESTAURANTS

Many in Shenzhen sense themselves to be without the supports and constraints that were once provided by extended family or local village life. And most respondents cherish this new psychological freedom. But hunger for a sense of belonging continues, and for some, even intensifies, in this modernizing city. Here, through personally chosen participation in a loosely organized social network, spiritual seekers sustain one another in a new level of consciousness and reinforce an emerging spiritual identity.

Shenzhen brings together people from many different parts of China. This mobility and heterogeneity of population has affected the experience of this common religious heritage. While most Shenzhen respondents resist formal identification with any particular religious institution, the communal dimensions of spiritual practice remain strong. But in this new urban setting, the communal practices of Chinese religiousness are organized differently.

Many respondents assemble regularly with fellow searchers. These gatherings function more as a loosely organized network than as a formally constituted membership group. Vegetarian restaurants are frequent settings for these gatherings. In addition to the large restaurant depicted earlier, several others serve as important locations for those in the spiritual search.

Another example: a small storefront restaurant nestled in a downtown high-rise building comfortably accommodates perhaps thirty people at its several round tables. Open to the general public, the restaurant welcomes passersby along with more regular customers. A bookshelf stretches along one wall, stocked with a selection of spiritually oriented books that the restaurant owner makes available to patrons for loan or purchase. At one end of the room a video screen continuously displays a series of calming nature scenes, interspersed with brief readings and recitations from spiritual texts. In another corner, a small altar has been set up and many patrons stop on their way in or out of the shop to offer a gesture of respect. A notice board lists activities in which people may be interested: a lecture in the area; a ritual gathering planned for the future; an ecological project inviting volunteers.

The restaurant was not established by a religious organization and exists without any outside investment. The manager, a layman without formal religious training or membership, indicates that operating this restaurant is part of his own spiritual practice. Several respondents gather here regularly to share a vegetarian meal and to discuss their spiritual reading and practices. Sometimes the restaurant owner will invite a local monk or a visiting international author to make a brief presentation. More often the discussion develops informally, as customers linger after their meal to share concerns and speak about their spiritual practices.

HEIGHTENED AWARENESS OF PERSONAL AGENCY IN BELIEF AND PRACTICE

In these self-selected gatherings we may have evidence of a new dynamic in the relationship between individual and group, one that characterizes a shift toward modern consciousness. In China's rural past, entire families or villages lived within a shared spiritual perspective. Commonly held values served as the screen through which personal experience was filtered. The group thus provided and secured the meaning system for its members. When individuals were embedded in this surrounding culture, there was neither need nor opportunity for conscious awareness of spiritual choice.

At this new stage in China's history, middle-class Chinese are consciously endeavoring to interpret their lives for themselves. No longer embedded in the assumptive world of village life, and less subject to the constraints of family network and work unit, these people are insistent that they wish to find the sources of spiritual nourishment that are appropriate for their lives and temperaments. As one respondent asserted, "What I believe is nobody's business but my own."

In Shenzhen, as is typical of rural China, most respondents do not join an established religious group or identify exclusively with a single sect or master. But respondents here gave personal reasons to justify their eclectic approach. Some suspected that the officially registered religions remain too close to the government,

BOX 1.4 The Spiritual Vacuum

With Mao's victory at mid century and the establishment of Marxism-Leninism-
Mao Zedong Thought as official ideology, the ancient heritage of Confucian
values, already under severe scrutiny as contributing to China's stagnation, was
threatened with bankruptcy. By the onset of Reform and Opening policy in the late
1970s, many Chinese were turning away from now discredited moral ideals of
Marxism; thus a second spiritual bankruptcy loomed.

Between these two sobering depletions of moral capital came the cataclysm of
the Cultural Revolution. The events of this horrendous decade badly compromised
the capacity for mutual trust among Chinese, thus undermining social capital at its
core. Moral reciprocity, which long lay at the heart of China's deepest spiritual
values, was severely jeopardized.

These events conspired to produce what many critics described as a "spiritual
vacuum." Observers both within China and outside asked searching questions:
Were China's deep reserves of humane spirit and moral ideals, accumulated and
reinvested over millennia, now bankrupt? Would the moral currency needed to
build China's future as a modern state have to be borrowed from the West? (See
Jiwei Ci, *Dialectic of the Chinese Revolution: From Utopianism to Hedonism*,
Stanford, Calif.: Stanford University Press, 1994.)

---

too susceptible to party control. Having only recently escaped the all-encompassing
control of the state-sponsored work unit, they resisted affiliating with another institution that seems to depend on government approval.

But most offered another explanation. For people in Shenzhen, a dominant feature of life is the exhilaration of personal choice. In the realm of the spirit, as in
much of the rest of their lives, personal choice has become the standard. Respondents
wanted to make clear that their new moral convictions and ritual practices, too,
represented personal decisions. These decisions are personal because they were not
made in deference to social pressures exerted by family and village life. Their religious choices are personal because these were not coerced by government control or
political orthodoxy.

For many in Shenzhen today, spiritual practice is a matter of personal decision.
And the decision is made with keen awareness that it is both intentional and
voluntary. But the selectivity manifested here is not the religious individualism
more evident in North America. In Shenzhen, the personalized quality of spirituality is less a private journey of the interior life and more a heightened awareness of
personal responsibility.

Conclusion

Indications abound that the moral capital of China's cultural and spiritual heritage
is far from bankrupt. Taiwan, where cultural reconstruction has been somewhat

less inhibited, offers striking examples. Buddhist and Daoist organizations in Taiwan have collectively brought traditional values back into play in a rapidly modernized civil society.[14] With the transition to economic prosperity and political democracy, these religious organizations were compelled to reimagine their moral capital and how their spiritual resources might serve society. Thus, after the disastrous earthquake in Taiwan on September 21, 1999, the leader of the Dharma Drum Mountain Buddhist temple appeared frequently on television, encouraging the Taiwanese "not to think of the disaster as the result of bad karma for previous sins but as an important opportunity to make Taiwan safer and better for future generations."[15] Rather than interpret this national tragedy through a negative lens focused on a guilty past, this religious leader offered a positive perspective focused on a hopeful future. The core of his expressed concern was civic compassion rather than punitive personal karma.

Another indication of China's moral capital being reimagined in modern guise is taking place in discussions about the role of NGOs on the mainland. Though the government has long been suspicious of these organizations, a number of Chinese scholars are encouraging political leaders to recognize how these not-for-profit groups contribute to the nation's moral well-being and to the "harmonious society" that the government promotes. In a previous work, for example, the senior author of this essay has linked the Chinese tradition of doing good—an aspect of cosmic recompense—with the contributions of NGOs to China's future.[16]

Award-winning author Frances Fitzgerald has discovered a similar return to religious moral capital in an Asian neighbor of China. Returning to Vietnam, about which she had written twenty-five years ago, Fitzgerald was struck by the resurgence of interest in religious practices that an earlier socialist regime had severely curtailed: "There has been an astonishing revival of traditional social and religious practices throughout the country."[17]

The rapid development of a market economy in Vietnam has not signaled the demise of its traditional religiousness. Instead, economic opportunity seems to have quickened the impulse of spiritual renewal. And, Fitzgerald notes, "In Vietnam the revival of rites does not mean a return to the past... people may go to pagodas to pray for good health or fortune, but they also go to health clinics and learn business skills." As is the case with the Chinese in Shenzhen, the return of Vietnamese to the moral capital of their heritage does not represent a regression. These modern citizens are adopting and adapting practices from their past and weaving them into a contemporary spirituality. "The Vietnamese are going back to tradition and forward at the same time. More precisely, they are reclaiming and refashioning their traditions in order to move on."[18]

Important questions remain. Will the heritage of Chinese popular religion—its common spiritual heritage—that has for centuries thrived as an intensely localized and traditional phenomenon, make a successful transition to the cosmopolitan settings of the new China? Will this traditional symbol system survive as a reservoir of personal and communal meaning in modern urban environments?

Shenzhen findings suggest that the images and practices of China's local and common religion, which flourish largely under the radar of government surveillance, provide a vocabulary though which modern urban Chinese are fruitfully exploring issues of life meaning and destiny. This spiritual heritage may well remain as moral capital funding the future of the new China.

Notes

We are grateful for permission granted to draw on our earlier discussion of findings from the Shenzhen research: see "Fate and Fortune: Popular Religion and Moral Capital in Shenzhen," *Journal of Chinese Religions* 32 (2004): 83–100; "Adopting and Adapting China's Common Religious Heritage," *Nova Religio* 9.2 (2005): 50–61.

1. See Ian Buruma, *Bad Elements: Chinese Rebels from Los Angeles to Beijing* (New York: Random House, 2001), 250, 252.

2. For general discussions of the recent changes in Chinese society and culture, see Ian Buruma, *Bad Elements,* and Rob Gifford, *China Road: A Journey into the Future of a Rising Power* (New York: Random House, 2007).

3. See, for example, Robert P. Weller, *Unities and Diversities in Chinese Religion* (Seattle: University of Washington Press, 1987), as well as the contribution of Kenneth Dean, "Local Community Religion in Contemporary Southeast China" (pp. 338–358), and Lizhu Fan, "The Cult of the Silkworm Mother as a Core of Local Community Religion in a North China Village," *China Quarterly* 174 (2003): 359–372.

4. K. S. Yang and David Ho, "The Role of Yuan in Chinese Social Life: A Conceptual and Empirical Analysis," *Asian Contributions to Psychology,* ed. Anand C. Paranjpe, David Y. F. Ho, and Robert W. Rieber (New York: Praeger, 1988), 270. Sociologist Li Peiliang reports that a survey of 550 persons in Hong Kong in 1974 showed that more than 50% believed in the importance of establishing good *yuanfen* with one's physician. (Here *yuanfen* refers to the "chemistry" or friendly feeling between persons; as such, it is both a "fortunate" relationship and one that people have some responsibility to influence.) Li argues that such an attitude is both positive and rational: having a comfortable relationship with one's doctor will likely lead to better care and a healthier life.

5. Cynthia Brokaw and other scholars prefer to translate *baoying* as "moral retribution" (though Brokaw does occasionally use the word *reciprocity*; see *The Ledgers of Merit and Demerit: Social Change and Moral Order in Late Imperial China* [Princeton, N.J.: Princeton University Press], 28). The term *retribution* carries negative nuances, suggesting that *baoying* functions more characteristically as punishment than as positive reward. In our judgment, the term *recompense* better expresses the distribution of both reward and punishment.

6. Brokaw defines this belief as "the faith that some force—either a supernatural force like heaven or the gods, or an automatic cosmic reaction—inevitably recompensed human behavior in a rational manner: it rewarded certain 'good' deeds, be they religious sacrifices, acts of good government, or upright personal conduct, and punished evil ones" (p. 28).

7. Judith Berling, "Religion and Popular Culture: The Management of Moral Capital in The Romance of The Three Teachings," in *Popular Culture in Late Imperial China,* ed. David Johnson, Andrew J. Nathan, and Evelyn S. Rawski (Berkeley: University of California Press, 1985), 188–218.

8. Ibid., 208, 218.

9. See John Coleman, "Under the Cross and the Flag: Reflections on Discipleship and Citizenship in America," in *American Catholic Social Teaching*, ed. Thomas Massaro and Thomas Shannon (Collegeville, Minn.: Liturgical Press, 2002), 128.

10. Francis Fukuyama, *Trust: The Social Virtues and the Creation of Prosperity* (New York: Free Press, 1995), 11.

11. Ibid., 325.

12. Daniel Overmyer, "God's, Saints, Shamans, and Processions: Comparative Religion from the Bottom Up," *Criterion* 34 (2002): 7.

13. Overmyer, "Gods, Saints, Shamans, and Processions," 4.

14. Madsen, *Democracy's Dharma: Religious Renaissance and Political Development in Taiwan* (Berkeley: University of California Press, 2007).

15. See the preface to Madsen, *Democracy's Dharma*, xviii.

16. See, for example, the volume *Quanqiuhua xia de shehui bianqian yu fei zhengfu zuzhi* (Social Change and NGOs in a Context of Globalization), ed. Fan Lizhu (Shanghai: Shanghai People's Press, 2003). In this volume Julia Huang describes how the Buddhist Compassion Relief Foundation in Taiwan is creating ways of religious service to civil society in a newly globalized context. See her essay, "Global Engagement and Transnational Practice," 496–515. Also see Robert P. Weller, ed., *Civil Life, Globalization, and Political Change in Asia: Organizing between Family and State* (London: Routledge, 2005).

17. See her essay "Silk Robes, Cell Phones," *Smithsonian Magazine* (January 2002): 90. Also see her book *Vietnam: Spirits of the Earth* (New York: Little, Brown, 2001). For a comparison of China with Vietnam, which has been going through similar social changes, see Frances Fitzgerald, *Vietnam: Spirits of the Earth* (New York: Little, Brown, 2001).

18. Fitzgerald, *Spirits of the Earth*, 92.

Communal Worship and Festivals in Chinese Villages

Wai Lun Tam

"Every five or ten miles, local customs are not the same."

Introduction

The Chinese word *shehui*, which is used to translate the English word for *society*, refers to a religious activity. The term is a combination of two characters: one meaning "the shrine of the earth god," and a second meaning "an assembly." In ancient China, the term *society* referred to the assembly for welcoming and parading the gods during the spring and autumn sacrifice to the deity of the soil.[1] In short, the Chinese word for *society* means "temple festival"—the temple festivals of the deity of the soil. Later it came to mean temple festivals in general. It is not accidental that the Chinese coined the word for *society* on the basis of temple festivals.

Chinese religion has long been understood in terms of the Three Teachings: Confucianism, Daoism, and Buddhism. An obvious problem of subsuming Chinese religion under the category of the Three Teachings is that only a tiny minority of the Chinese population are formal members of the Buddhist or Daoist communities, while there is even less of a "Confucian" community. In this connection, the eminent Chinese scholar Hu Shih (1891–1962) claimed that China had no native religion, just customs, and that its only real religion was an import, namely, Buddhism. A deeper implication of representing Chinese religion as the Three Teachings is that it is compatible with a Western model of religion and is readily interpreted from a Eurocentric Christian perspective and, thus, serves to perpetuate Eurocentric values. This means that priority is given to canonical texts, to a focus on doctrinal belief, to an understanding that the goal of religion is transcendence, and to an emphasis on intellectual activity such as philosophy or theology.[2] Proceeding from such a normative viewpoint will lead to a misunderstanding of non-Western traditions such as China's (see chapters 4 and 10).

In this chapter, we will explore an alternative way of studying Chinese religion. Recognizing the contextual nature of all cultural practices, including religion, we propose to examine Chinese religion in a local and rural setting. Inasmuch as 95% of the Chinese population traditionally lived in villages and, despite the rapid urbanization process, over half of the population (57%) still live in villages, it is clear that any examination of Chinese religion sensitive to its context could lead us only to the countryside. If elite traditions characterized by texts and philosophies, as represented by the Three Teachings, are not the dominant modality of Chinese religious expression and most religious behavior, an alternative way to study Chinese religion should be on-site ethnographical observation and description of religion at the grassroots level. The vast area and enormous diversity of culture in China, as well as our limited resources, however, prevent us from considering the whole of China. This chapter focuses on southeast China, especially the mountain areas of the provinces of Jiangxi, Fujian, and Guangdong, where the scale of destruction of traditions during the Cultural Revolution (1966–1976) was relatively smaller than elsewhere. The situation is significantly different in other parts of China.

An important note on the use of vocabulary when doing fieldwork on Chinese religion in Chinese villages is that *customs* is a much more useful term to use in the field than *religion*. As it is commonly known, the term *religion* in China is typically understood as referring to the five officially recognized institutional religions (Buddhism, Daoism, Islam, Catholicism, and Protestantism). Therefore, if we actually visit a Chinese village and ask about *religion*, we will never get to the real religious life of the villagers. Instead, we will be referred to a church or a monastery in the county seat. If, however, we ask the villagers about their customs, real conversation on religion and local community will begin.

As the saying goes, "So many countries, so many customs." In China, we perhaps should modify it to say, "So many villages, so many customs." In fact, there is a Chinese idiom that says, "Every five or ten miles, local customs are not the same." Sometimes it is not only customs that differ in two given villages; even their dialects are not the same. It would be an exaggeration to say that every village in China has its own customs and dialect, but it would not be difficult to find two neighboring villages that have different customs and dialects. This gives us some idea of the kind of diversity, complexity, and variety we are dealing with in Chinese villages.

Architecture, Fengshui, and the Use of Space in Chinese Villages

We will start our investigation by examining the structure and orientation of vernacular houses in southeast Chinese villages. The first thing we notice when we visit a Chinese village is the buildings. Since the Reform and Opening policy was launched in 1978, Chinese villages, especially those in the South, have been experiencing huge changes. These changes were brought about by the massive migration of the working population of the village to work in the factories in booming coastal cities such as

FIGURE 2.1 *Donglong village, Jiangxi province. (Photo Wai Lun Tam)*

Shenzhen, Guangzhou, and Xiamen. Only old people and mothers with children
are left in the village, and many of the village houses are virtually empty. In the
course of time, those working in the factories of the coastal areas send remittances
back to their villages to build new village houses of two to three stories. As a result,
three types of houses can be discerned, standing side by side, in contemporary villages in the South: traditional ancient gray brick or stone houses built before the
Communist liberation in 1949; old clay houses built during the 1960s and '70s; and
new multistoried houses built in the 1980s, '90s, and after. Our estimation, however,
is that over 60% of Chinese villages are still traditional in appearance, dominated
by mostly single-story bungalow-style houses.

   In the very appearance of a village, we see the major role played by Chinese geomancy or fengshui. Fengshui represents the Chinese concept of space (see chapter
7). It is a symbolic system for gaining and keeping control of land and water,
resources that are critical to survival and prosperity in the agricultural society of
traditional China. Manipulation of fengshui is said to bring the village prosperity
and fertility. Lineage registers, in which lineages (extended families going back several generations) record their genealogies, usually contain descriptions of the configuration of the whole village and the grave of the ancestor from a fengshui
perspective. The basic idea of Chinese geomancy, as indicated by the compound
word fengshui, is about capturing chthonic energy (energy represented by *qi* or *feng*,
literally: "wind") and water (*shui*, literally: "water"). The chthonic energy to which

fengshui pays so much attention also takes the concrete form of water needed for agriculture and male children that stand for manpower for agricultural production. Thus, fengshui expresses the most coveted goods in villages; namely, vitality and fertility.

Except for the striking differences between the traditional and the newer houses, the architecture in villages is actually quite uniform. This is due to a fengshui concern. We are constantly told that a house in a village should not stand out from the rest or it will be blamed for any misfortune anywhere in the village. A house standing out from the rest is said to look like a man carrying a heavy load of buckets with a pole. A building protruding from the rest is said to look like a tumor and symbolizes one (because like produces like; or, an effect resembles its cause). Hence the height of the individual houses in a village should be standardized. This principle of standardizing the height of houses in a village also gives us a glimpse of the Chinese value system. Priority is attached to the group, with the group being put before the individual.

The other obvious aspect of architecture in Chinese villages is the presence of large entrance gates in front of villages, big houses, and temples.

These gates are oriented to capture the chthonic energy. This is, again, related to a fengshui belief that states that the gate of a building is four thousand times more important than the building.

FIGURE 2.2 *Lineage hall gate at Qigong village, Guangdong province. (Photo Wai Lun Tam)*

The ideal geomantic condition of a village is such that it is surrounded on all sides by rising terrain. This same principle applies to a single house, a temple, a graveyard, or a village. There is no fundamental difference between secular and religious buildings (including graves and temples). A good site is one that captures most of the earth's energy currents. Houses are built around the "dragon node" where there is a concentration of energy, or an accumulation and concentration of *qi*. The first principle of Chinese fengshui is, therefore, to locate the earth energy or the *qi*. In fengshui, it is believed that the earth energy flows along the rising terrain. When a mountain opens up to flat land surrounded on all sides by such terrain, this is a first sign of a good site.

The basic configuration of a good fengshui location consists, therefore, of a group of mountains leading to a valley. In fengshui, the mountains are imagined in the form of a dragon due to undulations that resemble the rise and fall of a dragon's body. The earth energy that flows along a group of mountains is called dragon arteries or dragon veins. The last mountain of a group of mountains leading to a valley is called a back mountain because a village, house, temple, or grave will be built in front of it, thus backed by the mountain.

After locating the flow of *qi* by observing the terrain, the next step is to locate the point where the *qi* is most concentrated. In Chinese fengshui, water flowing crosswise is the means to retain advancing *qi*. It is also believed that where earth energy concentrates, the terrain will miraculously appear in the form of an armchair, that is, a central area surrounded on three sides. The belief is that most of the currents of energy flow through this area, and it is called the "dragon node," the spot where houses, temples, or graves should be built. Directly in front, there should be a large area of open flat land surrounded by small mountains on both sides; there should be another mountain in front, but far away. This flat land is also known as the "Hall of Light." The mountain on the left is usually called "Azure Dragon," and the one on the right "White Tiger." The mountain in front is called "Vermillion Bird," while the mountain at the back is called "Black Tortoise." These are the necessary and sufficient conditions for a good site with ideal geomantic conditions.

A fengshui master will sometimes summarize a basic configuration for ideal geomantic conditions by referring to the presence of the four animals: dragon, tiger, bird, and tortoise. This actually means a flat land surrounded by rising terrain. So far we have been concentrating on *qi* that is associated closely with mountain terrain. Another basic factor for a good site is water—ideally, water flowing from the back mountain along both sides of the site in a zigzag path and then flowing crosswise in front so as to stop the *qi* from flowing away. Trees are usually planted at the water exit—that is, where the water flows away from the house, temple, village, or grave. This is a device to help retain the water because, as the Chinese saying goes, "water stands for wealth." Trees are planted, and in addition a small shrine is usually found at the water exit to guide the water. When there is no water flowing crosswise, a pool may be dug as a replacement.

FIGURE 2.3 *Fengshui Geomorphology: 1. Dragon vein; 2. Back mountain; 3. Dragon's lair; 4–6. Inner, central, and outer Hall of Light; 7–8. Azure dragon (left); 9–10. White tiger (right); 11. Desk ridge; 12. Surrounding ridges; 13. Bowing front hill; 14–15. Side ridges. (Photo Wai Lun Tam)*

Once a site is chosen according to the above-mentioned principles, the final step is to choose the orientation. We were told that in considering the geomantic conditions of a site, the shape or landscape configuration accounts for 70% and the direction for 30%.

Fengshui in a village involves different rituals. Because the dragon represents the energy of the earth, once every few years a "dragon pacifying" ritual for revitalizing the chthonic energies will be performed.

Although one can also perform the dragon pacifying ritual for an individual house, it is more commonly performed at the lineage hall or a temple of a village. In some counties, dragons are paraded from the "back mountain" to their village.

Although the dragon dance today is used as a carnival performance to mark any important event, or as an urban recreational activity, the dragon dance in a village reminds us of its origin, which is closely related to the fengshui belief.

Fengshui in a village is also closely related to exorcism. After locating a good site, a geomancer often acts as a demon expeller as well, by killing a cock and sprinkling its blood on a building site. At the time of a burial and when a new house or temple is being built, a geomancer performs a ritual to "yell for the dragon," which helps to energize and consecrate a newly found site. It involves

FIGURE 2.4 *Dragon pacifying ritual. (Photo Wai Lun Tam)*

FIGURE 2.5 *Dragon dance at Liangcheng, Fujian province. (Photo Wai Lun Tam)*

burning a contract to announce the new owner of the site to the nether world. At times, geomancers will be possessed by the gods to help them locate a good feng-shui spot.

Some scholars argue that fengshui is an amoral and competitive system of prac-tices: families and lineages use it to direct energies for their own benefit, while diverting benefits away from others.[3] However, many geomancers are strong believers in the system of cosmic recompense described in chapter 1. This means that they would hesitate to find a good site for someone who does not deserve one, because punishment, in the form of misfortune, would befall the geomancer. Indeed, if his client has no moral merit, the cost for a good fengshui site would be deducted from the geomancer's moral merit.

Lineages, Ancestor Worship, and Lineage Halls

The geographical location of Chinese villages is a deliberate decision that is closely related to the fengshui concerns and local history of the villagers. As a rule, all lineages in the villages of South China trace their ancestry to immigrants from the North. Most claim to have arrived during the Song dynasty (960–1279). Each lineage has a legend describing its founding. These legends typically follow a pattern and always have to do with fengshui. The first settler of the lineage, usually a scholar official, passed by the area, sometimes during an official trip to the South; attracted by the good fengshui, he decided to settle down. Sometimes the story starts with a migrating lineage from the North. The migration is nor-mally triggered by overpopulation in the original village. The story goes on to state that the ancestor's carrying pole broke when he entered the area during his trip to look for a new place to settle. This is interpreted as a supernatural sign from an ancestor or protector deity, an indication that he should stay in that spot. In other cases, the founder of the lineage received instruction from a local deity in a dream, telling him to settle down when he passed through the area. The foundation legends of lineages arriving later than others usually tell stories of herding ducks. A lineage founder might be the servant of another already settled lineage, who, alerted by the ducks' prodigious egg production, an indication of good fengshui, built his first hut on the site where the lineage then developed. The site might also later become the ancestral hall of the lineage. In another fre-quently encountered story, the founder of the lineage arrived as an indentured servant who had been slighted by his wealthy employer. A geomancer took pity on him, telling the founder the best site on which to build his first hut, and due to this good fengshui, the lineage grew strong. The ancestral hall built for the first settler of the lineage and other ancestors is an important focus of religious culture in Chinese villages.

Each Chinese village may consist of one or more lineages. A lineage is an extended family going back several generations. The founding ancestor of a lineage, as well as the descendants of all his sons, are collectively venerated in a building called a *lineage hall*. Today, lineage halls in contemporary South China are often called "senior citizens' centers." This shift resulted from villagers' negotiation with the local government to keep their lineage hall without labeling it as a place for "feudal" or "superstitious" activity. This is a new development, of course, but the lineage hall in a Chinese village is itself a relatively recent development. In early days, during the Qin dynasty (221–206 BCE), commoners were not allowed to have their own lineage halls. When their parents died, they would venerate them in their own homes. Another option for commoners was to venerate their ancestor in a graveyard or in a Buddhist temple. Sometimes a Buddhist shrine would be built next to the graveyard and monks hired to see to the veneration of ancestors. Until the Ming dynasty (1368–1644), only high-ranking officials could build a lineage hall, for the veneration of up to four generations of their ancestors. Even today, we can find relics of flagpoles that stood in front of most lineage halls, signs indicating the success of some lineage members in the Civil Service Examination in times past. A section to record the official titles of all lineage members who held official position in the court is a must in all lineage registers. It was not until the Qing dynasty (1644–1911), however, that the building of lineage halls by commoners became a widespread phenomenon in China.

FIGURE 2.6 *Ancestors' tablet at Xicun village, Guangdong province. (Photo Wai Lun Tam)*

FIGURE 2.7 *Statues of lineage founders, Dachenggang, Guangdong province. (Photo Wai Lun Tam)*

Lineage halls may be arranged in a great variety of ways. We found lineage halls with a single tablet to represent all the ancestors and others with dozens of tablets representing individual ancestors.

Although the criteria to determine whose ancestor's tablet could be put in the lineage hall is solely a financial one in contemporary times, we were told that in the past the social status and contribution to the lineage of one's ancestor had to be taken into consideration. At times, an image of a god may be found in the lineage hall, violating a general principle that the lineage hall is a place to venerate ancestors, not to worship deities. Closer examination reveals that these images belong to ancestors who became immortalized as gods. Ancestors who became gods were frequently former Daoist masters, knowledgeable in Daoist magic and able to fight against evil forces even before they died. In one lineage in northern Guangdong, however, we found an image of the first settler of the lineage being venerated in the lineage hall together with the tablets of other ancestors.

The image of an ancestor is sometimes replaced by a portrait. In both Guangdong and Fujian, we found cases of ancestors represented by a portrait, rather than by wooden tablets. In individual homes, gods are usually represented by a list of names on red paper, in front of which a tablet is put for the ancestor. The list of gods might contain anywhere from seven to twenty-one names. In some cases, the gods worshipped at home are not represented by written lists, but by actual images worshipped together with the ancestor's tablet.[4]

Lineage halls are used for the purpose of "red" and "white" life cycle rituals in the village. "Red" rituals refer to weddings, celebrations for old people's birthdays (usually over sixty) and the birth of a baby. The focus of these celebrations is a communal meal at the lineage hall. A "white" ritual is a funeral. A funeral ritual in a village lasts for two to three days, when priests are invited to perform the rituals.

On the first day, relatives will pay a visit to offer condolences. A big, satisfying meal for all is usually served in the lineage hall.

Ancestors are venerated during the last day and first day of the lunar year, when family members will bring offerings and burn incense in the lineage hall. Communal sacrifice to the ancestors takes place in the autumn and in the spring. Autumn veneration is usually performed on the Double Nine festival (the ninth day of the ninth lunar month) and spring veneration on the Qingming festival (literally, Clear and Bright Festival, a traditional Chinese festival on the one-hundred-fourth day after the winter solstice, or the fifteenth day from the spring equinox, which usually occurs in April). These are days when all the lineage members gather at the lineage hall to perform group veneration of their ancestor. Members who work far from the village return on these special days. For a large lineage, members from the same lineage branch will arrive together, accompanied by a hired lion dance troupe.

FIGURE 2.8 *Funeral in a lineage hall, Taining Fujian province. (Photo Wai Lun Tam)*

FIGURE 2.9 *Lion dance troupe in a lineage hall, Taining, Fujian province. (Photo Wai Lun Tam)*

Counting the number of lion troupes can, therefore, give us a rough idea of the number of branches in the lineage, again indicating the size of the lineage. The ancestor veneration in the lineage hall will usually take place in the morning. It consists of offering incense, food, and wine to the ancestors and a reading of a memorial to the ancestors by an elder member of the lineage. The ritual will be followed by a visit, known as "tomb sweeping," to the graveyards of the ancestors. The whole lineage will first visit the grave of the first settler and then break into groups according to lineage branches. The grave of the immediate ancestors will be visited last.

Gods, Ancestors, and Ghosts

As Mao Zedong (1893–1976) observed, both the lineage and the worshipping of gods were two basic constituents of traditional Chinese society.[5] The former was informed by Confucian ideology. The latter was constructed from the cultural resources of both Buddhism and Daoism. Scholars such as Francis L. K. Hsü (1909–1999) thought that lineages constituted the essential social fabric of China. Hsü is right to speak of life in South China as lived "under the ancestors' shadow."[6]

Lagerwey, however, claims that the ancestors, in turn, lived "in the shadow of the gods" who represented a public dimension of life that circumscribed and transcended the private life of the lineage.[7]

When we come to the religion of the village, local gods dominate the scene. Based on field observation, Lagerwey classifies village gods in South China hierarchically in three groups: (1) those with neither open-air altar nor temple; (2) those with an open-air altar; and (3) those with a temple.

The first type, which are sometimes called "Uncle King," are the spirits of rocks, fields, trees, or bridges. Sons and daughters with bad health are sometimes contracted out in adoption to tree or stone gods. Some may even be given names that include the character for "trees" or "stones," or other associated characters.

Elsewhere, sons and daughters are contracted out to Guanyin (Avalokitesvara) or other local deities. Parents of such adoptive children usually have to worship the divine foster parent annually, along with the child, and "ransom" the child when he or she reaches the age of sixteen. Local ritual specialists will be hired for this job.

Gods with open-air altars are usually called "Duke-King," or "Big King." Very often they are the protectors of a village, with their altar situated at and guarding the place where the river flows out of the village. At the start of the New Year, villagers pray there for good fortune. In the winter solstice, they thank the god, usually by performing a great communal sacrifice.

FIGURE 2.10 *Child Sale Contract with a Tree, Yangshan, Guangdong province. (Photo Wai Lun Tam)*

There is great variety with regard to the deities in a temple. Gods enshrined in a temple are, generally speaking, higher level gods, but such a temple could also be a small shrine for the earth god, or a temple for a single local deity. In most temples, gods are represented by images, but they can also be represented by a written tablet, or in some cases by a piece of red paper containing a list of the gods' names. Sometimes, only an incense burner and offering cups are found in the ruins of temples destroyed during the Cultural Revolution. At the other extreme, there can be as many as sixteen or more deities on the altar of a temple. In Jiangxi, there are temples where only the head of a god or his masks are worshipped; these depict generals who were beheaded. Masks of the gods will be worn for a ritual dance at the start of the year.

There are two main categories of temples: (1) altars and temples, and (2) monasteries and cloisters. The first category consists of three types: altars for local gods; temples for more widely known and higher-ranking gods, such as the city god, the renowned Empress of Heaven (Tianhou), and Lord Guan; and shrines for historical worthies and meritorious officials that reflect the Confucian ideology of righteousness and state loyalty. The temples of higher level gods are likely to be found in townships rather than villages. The second category refers to Daoist cloisters and Buddhist monasteries. They are frequently established in the surrounding hills and are normally occupied by monks, nuns, or lay female religious specialists known as "vegetarian mothers." They perform both village funerals and the communal ritual sacrifices.

This account of village gods would be incomplete without a mention of their opposite, the ghosts or demons. If gods occupy different vital points in the villages, ghosts, their opposite, are not tied to a single spot, but wander and make surprise appearances in solitary places. By definition, ghosts are the spirits of those who are not venerated as ancestors. Either they do not have any offspring to venerate them or, because they died violently, custom forbids their descendants from giving them offerings. One of the main purposes of the communal sacrifice is precisely to subdue the wandering ghosts of the area. A sacrifice is offered first, followed by an exorcism to drive away any uncooperative ghosts. The Ghost Festival, on the fifteenth night of the seventh lunar month, is the day when ghosts come out from the lower realm. Every family will prepare ritualistic food offerings and burn incense, joss paper, and papier-mâché imitations of items such as clothes, gold, and other fine goods to be burned for the ghosts on that day.

Rituals, Festivals, and Priests

The first and fifteenth day of each month and the last and first days of each lunar year are traditional dates for worshipping gods. Apart from these dates, one will find few visitors to most village temples. An exception is the birthday of the principal deity of a temple, when the temple is jam-packed with worshippers. Other important dates are the final day of the renovation of a temple and the day to redeem a communal vow pledged before the gods.

After praying to the gods by burning incense, worshippers typically draw divination sticks to learn their fate (see chapter 1). The number of divination sticks varies from 12, 28, 36, 50, or 100, but the most common number is 100. The divination sticks are put in a canister that is shaken backward and forward until one strip rises above the others and falls to the ground. It is believed that when one shakes the canister, the deity of the temple comes forward to pick the strip for the worshipper. In some temples, mostly found in Taiwan, a big canister holding long strips is used.

Instead of shaking the canister, one goes forward and picks up the strip randomly without looking at the number marked on it. Each strip carries a number that corresponds to an answer that is printed on a piece of paper, or sometimes printed on cloth, or carved on a block and hung on the temple wall. The answers are framed as poetry and are usually classified according to category: family, health, fate, wealth, fame, marriage, offspring, livestock matters, and so on. One should finish one's divination by putting some money into the donation box of the temple. A diviner is usually needed to give an interpretation of the obscure meaning of the poem; in this case, he also receives a small reward. A study of a system of 100 divination sticks has shown that there are 13 good, 69 medium, and only 18 bad divination results; 60 sticks exhort one to go the right way and to do good.[8]

FIGURE 2.11 *Canister holding divination sticks. (Photo Wai Lun Tam)*

Divination blocks are used to check that the divination slip that has come out is the correct one. If it is not, the shaking process or the picking is repeated. Divination blocks are moon-shaped pieces of wood that are used to communicate with the gods. They are held at chest level usually from a kneeling position and dropped to the ground. One side of the block is convex and the other is flat. When they both land flat side up, one must ask again. When the blocks both land flat side down, the answer is no. When they are one up and one down, the answer is yes.

As mentioned earlier, it is common for a village or a group of villages to pray for good fortune, to make a pledge before their gods for a wish of prosperity and health at the start of a New Year. In the winter solstice, they thank the god, usually by performing a great communal sacrifice. Depending on the economy of a village, the service will last from two to seven days (see chapter 4). A three- to five-day event is most common when local ritual specialists are invited to perform the communal sacrifice. An organizing committee takes care of the whole event, including raising funds to build a temporary shed for the event and to hire the ritual specialists. The organizing committee also acts as a representative of the whole village, and its members take turns participating in every session of the whole ritual. For the rest of the villagers, a female member of each family will come with a basket of offerings for the individual worship of the gods on the main day of the event, usually coinciding with the birthday of the god.

FIGURE 2.12 *Deity on parade during festival, Donglong, Jiangxi province. (Photo Wai Lun Tam)*

A parade of some kind is usually organized during a communal sacrifice, during which the statue of the god is taken on a tour through his domain.

The route of the procession always coincides with the boundaries of the village's territory. Thus, the procession of the gods also serves to mark off the village's territory and, at the same time, has the function of demonstrating and reinforcing the economic and social power of its community. Like military exercises in modern countries, it shows neighbors the power of both the gods and the people (represented by the youths carrying the gods). The festival procession at once unifies the group and acts as the focus of local identity.[9]

The more complex rituals are conducted by priests, who are hired by villagers to perform their services. Most of them are part-time workers, agricultural laborers during the peak farming season and ritual specialists during the slack season. Scholars usually call them Daoist priests, although they often do not identify themselves as such.

Many priests in South China belong to the Lüshan tradition. This tradition can be easily identified, as the ritual specialist has to cross-dress as a woman when performing ritual. This is because the founders of the tradition were three ladies whose surnames were Chen, Lin, and Li. The ritual implements they use consist of horns and ritual knives.

FIGURE 2.13 *Lüshan Daoist priest in Gutian, Fujian province. (Photo Wai Lun Tam)*

FIGURE 2.14 *Buddhist priest, Huanghua, Guangdong province. (Photo Wai Lun Tam)*

In other cases, the Daoist and Buddhist gods are represented together by writings on a tablet.

A closer examination shows that many of them actually have a clear Buddhist identity, demonstrated by the setting of their ritual altar and their clothing during performance of a communal sacrifice ritual in the village.

A reading of their ritual memorials submitted to the god also shows their self-identity as Buddhist ritual specialists. Some of them have two identities, both Buddhist and Daoist. These Buddho-Daoist ritual specialists will change identity according to the ritual they perform. Indeed, Daoist rituals are seen as most effective for exorcising ghosts, whereas Buddhist rites are more concerned with the universal deliverance of souls.

Conclusion

There are two main aspects of village religion in China: seasonal sacrifice to ancestors in the lineage hall and religious festivals in the territorial temples. The former represents a "private" dimension of village life associated with family and lineage,

FIGURE 2.15 *"Hot and noisy" crowds at a festival, Lianzhou, Guangdong province. (Photo Wai Lun Tam)*

whereas the latter represents a "public" dimension that circumscribes and transcends family and lineage.

The overall rhythms of traditional Chinese life are marked by customs that divide the year into "ordinary time" and "festival time." Festival time is a time to relax and is filled with a carnival spirit, or in Chinese, a "hot and noisy" experience.

This applies to both lineage activities and communal temple rituals. These are important cultural resources of indigenous traditions that witness to the creativity, vitality, and diversity of the Chinese culture. They not only represent a precious heritage of intangible culture but are also an important cultural resource to resolve problems brought on by modernization and globalization. As Lagerwey once said,

> If I had to single out our one most important discovery, it would be the virtually infinite variety of local culture, even from one village to the next, let alone from one region to the next.... It is the cultural richness of these expressions of popular creativity that is, for me, the defining feature of these societies, especially when compared with the increasingly homogenized, not to say tasteless culture produced by the globalizing economy.[10]

Notes

This chapter is a partial result of the research project "Religion and Society in Southeast China" (RG008-P-05) supported by a grant from the Chiang Ching-kuo Foundation for International Scholarly Exchange 2006–2009. The author would also like to express his gratitude to Ms. Barbara Bayne of Ontario, Canada for her helpful suggestions on style.

1. *Hanyu da cidian* (The Dictionary of Chinese) (Shanghai: Xinhua Shudian, 1991), 7:833, s.v. "She."

2. Jordan Paper, "Religious Studies: Time to Move from a Eurocentric Bias?" in *Religious Studies: Issues, Prospects and Proposals*, ed. Klaus K. Klostermaier and Larry W. Hurtado (Atlanta, Ga.: Scholars Press, 1991), 76–77. See also his *The Spirits Are Drunk: Comparative Approaches to Chinese Religion* (Albany: State University of New York, 1995), 7.

3. Ole Bruun, *Fengshui in China: Geomantic Divination between State Orthodoxy and Popular Religion* (Copenhagen: NIAS Press, 2003), 132, 175.

4. See, for instance, David K. Jordan, *Gods, Ghosts, and Ancestors: The Folk Religion of a Taiwanese Village* (Berkeley: University of California Press, 1972).

5. Mao Zedong, *Mao zedong xuanji* (Collected Works of Mao Zedong) (Hong Kong: Sanlian shudian, 1968), 31.

6. Francis L. K. Hsü, *Under the Ancestors' Shadow: Kinship, Personality and Social Mobility in China* (Stanford, Calif.: Stanford University Press, 1948, 1967).

7. John Lagerwey, "The Structure and Dynamics of Chinese Rural Society," in *History and Socio-economy: Proceedings of International Conference on Hakkaology*, ed. Cheng-Kuang Hsu (Taipei: Institute of Ethnology, Academia Sinica, 2000), 4–5.

8. See Wu Lizhen, *Xianggang Huang daxian xinyang* (The Faith of the Immortal Wong Tai Sin in Hong Kong) (Hong Kong: Sanlian shudian, 1997).

9. See John Brim, "Village Alliance Temples in Hong Kong" in *Religion and Ritual in Chinese Society*, ed. Arthur Wolf (Stanford: Stanford University Press, 1974), 93–103.

10. John Lagerwey's concluding remarks in a two-volume collection of essays published in his Traditional Hakka Society Series, vols. 1 to 10. See John Lagerwey, *Kejia chuantong shehui* (Beijing: Zhonghua shuju, 2005), Part II: *Lineage Society and Its Customs,* "Introduction," 518–520.

The Religious Life of Ethnic Minority Communities

Philip L. Wickeri and Yik-fai Tam

The best-selling Chinese novel *Wolf Totem* is set against the background of a student's experience of life among the Mongol people during the Cultural Revolution era (1966–1976). Drawing on his own experiences as a youth sent down to be "re-educated" in the grasslands of Inner Mongolia, Jiang Rong writes about the Mongols, their nomadic freedom, their attachment to nature, and their spirituality.[1] The wolf totem is an object to be both feared and revered, a symbol of nomadic freedom, but also a challenge to the supposed "sheepishness" of the Han majority. The novel reflects a romanticism about the culture of the Mongol people, and has provoked a variety of responses in China and overseas. Is it a call to Chinese nationalism or a celebration of the freedom of an ethnic minority? Does it proclaim an ethnocentric ideology or is it a wake up call to China's looming environmental problem? Beyond all the controversial interpretations, *Wolf Totem* tells an engaging story about the encounter between the Han Chinese and the culture and religion of the Mongol people, one of China's fifty-five recognized ethnic minorities.[2]

China's minorities have been much in the news in recent years. Television images of robed Tibetan monks demonstrating on the streets of Lhasa and protestors from the predominantly Muslim Uyghur minority in China's far west have focused world attention on ethnic religious communities in China. Such stories reflect the potentially explosive aspects of the encounters between Han Chinese and minority religious communities, a subject that is discussed elsewhere in this book in terms of the challenges they pose for political authority. But the religious life of ethnic minorities in China is a subject that is both deeper and more extensive: Naxi people in southwest China performing age-old shamanistic rituals; growing numbers of Muslims coming to terms with Islamic life in a globalized world; Lisu and Miao Christians worshipping in newly established Protestant and Catholic churches in the mountains of Yunnan; Tibetan Buddhists maintaining their temples and continuing traditional religious practices despite decades of repression. To gain perspective on these headline-grabbing events, we need to consider more carefully the religious practices and beliefs of China's diverse minorities.

The overwhelming majority of China's population of just over 1.3 billion is Han Chinese, and they are the focus of most of the chapters in this volume except this one. This chapter surveys the variety of religious traditions, communities, and practices among the minority ethnicities of China. We will move from coastal and inland China to the periphery, the borders and mountainous areas where most ethnic minority groups live. In the previous chapter, the Chinese idiom "Every five or ten miles, local customs are not the same" was introduced to emphasize the diversity of religious practices in rural villages. If this is the case with majority Chinese religious communities, it is even more so for ethnic minorities in China and their religious practices. From far western Xinjiang Autonomous Region to the island of Taiwan, and from the Siberian border in the northeast to the mountains of the southwest, minority communities in China have been shaped by their religious traditions, some of which date back many millennia. These traditions include a wide array of inherited and acquired religious practices, including indigenous religious beliefs and various expressions of shamanism, as well as different forms of Buddhism, Daoism, Islam, and Christianity. Some of the religious traditions are unique to the minority groups, while others are contextualized adaptations of majority Han religious practices. As is the case with all Chinese religious communities, the minority religions have experienced a revival over the last three decades.

Minority groups in mainland China are found mostly in the border regions on China's periphery, in sparsely populated provinces and autonomous regions that constitute more than 50% of China's landmass. These areas are today marked by boundaries separating different countries, but national boundaries are of recent origin, and they have been porous and fluid even in modern times. For some ethnic groups, attachment to the land has both religious and political significance. Minority peoples in the southwest are related to ethnic groups in Burma (Myanmar), Thailand, Laos, and Vietnam, and there continues to be much traffic and exchange back and forth. The same is true of the Islamic minorities in the far west who are related to their counterparts in the countries of Central Asia and beyond. Cultural Tibet once included a large part of the Qinghai-Tibetan plateau, and not just the present day Tibet Autonomous Region—as well as parts of the Himalayan regions of Kashmir, Nepal, Bhutan, and northeast India. In northeast China, Koreans and Mongols are related to peoples across their borders that now live in separate countries. As we shall see, the transnational nature of ethnic minorities has deep significance for the people themselves as well as for the Chinese government.

The government of the People's Republic of China recognizes fifty-six ethnicities in China, the majority Han Chinese and fifty-five national ethnic minorities. According to the 2000 census, ethnic minorities numbered about 106 million people, or almost 9% of the Chinese population. The real picture is a great deal more complex, for the self-perception of minority ethnic groups is often at odds with their official classification. For example, there are many subdivisions or branches of minority groups, with their own languages and cultures that could easily be regarded as separate ethnicities in their own right. There are also "unrecognized minorities" (including the Jews and the Sherpas), several hundred of which have applied for official recognition; and almost 800,000 individuals who are listed as "unclassified."[3]

The very conceptualization of what it means to be an ethnic group or a "minority nationality" is a contested category of understanding. Scholars emphasize the social and historical construction of ethnic identities, and warn against the "exotic representation" of minority groups in China. Ongoing debates about the "essential-izing of ethnicity" are now common in academic conferences in the West. The idea of the "Han people" has had different meanings at various periods in history, and some studies question whether Han people themselves can be regarded as an undif-ferentiated ethnicity. Chinese have historically viewed all minority communities as "the other," culturally and religiously. This means that in many different ways, minorities have been oppressed and subject to prejudice and discrimination, despite legal safeguards and government-sponsored affirmative action programs. Some scholars have advanced alternative understandings of cultural ethnicity in China. There is clearly a more complex and nuanced view of the minority situation in China than what is implied in the existing identification of fifty-five minority ethnic groups.

While recognizing this complexity, our chapter focuses on the religious practices and beliefs of some of the officially recognized minority groups, about which there is a scholarly consensus. After an overview of the Chinese context and the diversity of minority religious practices, we consider the religions of a few groups in greater detail.

Minority Religious Communities in the Chinese Context

Ethnic religious communities in the People's Republic of China face situations that are in many ways similar to minorities in other countries. (In China, ethnic commu-nities are not designated as "indigenous" peoples in the sense that that term is used elsewhere.) They negotiate issues of identity and assimilation with the majority (Han) culture; they face challenges in maintaining religious beliefs and practices in a world of modernization and economic development; they live out and express religious and ethnic identities that are both contextual and transnational at the same time. Minorities in China respond to these challenges in a variety of ways, even within the same ethnic group. There is a continuum between what might be termed a "pure" religious or ethnic expression (if this were possible) and total social integration and assimilation (if that were possible), with a great many mediating positions. All of these have a political dimension that must be considered in any discussion of religion in China.

Throughout the twentieth century, the Chinese government had one overriding interest in dealing with questions of ethnicity: maintaining a unified China. Given the history of religiously inspired ethnic rebellions and the complex international politics of Chinese border regions, the government's preoccupation with national unity is not difficult to understand. Chinese Communists inherited policies aimed at establishing a unified, multiethnic country from the government of the Republican era (1911–1949), but these became much more strictly enforced in the People's Republic of China. In the 1950s the new regime consolidated its power in ways that involved the unification of minority areas and the assertion of government control over every aspect of popular religious life. This intensified in the Cultural Revolution era (1966–1976) when all religious practices were suppressed. Mosques, temples, and churches were closed; monks, nuns, and priests were secularized or, in some places, forced to take spouses; religious leaders were paraded through the streets and humiliated, imprisoned, or even executed. This period came to an end in the late 1970s with the accession of Deng Xiaoping as paramount leader. The Reform and Opening era initiated an unprecedented period of religious tolerance and ethnic autonomy, which has in turn made possible the revival of minority religious communities.

Over the past thirty years, there has been a renewal of the public expression of religious belief and practice all over China. The government policy of "ethnic autonomy" for minority areas has been restored and developed further, and this has had a positive impact on cultural and religious life, despite continuing ethnic tensions. There are today 5 autonomous regions, almost 100 autonomous counties, and hundreds of autonomous villages and townships. The administration of these areas has afforded a measure of tolerance for religious belief and practices. China has changed a great deal since the late 1970s, but there are still strict limits to the full exercise of religious freedom. Religion is not allowed to interfere with politics or education; political control is maintained through official religious organizations and designated leaders who are acceptable to the government; and all activities that might promote "splittism" or political independence, especially among the Islamic minorities and Tibetan Buddhists, are closely monitored. In the case of minority religious communities, religion and politics are not easily separated.

At the same time, more open policies have made possible the growth and revival of religion. This has been assisted by permissive government attitudes to minority cultural and religious life. Ethnic minorities enjoy certain privileges. In contrast to the Han majority, minority families are allowed to have more than one child, for example, and minorities are given preferential treatment on the university entrance exams. China's concern for improved international relations with Islamic countries that supply oil and other natural resources that are essential for economic development, as well as an interest in promoting international tourism, have also shaped more tolerant policies. In addition, minority religious communities have benefited from increased attention to the academic study of religion in institutions such as the Central Nationalities University in Beijing and regional universities and centers for social scientific research.

Rapid economic development and the integration of China into the global market challenge minority religious communities in different ways. In some cases, religion may help to foster economic modernization. Korean Chinese are the wealthiest and best-educated ethnic group in the country, in part due to the interest that South Korean Christians have had in investment and economic development in northeast China. Religion has also helped to preserve tradition and inhibit economic progress, particularly in the case of some indigenous traditions. There are important regional variations in terms of intra-ethnic relations and government policy. The loosening of central control has resulted in greater religious pluralism as well as increasing contact with transnational religious communities, whether Buddhist, Islamic, or Christian. This has led to political tension and sometimes conflict between minority religious groups and the government. It has also created new opportunities for dialogue among religious communities, both nationally and internationally.

The Diversity of Religious Practices

The religious map of Chinese ethnic minorities is extremely complicated. Most of the ethnic minorities at one time had their own indigenous religious traditions. Although those traditions have survived only to a limited extent, religious and cultural practices in minority communities continue to reflect indigenous beliefs and traditions. A great many ethnic groups converted to different forms of Buddhism and Islam centuries ago, whereas others have converted to Protestant or Catholic Christianity more recently. Some minority religions are locally adapted forms of majority (Han) religious practices, but others are distinctive expressions of a given culture or ethnic group. Some minority nationalities collectively belong to a single religion, whereas others reveal more diverse religious affiliations that vary from place to place.

Various forms of shamanism and indigenous religious practices continue in a number of minority groups. The best known among these is the *dongba* religion among the Naxi in Yunnan, which is discussed in the case study that follows. Shamanism, as depicted in the novel *Wolf Totem*, is also practiced by the Mongols. Other ethnic minorities, including the Oroqen, Ewenki, and Daur, practice different forms of animism and shamanism. Even when minorities have converted to other religions, one can continue to see elements of indigenous religious beliefs in their new beliefs and practices.

Daoism is regarded as the only indigenous tradition among the five "world religions" (Daoism, Buddhism, Islam, Catholicism, and Protestantism) with formally recognized religious organizations in China. Among Chinese minorities, Daoism is particularly prominent among the Zhuang, the largest of the fifty-five ethnic minorities. Its population of more than seventeen million lives in the Guangxi Autonomous Region and neighboring provinces. Although shamanistic and animistic practices are not uncommon, their dominant religion is Daoism. Historical records show that Daoism and its related practices have been popular in the Guangxi region since the fifth and sixth centuries. Daoism is also prominent among the Yao people. It is also practiced by the Maonan people (in Guangxi), and to a lesser extent among other minorities in the southwest. Many of these Daoist ethnic groups are also widely dispersed in the hills and mountains of Vietnam, Laos, Thailand, and Burma (Myanmar).

Buddhism was introduced into Tibet in the early centuries of the Common Era, and after successive times of decline and revival, was firmly established by the eleventh century. Buddhism in Tibet was influenced by the indigenous Bön religion, but it was given formal religious, philosophical, and institutional expression by locally adapted Indian Buddhism. The overwhelming majority of Tibetans in China today (about 5.4 million) practice Tibetan Buddhism, and it would be impossible to separate Tibetan culture from the religious life of the people. Today, Tibetans live in the Tibet autonomous regions as well as in Qinghai, Sichuan and other areas. Historically, Tibetan Buddhism has also been especially important in Mongolia, where it incorporated elements of indigenous shamanism. To a limited extent, it is also found among the Yugur, the Tujia, and the Manchus.

The region known as the Tibet Autonomous Region was formally incorporated into the People's Republic of China in 1950. After a failed uprising against Chinese rule in 1959, the Dalai Lama, Tenzin Gyatso, who was the political and religious leader of the Tibetans, fled to India with a large group of followers. There they established a government in exile that has become a center of Tibetan religion and culture, as well as a focal point of opposition to Chinese rule. The Chinese government has continually criticized the Dalai Lama and Tibetans in exile for engaging in political activities aimed at promoting Tibetan independence. The Dalai Lama enjoys enormous international prestige, especially after he received the Nobel Peace Prize in 1989. Besides this community in Dharamsala, Tibetan Buddhists are also found in Nepal, Europe, North America, and other parts of Asia.

Mahayana Buddhism is practiced among a number of southwestern minorities including the Zhuang, the Dai and the Bai people, who have contact with Han Chinese Buddhism. The Dai are predominantly Theravada Buddhist, and the Hani, Wa (or Va) and other minorities also have Theravada communities, and maintain communication with Buddhist centers in southeast Asia. Buddhism has almost disappeared among the Koreans in the northeast, who have become Protestant (and to a lesser extent Catholic) Christians in the course of the last century.

Muslim traders went to what is now northwest China within a few decades after the death of the prophet Muhammad in 632. By the time of the Tang dynasty (618–907), mosques could be found in the capital of Chang'an (Xi'an) and in many other cities and trading towns along the Silk Road. Today, there are Muslims in every Chinese city. They maintain mosques and run their own restaurants and other businesses. Muslims are most numerous in western China and particularly in the Xinjiang Uyghur Autonomous Region. Ten ethnic minorities are predominantly Muslim: the Hui, Uyghur, Kazakh, Kyrgyz, Tajik, Uzbeks, Tatars, Salar, Dongxiang, and Bonan. The Hui, who have been well integrated within China for many centuries, are the largest Muslim ethnicity (almost ten million people), followed closely by the Uyghur (8.4 million). Estimates vary, but scholars agree that there are at least twenty to thirty million Muslims in China (more than 2% of the population), almost all of whom are from the above-mentioned ten minority nationalities.

There is an enormous ethnic, linguistic, and religious diversity among and often within Muslim ethnic groups in China. Most Muslim groups speak Turkic languages, but most Hui are Chinese speaking, and the Tajik are in the Persian language family. Many Chinese Muslims read and speak Arabic or Turkish. Most are Sunni, including those belonging to the different Sufi orders, but there are different forms of Shiite and Wahhabi traditions within the ten minority nationalities as well. China now has the largest Muslim community in East Asia, and its Muslim population surpasses that of Saudi Arabia.

Oriental Orthodox Christian traders, missionaries, and priests (from the East Syrian Church of the East) came to China in the Tang dynasty, from the seventh to tenth centuries. Like Muslims, Manicheans, and Jews, they traveled the Silk Road and established churches and Christian communities. At different times in China's history, many Mongolians and Turkic-speaking peoples were predominantly Christian. A Russian Orthodox mission was established in China in the seventeenth century, and there are still small Orthodox Christian communities in the Chinese Russian minority. Catholic missionaries worked among minorities in Tibet, Yunnan, and Sichuan beginning in the seventeenth century, and there are still churches among Tibetans that date from that time.

Protestant and Catholic missionaries worked in minority ethnic communities all over China in the nineteenth and twentieth centuries. Today, there is a strong Christian presence among minority groups in northeast and southwest China, and among the aboriginal groups in Taiwan. The majority of the Miao and Lisu are Christians, and there are significant Protestant and Catholic minorities in other ethnic groups. In the last twenty years, small Protestant communities have been started among most of the national minorities by evangelists from China and missionaries from overseas.

Buddhist, Muslim, and Christian communities in China are shaped by their cultural contexts as well as by transnational religious movements. At the mosque in Lhasa, Hui Muslims chat with each other in Tibetan, not in Chinese. In Yunnan, recently converted Tibetan Protestants were evangelized by the Lisu, and still worship and read the Bible in that language. Muslims from the People's Republic of China have been going to Mecca on the Hajj since 1984. There are also regular travelers who go from Dharamsala to Lhasa and back, along the borders between China and Southeast Asia, and who do missionary work among South Koreans along the border between China and North Korea. All of this has implications for

BOX 3.1 Korean Missionaries in China

Korean Christian missionary work began in northeast China and in Shandong in the first part of the twentieth century. In the late 1970s, Korean Protestant churches began sending missionaries all over the world. In the process, South Korea became the most important Protestant missionary-sending country after the United States. Foreign missionary work is illegal in China, but South Koreans have been particularly interested in proselytizing among the Han Chinese and the ethnic minorities. Going to China as language students, teachers, businessmen, and doctors, Koreans began working in the northeast, but they soon moved to Beijing, Shanghai, and cities on the east coast. Their numbers grew, and an estimated 5,000 Koreans are working as "underground missionaries" in China. Today, Korean missionaries can be found in virtually every city in China, evangelizing Tibetans in Lhasa, Uyghurs in Urumchi, and Koreans along the North Korean border. Some Chinese Christians are critical of these efforts, and even some church leaders in South Korea have begun to question how effective such missionary work has been.

the appropriation of minority religious belief, movements of ethnic solidarity, and the political impact of religion on China as a whole.

We now turn to a consideration of religious belief and practice in four different minority communities. These do not exhaust the wide range and different modalities of religious expression, but they do illustrate the enormous religious diversity within ethnic minority communities in China.

Dongba among the Naxi People

The Naxi people (310,000 in all) are found primarily in northwestern Yunnan and southeastern Sichuan. They speak a Sino-Tibetan language, and their religion is known as Dongba, which is basically a type of shamanism that has been influenced by Tibetan Bön religion, Buddhism, and Daoism. *Dongba* refers to the title of their priests, and literally means "wise man." The Dongba are the priests of various rituals and interpreters of the holy text, which is also known as *Dongba*. The ancestral founder of the Dongba religion was a Tibetan shaman who probably lived in the eastern part of Tibet around the twelfth century. According to Dongba tradition, he was known as Dingba Shilo.

The indigenous religious culture of the Naxi is similar in many respects to that of the Han described in chapter 2. The main difference is that the priests, instead of practicing Buddhist or Daoist liturgies like their Tibetan and Han neighbors, have their own Dongba ritual tradition, and ritual texts composed in a unique hieroglyphic script. Naxi people believe that there are spirits in natural phenomena and objects. The Dongba priests act as mediators between the spirits and humankind. In different Dongba rituals, the priests communicate with spirits found in natural

FIGURE 3.1 *Dongba shaman. (Hui Yan/FOTOE)*

phenomena as well as with ghosts. They are also exorcists and ritual performers for curing illnesses and seeking spiritual blessings in the community and in personal life.

The Naxi believe that the *Baidi* (White Land) in northwestern Yunnan province is their holy land. They have a saying, "Unless one goes to Baidi, one is not a real Dongba." Zhongdian County, the Tibetan autonomous county in which Baidi is located, was renamed Shangri-La County in 2001, largely to encourage its potential as a tourist destination.

Dongba is not a highly institutionalized religion. Priests perform their religious roles and functions as individuals or in small groups. They do not form a hierarchical order, and they pass on their religious roles and knowledge through family tradition. Sons learn their knowledge and practices from their fathers and pass these on to their descendents. There are temples scattered among different settlements and villages, which do not form any structural relationship with each other.

Naxi religion and culture are protected by the Chinese government, and the Naxi community in Lijiang, Yunnan, is a popular tourist attraction. Their unique writing system records Naxi religious beliefs and cultural practices. It resembles hieroglyphic scripts of earlier cultures and is the only such pictographic script still in use in the world today.

Tibetan Buddhism

Known as "the roof of the world," the Tibetan plateau is a difficult place in which to live. Despite the harsh conditions, Tibetans are proud of their cultural heritage and traditional lifestyle. Most of them live in widely scattered settlements. Lhasa, the capital of the Tibet Autonomous Region, was actually a city of only two main roads just a few decades ago. It is now a crowded urban area with a booming economy. The relationship between Han Chinese and the Tibetan people has not improved because of the economic development and the modernization, however. Although Tibetan people have benefited from the developing economy, the concern about losing their cultural and religious identity, especially among a new generation of Tibetans, is evident, even to the casual observer.

Tibetan Buddhism is a religious tradition practiced by the Tibetans, the Mongolians, and other neighboring peoples such as the Bhutanese. It is a complex tradition that has been influenced by Indian Tantric practices and Mahayana Buddhism, as well as beliefs and practices of the indigenous Bön religion. The current practice of Tibetan Buddhism is actually a combination of elements from various traditions.

According to the Tibetan tradition, two princesses (one from Nepal and the other from China) were married to the Tibetan ruler and brought different Buddhist schools and practices to Tibet in the first centuries of the Common Era. Yet, the Buddhist influences were mainly confined to the imperial court. Monasteries were built and translations of sutras from India and China began, but the majority of the Tibetan people did not know about this religion. Royal patronage of Buddhism was stopped with the accession to the throne of a new ruler who favored the native Bön religion. The second wave of introduction occurred in the tenth century and successfully penetrated into the cultural structures of the Tibetan people. It was in the thirteenth century that the leader of the Gelugpa school, who had converted the Mongolian khan (ruler), received from him the honorific title of Dalai Lama. Literally, the title *Dalai Lama* means "religious teacher whose wisdom is as deep and vast as the ocean." Gradually, he became both the religious and political leader of the Tibetan people.

Tibetan Buddhism forms a significant part of the Vajrayana Buddhist tradition. It is also known as Tantric or Esoteric Buddhism or the Diamond Vehicle. It is known as Esoteric Buddhism because it considers that the ultimate Truth of the Dharma is not communicable through language or in public. It can be passed on between masters and disciples only through different ritual activities, such as the fire ritual, and gestures, such as hand signs. The Sanskrit term *Vajra* literally means "thunderbolt" (a legendary weapon used by Buddhist deities) or "diamond." It is used to describe the utmost effectiveness of this form of Buddhism in destroying any obstacles to achieving final enlightenment. Vajrayana Buddhists believe that the dharma is communicated to humankind in two ways: the historical way and the Tantric way. The historical way refers to the Buddhist teachings that rely on studying the doctrines and ideas of sutras.

The Tantric way refers to the yogic and tantric practices that culturally originated in Hinduism. It is believed that there exist certain forms of spiritual energies within the human body. Tantric ritual practices are learned and used to meditate on these energies in order to speed up the process of enlightenment. These were also influenced by the native Tibetan Bön religion. There are three typical kinds of religious practices in this esoteric Buddhist tradition: mudra, mantra, and mandala. The mudra is ritual or symbolic gesture, in other words, hand signs. The mantra is a ritual word, phrase, or formula said to communicate the essence of true Buddhist teachings. The mandala is visual diagram, usually in circular form, with colorful patterns that can help practitioners to meditate.

Pilgrimage is an important religious activity for Tibetan Buddhists. On the different routes from the scattered towns to Lhasa, one can see small groups or individual Tibetan Buddhists bowing and kneeling along the roads. They chant mantras or sutras all the way to their destination. For most of the pilgrims, who are laypeople as well as monks and nuns, the journey will take many months to finish. They recite their mantras using prayer wheels and rosaries. Mantras, prayers, and sutras are carved on prayer wheels set in temples and available for visitors. The most common mantra is "Om Mani Padme Hum," which can be interpreted in many different ways. It is a prayer to Chenrezi (the Tibetan title of the Bodhisattva of Great Compassion, who is known as Guanyin in Chinese—see chapter 6). Tibetan Buddhists chant mantras and pray spontaneously throughout the day.

Tibetans believe that the Dalai Lama is actually the incarnation of Chenrezi, and that the present Dalai Lama is the fourteenth in this line. In Tibetan homes, a picture of the Dalai Lama is one of the most sacred religious objects, even though the government forbids the public display of such images. The term *lama* means religious teacher and is usually used as an honorific title for eminent Tibetan monks. The two most important lamas in Tibetan Buddhism are the Dalai Lama and the Panchen Lama. Tibetans believe that Dalai and Panchen are incarnations of the Bodhisattva of Great Compassion and the Amitabha Buddha, respectively. They are the leaders of two different sects within the Gelugpa school of Tibetan Buddhism. There are three other important schools: Nyingma, Kagyu, and Sakya. The Gelugpa school is the newest but most important one. Tibetan Buddhists believe that eminent monks can achieve such a high level of consciousness that their consciousnesses can be reincarnated in another physical body after their death.

Traditionally, the Dalai Lama and Panchen Lama have also enjoyed tremendous political influence and authority in Tibet. As a result, for centuries, political factions in Tibet, as well as the Chinese government, have often tried to influence the process by which a child is identified as the reincarnation of the Dalai Lama and the Panchen Lama, and to control the upbringing and education of the child. Since the mid-1990s, a controversy over this issue has erupted between the Chinese government and Tibetans loyal to the Dalai Lama over the identification of the new Panchen Lama. (See chapter 11.) After the Dalai Lama approved the selection of one boy, the child disappeared and has not been heard from since. Another boy was then enthroned as the Panchen Lama by the Chinese authorities and he regularly appears in the Chinese media.[4]

Islam among the Uyghurs

The call to prayer is announced through electronic speakers from the towers surrounding the Id Kah Mosque in Kashgar. On Friday afternoons, men begin to gather in the courtyard and proceed into the Hall of Prayer. There they take off their shoes or sandals and unroll their prayer rugs. Some go to the mosque five times each day, but Friday afternoons are always a special occasion. Ten or twenty thousand Uyghurs gather, coming from the neighborhood, the city, and the surrounding towns. On special occasions such as the Corban festival, the number of worshippers can be double that number or even more. Women are not part of this public service of worship. The short service includes readings in Arabic from the Koran, as well as an order of daily prayers. After the service, the worshippers go into the surrounding park and courtyard to visit, sell their wares, and talk together.

The Id Kah Mosque is one of ninety in this southern city in Xinjiang. Built in 1442, the historic mosque is centrally located in a beautiful four-acre complex. It has a yellow brick facade, and intricate carvings and painted pictures adorn the ceiling and cedar pillars. Kashgar, which is known as Kashi in Chinese, is an important center of Uyghur religion, culture, and history. The westernmost city in China, it was once an important cultural and trading center on the Silk Road. In the last thirty years, Kashgar has become a favored tourist destination, as well as a commercial hub along the Karakorum Highway that links China, Pakistan, and the countries of central Asia. Despite the immigration of large numbers of ethnic Chinese to the Xinjiang Autonomous Region, Kashgar continues to be a Uyghur city, but with strategic and international importance for China.

The Uyghur people are the second largest Muslim ethnic group in China after the Hui, and arguably the least integrated minority. In contrast, the Hui have been almost totally assimilated and are often indistinguishable from the Han Chinese majority. Like all Muslims, the Uyghur do not drink alcohol or eat pork. Women are not prominent in the public life of Uyghur Islam, as they are in some other Chinese minority communities.[5] Many Uyghurs who are Communist Party officials continue in their religious practices, and they sometimes go to mosques for prayers. This is in spite of the fact that the party forbids religious practice among its members.

FIGURE 3.2 *Uyghur Muslims praying at Id Kah Mosque, Kashgar, Xinjiang province. (Song Shijing/FOTOE)*

The Uyghur regard themselves as part of the larger *ummah*, and they maintain important relations with the international Muslim community. They have taken part in the Hajj to Mecca since the mid-1980s, and some Uyghur students have been sent to study at the prestigious Al-Azhar University in Cairo. Many Uyghurs have families and relatives overseas. Still, there are enormous internal divisions within the Uyghurs. As is the case for all Chinese Muslims, the majority of the Uyghur are Sunni, but intense religious conflicts persist among Sufi and non-Sufi religious orders, and there are important regional religious variations among Uyghur communities. Although they became Muslim in the tenth century, religion is not the only marker of Uyghur identity. Language, history, and an attachment to the land are also important for the self-definition of the people in China and Central Asia.[6] The Uyghurs have their own self-constructed ethnogenesis and regard themselves as the "original people" of the Tarim basin.

The Chinese government keeps a close watch on the activities of the Uyghur and other Islamic groups and is particularly wary of pan-Islamic separatist movements. Rebiya Kadeer, a Uyghur businesswoman based in the United States, has a high international profile in the human rights community, and she now heads the World Uyghur Congress. Sporadic violent eruptions in Xinjiang have been attributed to Uyghur extremists. The most serious of these was in July 2009, when demonstrators took to the streets in Urumchi and other cities in Xinjiang in protest over a Han Chinese attack against Uyghur workers in a factory in southern China. The protests turned violent, and the fighting between Uyghurs and Han Chinese claimed 200 lives. This resulted in hundreds of arrests and the execution of a number of the alleged perpetrators. After September 11, China successfully pressed the United States to list one Uyghur group—the East Turkestan Islamic Movement (ETIM)—as a "terrorist organization." ETIM and other overseas-based Uyghur organizations have claimed responsibility for various bomb attacks in China in recent years. These attacks, and the Chinese government campaigns to "strike hard" against terrorism, have led to continuing tensions between Uyghurs and the Han, and to restrictions on Uyghur religious practices. (For more on these tensions, see chapter 11.)

International trade and increased electronic communications brought on by globalization add even greater complexity to the interaction of religion, ethnicity, and politics among the Uyghur and other Islamic minorities. It is likely that the tensions will increase rather than decrease in future years, even as Islam among the Uyghurs—and the Uyghur population as a whole—continues to grow.

Christianity and the Miao

It was just before sunrise, but the village church in the mountains of western Guizhou was almost full. Many of the Miao farmers had walked fifty kilometers or more to attend the Sunday service, and they had arrived the night before. They were young and old, more women than men. In the early morning hours, their children were just getting up. Everyone knew each other, and it seemed like the gathering of an extended family. At six, the adults began singing hymns, accompanied by a woman on a keyboard and led by a young man who was a teacher in the village school. Men and women sat on benches on opposite sides of the church. They held hymnals that had been printed locally on inexpensive paper. They also had Bibles in the (Miao) Pollard script, which had been printed at the Amity Printing Press in Nanjing. For many of the people, this was the only book they owned, and they had committed many verses to memory.

The service began at eight, led by a recently ordained pastor from this village. Prayers and Bible readings were followed by an hour-long sermon emphasizing the need to trust in the grace of Jesus Christ in all areas of life, and drawing on many examples from village life. When the service ended, the 200 or so people went out into the dusty village square for a simple meal of sweet potatoes, boiled eggs, peanuts, and pickled vegetables. Older women from the village did the cooking and made sure that everyone had enough to eat. The people lingered around the small circle of homes surrounding the church for several hours before they set out on their homeward journeys. They would all be back the next week.

There are similar scenes each Sunday morning in ethnic minority Protestant churches in townships and villages in the southwestern provinces of Sichuan, Guizhou, and Yunnan where the Miao Christians are concentrated. In addition to Sunday services and special services at Christmas and during the Chinese Spring Festival, Miao Christians organize weekly meetings for prayer, healing, and Bible

FIGURE 3.3 *Miao Christians gathering for church service in Yunnan province. (Deng Quyao/ FOTOE)*

study. According to the 2000 census, the Miao population is more than ten million, divided into three major linguistic subgroups.[7] Miao people are also found in southeast Asia and immigrant communities in North America, where they are known as the Hmong. But it is among the Miao of China that Christianity is now flourishing.

The indigenous religion of the Miao was shamanistic, practiced in different ways among a variety of Miao subgroups. Samuel Pollard (1864–1915), an English Methodist, began Christian work among the Miao in Yunnan and Guizhou in 1891. He built a hospital in Zhaotong, Yunnan, which is still in use, and later established a mission station in Shimenkan, fifty kilometers or so to the east in Guizhou province. There he and his wife settled down, established a mission station, and built a chapel and a school. Pollard began to work on a script for the Miao language; a complete Miao New Testament based on his work was published in 1917. Other English missionaries joined the Pollards and continued their work with the Miao until the 1940s.

Even in Pollard's time, Miao people themselves did the primary work of evangelization. They challenged the indigenous shamanism and religious beliefs of the Miao, and many incidents of interreligious conflict have been recorded. After a slow beginning, the church grew, especially among the Hua ("Flowery") Miao in mountain villages in the Yunnan-Guizhou border regions. Lay preachers not only started churches, but also taught literacy in village-based schools. Their Christianity was of that of their Wesleyan Methodist teachers, with simple services centered on the Bible, preaching, and hymn-singing. Christian faith appealed to the impoverished Miao, caught between Yi and Hui landlords, on one side, and the Chinese who regarded them as "barbarians" on the other. (Although the Miao people themselves have adopted it, the term *Miao*, meaning "seedlings," shows the disparagement in which they were held.) By the early 1930s, Miao were in positions of leadership in local governments and schools.

The Communist government closed the village schools in the early 1950s, and the churches came under increasing pressure. Many church leaders were imprisoned, and the Pollard script was banned. Churches were closed during the Cultural Revolution era (1966–1976), and areas such as Wuding County witnessed terrible violence against Christians well into the 1970s.[8] With the reopening of churches and Christian meeting points in the 1980s, the churches began to experience a revival. Bibles and hymnals were reprinted, lay leaders attended provincial training courses, and young people went for seminary training in Nanjing and Kunming.

Today, a contextualized Christianity among the Miao has grown from the roots that were established in the first part of the twentieth century. Women are often found in leading roles in local churches. Miao Christians are well known all over China for their singing and their devotion to the church. There will continue to be divisions between registered and unregistered churches, and between Christians and followers of indigenous shamanism. Many young Christians go off to the cities in search of jobs and a better education. They send money home, and visit when they can, and so the mountain churches are much stronger than they were before. Estimates vary, but in Yunnan, up to three-quarters of the Miao are said to be Christians. This means they are more than half of the officially recognized 600,000 ethnic minority Christians in the province,[9] far outnumbering the Han Christians in the region.

Conclusion

As we have seen, minority religious communities have experienced renewal and revival over the last thirty years, in a variety of forms and practices. Despite continuing pressures from government policy, ethnic tensions, and the challenges of economic modernization, the growth of religion in China's ethnic communities continues.

The religious pluralism present within the officially designated national minorities is both a challenge and an opportunity. In relationships with one another, particularly in the autonomous regions, pluralism presents an opportunity for interreligious dialogue in order to promote mutual understanding in a globalized world. Interreligious dialogue is now being encouraged by the government in certain places. It should be added that some religious beliefs and traditions tend to militate against dialogue, especially within the Christian and Islamic communities in China. For the minorities, the vastly different ethnicities and the many differences within recognized ethnic groups further complicate the picture.

Globalization and economic modernization may either encourage dialogue or work against it. As people are brought into closer contact, there may be an effort to understand one another's culture and religion, but closer contact may also result in increased tension that can lead to conflict and violence. Transnational religious movements, the growing importance of religion in international affairs, the attention to ethnicity as a global political force, and the rise of China as an economic and political power all have their impact on minority religious communities in the People's Republic. No discussion of religion and public life in China, therefore, can afford to ignore the many ways in which minority ethnic communities contribute to an understanding of how religion will shape our common future.

Notes

1. Jiang Rong, *Wolf Totem: A Novel*, trans. Howard Goldblatt (London: Penguin, 2008). Jiang Rong is the pseudonym of an author who is now a university professor in Beijing.

2. For an overview of Chinese ethnic minorities in the People's Republic of China, see Colin MacKerras, *China's Minorities: Integration and Modernization in the Twentieth Century* (Hong Kong: Oxford University Press, 1994) as well as the same author's *China's Ethnic Minorities and Globalization* (London: Routledge/Curzon, 2003). There are excellent but brief sections on minority culture and religion in both books. For essays on different approaches to ethnic identity in China, see William Safran, ed., *Nationalism and Ethnoregional Identities in China* (London: Frank Cross, 1998).

3. Dru C. Gladney, *Dislocating China: Muslims, Minorities and Other Subaltern Subjects* (Chicago: University of Chicago Press, 2004), 9.

4. For an overview of Tibetan Buddhism today, see Melvyn C. Goldstein and Matthew T. Kapstein, *Buddhism in Contemporary Tibet: Religious Revival and Cultural Identity* (Berkeley: University of California Press, 1998).

5. Among the Hui and other Muslim minorities, women play a more prominent role. There are even women imams and women's mosques. See Maria Jaschok and Shui Jingjun, *The History of Women's Mosques in Chinese Islam: A Mosque of Their Own* (Surrey: Curzon, 2000).

6. Dru C. Gladney, "Islam in China: Accommodation or Separatism?" *China Quarterly* 174 (June 2003): 457; also Gladney, *Dislocating China*, 219.

7. Norma Diamond, "Christianity and the Hua Miao: Writing and Power," *Christianity in China: from the Eighteenth Century to the Present*, ed. Daniel H. Bays (Stanford: Stanford University Press, 1996), 139.

8. See Philip L. Wickeri, "The Abolition of Religion in Yunnan," *The Terrible Alternative: Christian Martyrdom in the Twentieth Century*, ed. Andrew Chandler (London: Cassell, 1998), 128–143.

9. Xuezheng Yang, ed., *Yunnan zongjiao qingshi baogao, 2006–2007* (Kunming: Yunnan daxue chubanshe, 2007).

{ 4 }

Modalities of Doing Religion
Adam Yuet Chau

The previous chapters of this book presented a panoramic view of religious practices and ideas in different social contexts: large cities, rural villages, and regions inhabited by ethnic minorities. With the exception of some ethnic groups that overwhelmingly adhere to a single world religion such as Buddhism, Islam, or Christianity, the religious culture of the vast majority of Chinese defies easy categorizations and does not present itself as a neatly organized system. The great variety of practices and ideas, which appear in endless combinations and permutations, can be bewildering and confusing. One way of simplifying the picture is to look at how, in the long history of religious development in China, different ways of "doing religion" evolved and cohered into relatively easy-to-identify styles or "modalities." These are relatively well-defined forms that different people can adopt and combine to deal with different concerns in life; however, the contents within these forms can vary widely. These modalities of "doing religion" are as follows:

1. Discursive/scriptural, involving mostly the composition and use of texts
2. Personal-cultivational, involving a long-term interest in cultivating and transforming oneself
3. Liturgical, involving elaborate ritual procedures conducted by ritual specialists
4. Immediate-practical, aiming at quick results using simple ritual or magical techniques
5. Relational, emphasizing the relationship between humans and deities (or ancestors) as well as among humans in religious practices

These modalities are frameworks for religious practice and action. They both restrain and enable people to express their religious imagination in words, images, sculptural and architectural forms, and actions. At any one time in any corner of the vast late imperial Chinese empire—and to a great extent today as well—all of these modalities were available to be adopted by individuals or social groups, though factors such as class, gender, literacy level, accidents of birth and residence, position within different social networks, and temperament might channel some people toward certain modalities and not others. Most peasants in China have tradition- ally adopted a combination of the relational and the immediate-practical modal- ities into their religiosity; sometimes they adopt the liturgical modality and hire religious specialists when the occasion requires them, such as funerals and com- munal exorcisms. Illiteracy and lack of leisure would preclude them from most of the discursive and personal-cultivational modalities. The traditional educated elite tended to adopt a combination of the discursive and the personal-cultivational modalities, but they too often needed the service of the liturgical specialists.

This modalities framework focuses our attention on the ways in which people "do religion" rather than their religious conceptions, which can vary widely and in ways that defy any explanation; there are many flukes and accidents in the history of evolu- tion and interaction of religious ideas, and people's social experience and social struc- ture do not always determine the contours of their religious imagination. Studying people's religious conceptions is important, but it yields a bewildering diversity; on the other hand, there are only a limited number of forms (modalities) that permeate the Chinese religious landscape. The varieties of Chinese religious life have resulted from the elaboration of differences within these forms as well as the different configurations of various forms. The great variety in the symbolic contents of the Chinese religious world, as well as the limited number of forms (modalities) and their lasting stability and versatility, are both great achievements in the history of world religions.

A focus on form is of course not to say that studying the contents within the modalities is not important; far from it. But it is crucial to recognize the dialectic and mutually constituting relationship between form and content in any domain of sociocultural productions. Unless we understand the ways in which different reli- gious practices belong to different modalities of doing religion, we will not fully appreciate the actual significance of these various practices. If we see a particular society's religious culture as consisting of a particular configuration of various modalities of doing religion, then one of the first tasks is to identify the contours of these modalities. In the following sections, I shall illustrate each modality of doing religion found in Chinese religious culture with one or two paradigmatic religious practices that exemplify each modality. One thing I need to emphasize, however, is that these modalities are more or less ideal types, and that they often overlap.

The Discursive/Scriptural Modality

People are attracted to this modality because of the allure of Confucian, Buddhist, Daoist and other "great texts" (classics, sutras, scriptures, etc.). This modality often requires a high level of literacy and a penchant for philosophical and "theological" thinking. Key practices within this modality include compiling and editing scrip- tures or discoursing about the Way, or preaching, and its paradigmatic forms include reading, thinking about, discussing, debating, composing, translating, and commenting on religious texts. Also included in this modality is the composing of morality books using spirit writing and Chan/Zen masters' exegesis on *gong'an*, or dharma riddles.

The products of this modality are usually textual (or at least eventually appearing in textual forms) that range from a single religious tract to a whole set of scriptures and liturgical texts (e.g., the so-called Buddhist Canon or Daoist Canon compiled under imperial patronage). These texts form the basis of the classical "religious studies" approach to studying Chinese religions, which was derived from Western religious/theological exegetical traditions. Because of this textual bias, for a long time Chinese religious practices were understood in the West as exclusively this textually transmitted esoteric knowledge or, in the context of New Age or Orientalist consumption of exotic texts, "Oriental wisdoms."

Following are excerpts from what is perhaps the most widely published Chinese religious text, the *Tractate of the Most High One on Actions and Consequences*, which warns the reader about the operation of cosmic recompense described in chapter 1.

Besides following the advice contained in the text, one could attain religious merit simply by reading and rereading it, or by ritually chanting it, and also by printing it and having it offered for free distribution. For centuries, it has been published and distributed in millions and millions of copies by myriads of temples and

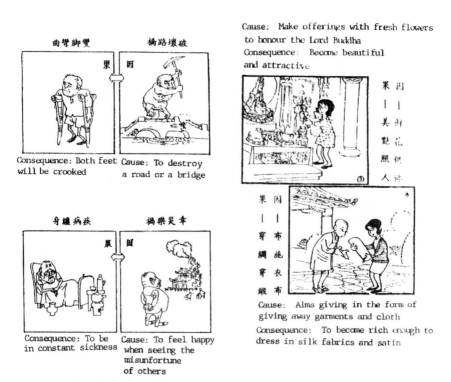

FIGURE 4.1 *A comic book on cosmic recompense, distributed in a Hong Kong temple. (Photo David Palmer)*

devotees, and it (or similar morality books) can typically be picked up today at any Chinese temple or vegetarian restaurant.[1] The author of the text is unknown, and it was likely produced through a spirit-writing séance several centuries ago.

Chapter I: The Workings of Good and Evil
The most high one says: "Disasters and blessings have no entry gates of their own; they are summoned by people. The effects of good and evil are like shadows following their forms."

And so heaven and earth have spirits who record crimes, and in proportion to the severity of their crimes, they shorten human lives appropriately. Because of this not only may a person's life be cut short, but he also becomes poor or destitute, his calamities are many; People all hate him; punishments and disasters follow him. Good fortune avoids him while evil stars persecute him. And when his span of years is complete, he dies. (...)

Chapter II: How to Be Good
Follow the right path, and retreat from the wrong one. Do not follow evil paths, nor sin in secret. Accumulate merit, show a compassionate heart in all things. Be loyal, filial, friendly, and brotherly; by correcting yourself, transform others. Pity orphans and be compassionate to widows, respect the elderly and be kind to the young. Do not even injure insects, grasses, and trees. Be saddened by other people's misfortunes and delight in their good fortune. Help those in need and rescue those in danger. Regard the gains of others as though they were your own. And regard the failings of others as your own failings. Do not expose other people's weaknesses, nor boast of your own strengths. Condemn evil and promote virtue, renounce much and accept little. Suffer humiliation without resentment; receive benefits as though startled. Extend help, but do not request compensation, help others without later regrets.

Chapter III: What Happens To Good People
When a person is known as virtuous, people all praise him. Heaven's Way protects him, happiness and wealth follow him, All evil forces stay away from him; gods guard him. Whatever he does is successful, and he can aspire to join the gods and immortals. He who would become a heavenly immortal must perform 1,300 good deeds. He who would become an earthly immortal must perform 300 good deeds.

Chapter IV: The Crimes of the Wicked
But sometimes there is someone who behaves without righteousness, and moves against rationality, who mistakes evil for ability, and inflicts injury on others, who secretly defames the virtuous, and behind their backs slanders his ruler or his parents, who ignores those born before him, and disobeys his

masters, who deceives the unknowing, and bears false witness against his fellow students, who lies, calumniates, deceives, and practices deceit, who exposes the failings of clan elders, who exercises power but not compassion, who is cruel, irrational, and self-willed, who does not distinguish right from wrong, and turns his back on those whom he should befriend, who oppresses those below him and claims their merit for himself, but cringes before those above him to win their favor, who has no feeling for favors received, but is tireless in remembering resentment, who makes light of heaven's ordinary people, but agitates and disturbs the empire's order...

Chapter V: The Fate of the Wicked

For crimes such as these, the masters of fate, depending upon the gravity of the offence, cut short a person's life by twelve years or by a hundred days. And after that the person dies. And if at death there still remain unpunished crimes, the bad luck is visited upon children and grandchildren.

And for all those who have wrongfully seized the property of others, they must compensate for it with their wives and children and other family members, even unto death. Those who do not die are inflicted with disasters of water, fire, theft, loss of goods, disease, slander, and more until it offsets their unlawful appropriations....

Chapter VI: Hope for Those Who Repent

When a person's heart is moved by goodness, although the goodness has not yet been achieved, nevertheless felicitous spirits are already following him. But when a person's heart is moved by evil, although the evil has not yet been achieved, nevertheless spirits of misfortune are already following him. A person who formerly did bad things but afterward repents and does no more evil, and continues in good behavior, then gradually he must obtain good fortune and happiness. This is called "changing disaster into good fortune."

Therefore a joyous man speaks what is good, thinks what is good, and does what is good; each day he does these three things, and in three years Heaven will bequeath to him good fortune. But an unlucky man is he who speaks what is evil, thinks what is evil, and does what is evil; each day he does these three things, and in three years Heaven will strike him with misfortune. Why would we not be diligent in following this?[2]

The Personal-Cultivational Modality

Practices such as meditation, *qigong*, internal or outer alchemy, the cultivation of the "Daoist body,"[3] personal or group sutra chanting, the morning and evening recitation sessions in a Buddhist monastery, merit-conscious charitable acts (e.g., volunteering to accumulate karmic merit), and keeping a merit/demerit ledger[4] belong to this modality. This modality presupposes a long-term interest in cultivating and transforming oneself (whether Buddhist, Daoist, or Confucian). The goals of this transformation and cultivation are different in each religious tradition: to become an immortal in Daoism, to be reincarnated into a better life or to achieve nirvana in Buddhism, and to become a man of virtue or to be closer to sagehood in Confucianism. But the shared element is the concern with one's own ontological status and destiny, something akin to a Foucaultian "care of the self."[5] In other words, the practices in this modality provide "technologies of the self."

Within this modality of doing religion there are both elite and popular forms. For many, working on scriptures itself constitutes a form of self-cultivation. However, ordinary and even illiterate people can pursue personal-cultivational goals without esoteric knowledge or high literacy or much religious training. For example, illiterate peasants can practice self-cultivation by chanting "precious scrolls," which are in metered rhymes and often memorized.[6] The simplest self-cultivation technique is the repeated utterance of the mantra *namo amituofo* (*namo amitabha*) thousands of times a day.

Charismatic movements sometimes precipitate out of these personal-cultivational pursuits. The modern *qigong* movement also exemplifies the personal-cultivational modality of doing religion.[7] When Falun Gong practitioners let the dharma wheel rotate in their lower abdomen day in and day out as instructed by their master Li Hongzhi, they are engaged in the personal-cultivational modality of doing religion. The key concepts in this modality are "to cultivate" (*xiu*) and "to craft" (*lian*).[8]

EXEMPLARY FORM: NEW AGE SPIRIT CULTIVATORS IN TAIWAN

Spirit mediumism has been a prominent aspect of Taiwanese religious life.[9] Spirit mediums are people who have succumbed to divine calling and agreed to be possessed by various kinds of deities in order to serve these deities and to help people with their problems. Their mode of operation typically belongs to the immediate-practical modality of doing religion (discussed later). But in the past few decades a new form of spirit mediumism emerged in Taiwan that has gained popularity. Ordinary people ranging from teenagers to the elderly, many more women than men, would gather in temples or other social spaces to get possessed by deities and to cultivate their own spirits. These people call themselves *lingji* (spirit mediums), though it is more appropriate to call them spirit cultivators to differentiate them from the better-known traditional spirit mediums, because the goal of their practice is to get in touch with one's "original spirit" and to cultivate this spirit to reach higher and higher forms of spiritual accomplishment. Not belonging to any formal religious organization (e.g., temple cult or sectarian group), these spirit cultivators gather in fluid, informal groups to meditate, seek to be possessed by deities such as the Taiwanese goddess Mazu, the Bodhisattva Guanyin, the Living Buddha Jigong, or even the Christian God, Virgin Mary, and Mao Zedong. Upon being possessed, the spirit cultivators will start burping, singing, chanting (speaking in stylized "heavenly language"), gesturing (e.g., with Buddhist mudras), and dancing, with various styles depending on the possessing deity and individual practitioner. The higher the level one is at, the wider the range of possessing deities will be. The ultimate goal of cultivating one's original spirit is to reach personal happiness, to reduce suffering, and to help build a harmonious and peaceful world. Unlike the traditional spirit medium, who typically works for a clientele and charges a fee, these spirit cultivators engage in these spiritual pursuits mostly for their own benefit (even given the professed purpose of benefiting the world at large). Self-consciously syncretic in nature, this innovative spirit-cultivation practice echoes the New Age practice of channeling found in the West and the many *qigong* innovations in mainland China.

The Liturgical Modality

> The characteristic form of the language of the two Testaments [in Christianity] is history...; the characteristic form of the language of the Covenant of Orthodox Unity [of Daoism] is ritual.
>
> —John Lagerwey[10]

> Ritual-events are machines that gather individual and social forces into specific configurations, activating distinct ways of perceiving, sensing, and knowing.
>
> —Kenneth Dean[11]

This modality includes practices such as imperial state rituals (e.g., the Grand Sacrifice),[12] the Confucian rites, the Daoist rites of fasting and offering, exorcism (e.g., a Nuo ritual drama), sutra chanting rites, Daoist or Buddhist rituals for the universal salvation of souls, the Buddhist grand water and land dharma assemblies, and funeral rituals. Compared to the personal-cultivational modality, practices in this modality aim at more immediate transformations of reality conducted in complex and highly symbolic forms, and are commissioned by and conducted for collective groups—be they families, clans, villages or neighborhoods, temple communities, or the state. This is the modality of the religious specialists (monks, Daoist priests, fengshui masters, Confucian ritual masters, spirit mediums, exorcist-dancers, etc.) and often involves esoteric knowledge and elaborate ritual procedures.[13]

EXEMPLARY FORM: THE DAOIST RITUAL OF OFFERING OR COSMIC RENEWAL (JIAO)

The ritual of offering or cosmic renewal is an exorcistic liturgical service conducted for the living by Daoist priests (see chapter 2). It is commissioned by communities or households on periodic cycles, or at the completion of a building or renovating a temple. Its purpose is to purify and renew the space or the temple of a community by driving away the demons. A typical *jiao* lasts for three days, but it can also be extended to five days or even longer.

In a *jiao* witnessed by the Daoist scholar Kristofer Schipper in 1969 to consecrate the renovation of the temple of Xuejia town in Taiwan, five lay members of the temple board of directors (who were all local notables and businessmen) were selected by throwing divination blocks (see chapter 2), to represent the community during the ritual service. The five directors were locked inside the temple with the Daoist priests for the entire duration of the liturgical service, which lasted five days and five nights, while outside the temple other priests conducted public rites for the masses. Priests and their acolytes conducted most of the ritual procedures inside the temple, while the directors stood quietly, and kneeled when required. At the beginning of the service, the priests and acolytes entered the sacred precincts, conducting sword dances and sprinkling holy water around in the four cardinal directions. The directors were then instructed to kneel, to inhale vapor from a bowl of vinegar into which a piece of hot iron had been dipped, and then to step over the vinegar and a pot of incense, and to march in procession around the ritual space. Suddenly, firecrackers exploded and filled the temple with smoke, and a masked demon surged into the sacred space, while the horns and percussive instruments produced a deafening noise. The demon jumped around frenetically, peering into all corners of the temple, until he saw the incense pot and grabbed it, and seemed about to flee with it. At this point the head Daoist priest appeared, holding his sword and his bowl of holy water. He gulped some water and spat it onto the demon, jabbed at it with his sword, and the two engaged in mock combat, attacking, pursuing, and dodging and stabbing, until, finally, the exhausted demon dropped the incense pot. At that point the priest blocked his way and "beheaded" the demon by removing its mask. The priest then began a triumphal dance, limping around and symbolically "sealing" the sacred space, and then "buried" the demon (i.e., the mask) in a secret rite in the northeast corner of the temple, called the "demon's gate."[14]

This was only the beginning act of the *jiao*, which lasted several days. The scholar of Daoist ritual John Lagerwey provides a meticulously timed sequence of ritual actions during the three-day *jiao* he observed November 19–22, 1980 in Taidong, Taiwan.[15] Within each named segment there are numerous complex ritual manipulations by different members of the Daoist troupe hired for the occasion. The basic program is as follows:

Preliminary Rituals (the Night before Day One)

1. Firing the oil to drive away dirt (21:05–21:40; 35 minutes)
2. Starting up the drum (23:03–23:14; 11 minutes)

Day One

3. Announcement (6:20–7:50; 1 hour and 30 minutes)
4. Invocation (7:52–8:49; 57 minutes)
5. Flag-raising (10:03–10:22; 19 minutes)

6. Noon offering (11:31–12:35; 1 hour and 4 minutes)
7. Division of the lamps (21:27–22:37; 1 hour and 10 minutes)

Day Two

8. Land of the way (6:28–8:18; 1 hour and 50 minutes)
9. Noon offering (11:36–12:53; 1 hour and 17 minutes)
10. Floating the water lamps (16:00–16:30; 30 minutes)
11. Invocation of the masters and saints (16:55–17:40; 45 minutes)
12. Sealing the altar (20:32–21:28; 56 minutes)
13. Nocturnal invocation (22:33–22:52; 19 minutes)

Day Three

14. Renewed invocation (6:43–7:52; 1 hour and 9 minutes)
15. Scripture recitation (8:30–8:50; 20 minutes)
16. Presentation of the memorial (9:30–10:26; 54 minutes)
17. Noon offering (11:00–11:30; 30 minutes)
18. Orthodox offering (16:30–17:44; 1 hour and 14 minutes)
19. Universal salvation (18:50–21:00; 2 hours and 10 minutes)

Each segment of the *jiao* consists of complex liturgical manipulations involving hand gestures, bodily moves (including dances), texts, talismans, swords, seals, scrolls, scriptures, costumes, and even tables and chairs. And the liturgical complexity of this modality often requires multiple ritualists for the job. For example, a large ritual occasion such as a *jiao* often requires more than a dozen ritualists, some in charge of the core liturgical work while others serve as ritual musicians.

There may be some occasions when a very large ritual event production would require the simultaneous service of dozens and sometimes even over a hundred Daoist priests. In Hong Kong, the Daoist community has had a long tradition of conducting large-scale "ritual congregations" or "dharma assemblies" to petition for blessings and to expel evil influences. For example, in 1997 the Hong Kong Daoist Association organized a "Ritual Congregation to Celebrate the Return of Hong Kong's Sovereignty to China and to Petition for Blessings." The service lasted for seven days and seven nights, and the Three Pure rites, the core of the entire service, were simultaneously recited by 250 Daoists, setting a record for the territory in terms of the scale of the event production. In the spring of 2003, during the height of the SARS epidemic in Hong Kong, the Daoist Association combined forces with sixteen different Daoist temples and altars to stage a "calamity-dispelling, misfortune-absolving, and blessing-petitioning ritual congregation" on behalf of the entire Hong Kong population. Again the service lasted seven days and seven nights, and 80,000 talismans to dispel plagues and ensure safety were distributed to people. The venue of this large service was on a soccer field in front of the famous Che Kung Temple in Shatin, the New Territories. One prominent Daoist temple was in charge of the main altar on each of the seven days, and an enormous number of scriptures were recited and chanted.[16]

BOX 4.1 The 2008 Beijing Summer Olympics as Ritual Event

Most premodern states had a very rich ceremonial system. The kings and queens in the West had their colorful court rituals (often fused with religious rituals; e.g., coronation, royal marriages and funerals), and the emperors in dynastic China also had an elaborate system of rites based on the long-standing Confucian understanding of the importance of a set of correct, patterned behavior on certain occasions. During late imperial times these imperial rituals were codified into five different categories: auspicious (e.g., state sacrifices); felicitous (e.g., marriages, festivals); martial (e.g., celebrating military victory); hosting (e.g., hosting foreign visitors); and inauspicious (e.g., funerals, disasters).

The emergence of the modern state saw the parallel processes of the disappearance of many premodern rituals and the appearance of new ones. There is a tendency toward the spectacularization of public rituals, the exemplary cases being Soviet processions and Nazi rallies. The modern Olympic Games have become the ultimate occasion for state ritual manipulations. Having wished to host the Olympics for decades, China finally was awarded host country status for the 2008 Summer Olympics. The symbolic meaning of this status is tremendous: it proves that China has finally come out of the shadow of its Maoist past and been fully recognized by the global community.

But the massive scale and heavy symbolic weight of the Olympics presented great challenges to the Chinese state. Because of its multifaceted nature, the Olympics is a state-orchestrated ritual event that incorporates elements from four out of the five old imperial rites: auspicious, felicitous, martial, and hosting. The Chinese state was anxious to make sure that everything went according to plan, the same way that imperial ritualists were anxious to ensure properly patterned ritual behavior on ritual occasions. But the international nature of the Olympics greatly complicated the process. Different actors with their own agendas have made the symbolically rich Olympic rituals subject to different interpretations and contestations. When Tibetan independence activists disrupted the international Olympic torch relay in several countries, many Chinese were angered and feared that the disruption would have inauspicious consequences for the Olympic Games. But the opening ceremonies were the grandest and most spectacular in Olympic history, and the games were a success—not to a small measure thanks to the Chinese government's understanding and orchestration of the games as a grand ritual.

The Immediate-Practical Modality

Practices in this modality also aim at immediate results but compared to those in the liturgical modality they are more direct and involve shorter and simpler procedures. There is minimal ritual elaboration. Examples include divination (oracle rod, moon-shaped divination blocks, divination sticks, coins, etc.), getting divine medicine from a deity, using talismans (e.g., ingestion of talismanic water), consulting a spirit medium, calling back a stray soul, begging for rain, ritual cursing, or simply offering incense. Because of its simplicity and low cost, this modality is the most frequently used by the common people (peasants, petty urbanites). The key concepts in this modality are efficacy (or miraculous power) and "to beseech for help."

EXEMPLARY FORM: "BEATING THE MEAN PERSON": RITUAL OF CURSING AND SPELLBINDING ONE'S ENEMY[17]

"Beating the mean person" is a form of sorcery common among the Cantonese and Tewchownese.[18] In its simplest form, a person who thinks that someone is bothering or hurting him or her can make a small cutout paper figure with the alleged enemy's name written on it (the enemy is the "mean person"), go out to the sidewalk after dark, invoke the power of a deity (with incense and offerings), and then beat savagely on the paper figure using a worn shoe or sandal while loudly cursing the enemy (not unlike practices involving voodoo dolls). The hope is that the enemy will be subdued and will no longer harm the person in question. A typical curse would go like this (loosely translated from the original Cantonese with an attempt to rhyme as in the original):

Beat your bloody head, so that you will never get ahead;
Beat your bloody mouth, so that your breath can't come out;
Beat your bloody hand, so that you will always have a lousy hand [at gambling];
Beat your bloody feet, so that your shoes will never fit;
Beat your bloody lungs, so that you will be stung and hung; . . .

FIGURE 4.2 *Hiring an old woman to "beat the mean person" under the Gooseneck Bridge, Hong Kong. (Xie Guanghui/CTPphoto/FOTOE)*

Though apparently quite common in the past and done by anyone with a grudge (because it is such a simple practice), nowadays in urban Hong Kong people who want to beat the mean person would hire a "specialist" (usually an old lady) to do it. The most famous place for beating the mean person is at the "Goose Neck Bridge" (the Gan Bridge in Cantonese), a dark place underneath the highway overpass between Causeway Bay and Wanchai. One can request and pay for the beating of a mean person any time of the year, even though in the spring, on the day of the "awakening of the insects" (March 6 or 7 each year), the need for a generalized anti-mean-people prophylactic treatment is the greatest and so is the effectiveness of such a treatment (similar to getting an immunization shot). On this day the site overflows with people requesting such sessions, and more "specialists" show up to meet the high demand. The cost of a "quick and dirty" session is around 50 Hong Kong dollars on an ordinary day, but more on the "Awakening of the Insects" Day.[19]

EXEMPLARY FORM: CONSULTING A DIVINATION ROLLER

The Chinese have developed divination techniques since antiquity. The oracle bones from more than 3,000 years ago are the best known (see chapter 9). The other well-known divination method is drawing divination lots, in which a worshipper with a particular problem goes to a temple, burns incense in front of the deity, and then shakes a box of divination sticks until one "jumps" out. He or she then consults the corresponding divination poem or message for the divine message and inspiration (see chapter 2). Here I will describe another divination method, which is widespread in north China.

The method involves the use of an oracle roller. And our example comes from the Black Dragon King Temple in northern Shaanxi province, where I conducted fieldwork in the 1990s. The roller is a short, fat length of wood with eight segments along its sides (so the two ends are octagon-shaped). It is about ten inches long, and a little thicker in the middle than at the ends. Each segment has a different four-character message inscribed in the wood. The consultee with a particular problem holds this roller in both palms and rolls it horizontally in a wooden tray about twelve inches wide and twenty-two inches long. When the roller stops, the characters on the top segment are the message Black Dragon King wants to communicate to the consultee. The eight four-character messages are as follows:

- Extremely auspicious
- Not so good
- Not clear how you would thank me for the help
- Go home soon if traveling
- Not in accordance with god's ways
- Pray with a sincere heart

- Bring the medicine with magical water
- Will get well after taking the medicine

The simplest application of this oracle is to ask a yes or no question. For example: "My brother and I are planning to take a trip to Inner Mongolia to sell some clothes. Your Highness the Dragon King, do you think we will make some good money? If yes, give us "extremely auspicious"; if no, give us "not so good." Then the consultee rolls the roller. If the god's answer is "Not sure how you would thank me for the help," the consultee either puts more money in the donation box or makes a vow, promising that he will bring a certain amount of incense money if he makes money on the trip with the Dragon King's blessing. Sometimes the consultee promises 10% of his profit or even higher. It is like entering into a partnership with the Dragon King. If the answer is "Not in accordance with god's ways," the consultee needs to reflect on whether his business plan is going to break the law or offend the god. Other yes or no questions can be: "Will I be married soon?"; "Will Grandma get better or not?"; "Will I get a promotion?"; and so forth.

The reference to medicine and magical water on the oracle roller indicates that this roller is the medicine oracle, most often used when consultees want to request the god's divine intervention in treating their own or their family members' illnesses. The Dragon King has another roller that is used only when, on increasingly rare occasions, there are requests for rain. It is called the rain oracle. On it the two medicine-related messages on the medicine roller are replaced by two rain-related messages: "will rain today" and "will rain within three days."

FIGURE 4.3 *Worshippers burning incense Baxian Temple, Xi'an. (Photo David Palmer)*

BOX 4.2 Burning Incense

The first thing that a Chinese person does when approaching a deity or spirit is to burn sticks of incense. Hawkers and shops sell incense and spirit money in front of every temple, and worshipers don't buy incense by the stick but rather by the bundle (though sometimes there are giant, person-tall incense sticks that one can buy by the stick). Normally one needs to put only three sticks of incense in the incense pot in front of a deity (though there are also those who light up the whole bundle at the same time), so many worshippers would leave the rest of the incense with the temple keeper so that he can keep the incense burning even when there are no worshippers. Other times the worshipper does need so many sticks of incense because there are often many deities enshrined in each temple and each should be offered incense. Most worshippers burn incense the way they do out of custom and without reflection, and they might not be able to tell an outsider what incense burning means exactly. But an investigator could venture some interpretations from its usage.

Burning incense is a sign of respect for the deity, and the fragrance of the incense is supposed to please the deity (the same Chinese word means both incense and fragrance). Typically the worshipper raises the incense sticks with both hands toward the deity statue in a gesture of respect before planting them into the incense pot; many murmur prayers or words of gratitude while holding the incense. Many worshippers bring offerings of fruits, meat, and other items to arrange on tables, and sometimes burning incense sticks are stuck onto these offerings as if the fragrance of the incense also transports the spiritual essence of the offerings up to the deities. Incense is also offered to ancestors and ghosts.

The Relational Modality

Chinese society is a hotbed of associational assemblages.

—Kenneth Dean[20]

This modality emphasizes the relationship between humans and deities (or ancestors) as well as relationships among worshippers. Examples are building temples, making offerings (i.e., feeding ancestors, deities, and ghosts), taking vows, spreading miracle stories (i.e., testifying to the deities' efficacy), celebrating deities' birthdays at temple festivals, going on pilgrimage, imperial mountain journeys, establishing religious communities, and forming affiliations between temples and cult communities. This modality also emphasizes sociality, the bringing together of people through ritual events and festivals. Obviously the other modalities all exhibit relational and sociality aspects, but the making and maintaining of relations and the production and consumption of sociality seem to be at the foundation of those practices that I have grouped under this modality. The key concepts in this modality are "social comings and goings" and social relations, or connectedness.[21]

EXEMPLARY FORM: THE "DIVISION OF INCENSE" IDIOM
AND GOING ON PILGRIMAGE TO "ANCESTRAL TEMPLES"

In southeastern coastal China and Taiwan, one of the most common ways of establishing a new temple is to go to an already established temple and to "divide" the incense and efficacy of the enshrined deity. This involves making a new statue of the deity, infusing this new statue with the incense fragrance of the older one, scooping up some incense ashes from the older temple's incense burner, lighting a lamp using the older temple's oil lamp fire, and bringing all these back to the new temple building to enshrine the new statue. From this moment on, the new temple and its enshrined statue will have an affiliation with the older temple that puts the new temple in a subordinate position. Even though the deity enshrined in the two temples is the same deity, each has its own power supported by a body of miracle lore testifying to its efficacy. And each statue is named after the place in which the temple is situated—for example, Mazu of Dajia, Mazu of Lugang.

In order to sustain and renew the power of the new statue, the new statue has to visit the "parent" temple periodically to recharge its power, thus necessitating periodic pilgrimage of members of the newer temple community to the older temple. These pilgrimages are called incense-presenting trips. Similarly, members of the older temple community organize periodic pilgrimages to *their* "parent" temple to recharge the power of *their* deity statue. Over time such relations of affiliation extended both vertically and horizontally (in a fashion resembling a pyramid) and can form an intricate and dense network of dozens if not hundreds of "higher" and "lower" temples and "brotherly" (or "mother-daughter") temples. Important temples with high claims of efficacy and a large number of affiliate temples would assert regional supremacy and become regional centres of pilgrimage, but the most important pilgrimage is always the one that centres on the so-called "ancestral temple," where all the other temples and their statues have been derived through varying degrees of direct connection.

The Mazu (Heavenly Empress; also known as Tianhou) temple pilgrimage network in Taiwan is the most famous and best studied among the incense-division temple networks.[22] The ancestral temple for the Mazu cult is on Meizhou Island in Fujian because that was where the apotheosized girl Lin Moniang first manifested her power and was worshipped. But because of Taiwan's geographical status as an island far from the Fujian coast, Taiwan's cultural and political separation from the mainland during the Japanese colonial period and the postcolonial period from the 1940s until now, and many other factors, the first Mazu temple in Taiwan assumed a quasi-ancestral temple status over the years. Even though there have been disputes between different temples over which is the first Mazu temple in Taiwan, for a long time it was the Chaotiangong in Beigang to which Mazu worshippers from all over the island converged annually to pay respect and to recharge their own Mazu statues' power. But what is interesting about these pilgrimage trips in terms of the relational modality of doing religion is that these pilgrims not only converge on Chaotiangong, but visit many other temples along the way, sometimes up to dozens, and not all of them Mazu temples, thus establishing relationships with members of various communities.

EXEMPLARY FORM: NEW MORALITY-BOOK COMMUNITIES

Reform-era China has witnessed the revitalization of Buddhist monastic life centered around the rebuilding of monasteries and temples, the growth of the number of monks, and the increased liveliness of rituals.[23] The printing and free distribution of morality books have also come back. These are Buddhist-themed booklets piled up at the entrances of monasteries for anyone to pick up for free. Many lay Buddhists sponsor the printing and distribution of these morality books as a means to accumulate karmic merit, and this practice has been around for more than a thousand years. There is, however, a new development in the courtyards of some of these monasteries. Some lay Buddhists come to the monasteries to preach their own understandings of the sutras in the courtyards and distribute their own morality books, which are sometimes books they have written. Other visitors gather around them to seek wisdom or just to see what they have to say. The monastic clerics tolerate them at best and try to keep them far away from the main halls where worshippers attend the dharma rituals, but some of these lay preachers are quite charismatic and develop followings of their own. Many admirers gather around these lay preachers on a regular basis in monastery courtyards, but they also go to the home of the lay preachers to discuss sutra teachings and share their insights with one another, forming a loosely connected but nevertheless real community brought together by a common religious pursuit. It is interesting to note that with this example, we witness the coming together of three modalities of doing religion: the discursive/scriptural modality (i.e., the writing of morality books), the self-cultivational modality (i.e., accumulating merit through printing and distributing morality books and developing one's "Buddhahood"), and the relational modality (i.e., new communities developed around lay Buddhist preachers).

Conclusion

Identifying the different modalities of doing religion can serve as a first step in examining Chinese religious practices in a new light. Scholars of Chinese religion have long followed the Three Teachings model of identifying and understanding Daoism, Confucianism, and Buddhism. But these "religions" are half reality and half reification. The neat and tidy categories quickly break down and become meaningless when we look at people's practices on the ground, where they don't care which deity belongs to which religion or which religious tradition inspired which morality book. What happens on the ground "religiously" is very much a congruence of local customs, historical accidents, social environment, personal temperaments, and configurations of modalities of doing religion.

Notes

1. Daniel L. Overmyer's *Precious Volumes: An Introduction to Chinese Sectarian Scriptures from the Sixteenth and Seventeenth Centuries* (Cambridge, Mass.: Harvard University Press, 1999) presents extensive examples of the discursive/scriptural modality of doing religion among sectarians in late imperial China. Terry F. Kleeman's *A God's Own Tale: The Book of Transformations of Wenchang, the Divine Lord of Zitong* (Albany: State University of New York Press, 1994) is a study and annotated translation of a Daoist morality book that narrates the legends of the deity Wenchang, patron saint of the literati during the late imperial times. The morality book was produced through the method of spirit writing, where supposedly the deity himself possessed the stylus that wrote the stories.

2. Translation by David Jordan, reproduced with permission from http://anthro. ucsdedu/~dkjordan/scriptorium/tayshanq/tayshanq00.html, accessed December 22, 2008.

3. See Kristofer Schipper's classic study *The Taoist Body*, trans. Karen C. Duval (Berkeley: University of California Press, 1994).

4. See Cynthia J. Brokaw's *The Ledgers of Merit and Demerit: Social Change and Moral Order in Late Imperial China* (Princeton, N.J.: Princeton University Press, 1991) on the invention and use of such a method in Song dynasty China.

5. Michel Foucault, *The History of Sexuality, Vol. 3: The Care of the Self*, trans. Robert Hurley (New York: Vintage, 1988).

6. Overmyer, *Precious Volumes*, passim.

7. Consult David A. Palmer's *Qigong Fever: Body, Science, and Utopia in China* (New York: Columbia University Press, 2007) for a sociological analysis of this phenomenal movement.

8. See Kristofer Schipper, *The Taoist Body*, on the cosmological justifications behind Daoist personal cultivation. Practicing *qigong* is mostly a personal-cultivational practice, though the large-scale *qigong* movement in China in the 1980s and 1990s grew out of a particular political and institutional environment.

9. This section is based on Alison R. Marshall, "Moving the Spirit on Taiwan: New Age Lingji Performance," in *Journal of Chinese Religions* 31 (2003): 81–99.

10. For a detailed historical and symbolic study of Daoist liturgical performance, consult John Lagerwey's *Taoist Ritual in Chinese Society and History* (New York: Macmillan; 1987). More on the same theme by Catherine Bell, "Ritualization of Texts and Textualization of Rituals in the Codification of Taoist Liturgy," in *History of Religions* 27 (1988): 366–392.

11. Kenneth Dean, *Lord of the Three in One: The Spread of a Cult in Southeast China* (Princeton, N.J.: Princeton University Press, 1998), 9.

12. Angela Zito, *Of Body and Brush: Grand Sacrifice as Text/Performance* (Chicago: University of Chicago Press, 1997), shows the relationship between the performance of imperial court rituals and their textualization by court ritualists, thus demonstrating the close relationship between the discursive and liturgical modalities.

13. Lagerwey, *Taoist Ritual*, passim.

14. Kristofer Schipper, "Comment on crée un lieu saint local," in Schipper, *La religion de la Chine: la tradition vivante* (Paris: Fayard, 2008), 305–327.

15. Lagerwey, *Taoist Ritual*, passim.

16. All information in this paragraph derived from Yau Chi On, "Xianggang daojiao songwen qifu fahui ji qi biwen jingwen" [The Hong Kong Daoist Ritual of Prayer to Expel Epidemics and Its Exorcistic Scriptures], in *Huanan yanjiu ziliao zhongxin tongxun* [Bulletin of the South China Research Centre] no. 32 (2003).

17. For more detailed studies on the "beating the mean person" ritual, consult Chiao Chien's "'Beating the Petty Person': A Ritual of the Hong Kong Chinese," *Special Issue on Anthropological Studies of China, New Asia Academic Bulletin* 6 (1986): 211–218 and a research report on the website http://www.cciv.cityu.edu.hk/website-2006-2007-a/?redirect=/~cciv/product/fest/gano/index.php (Chinese Civilization Centre, City University of Hong Kong; in Chinese), accessed on 25 April, 2011.

18. The information in this section is based on various websites on the practice of beating the mean person, especially one provided by the Chinese Civilization Centre at the City University of Hong Kong, which includes an audio segment of a professional old lady's beating the mean person curse (see note 17 for web link).

19. See the online article in note 17 for details of the session.

20. Kenneth Dean, *Lord of the Three in One*, 34.

21. Adam Yuet Chau's *Miraculous Response: Doing Popular Religion in Contemporary China* (Stanford, Calif.: Stanford University Press, 2006) is particularly useful in explaining the importance of the immediate-practical and relational modalities of doing religion, which are prominent in most agrarian deity cults.

22. Steven Sangren, *Chinese Sociologics: An Anthropological Account of the Role of Alienation in Social Reproduction*, London School of Economics Monographs on Social Anthropology, Volume 72 (London: Athlone Press, 2000).

23. Here I am relying on the work by the anthropologist Gareth Fisher, "Morality Books and the Re-Growth of Lay Buddhism in China," in Adam Yuet Chau, ed., *Religion in Contemporary China: Revitalization and Innovation* (London: Routledge, 2011). Fisher conducted fieldwork in a number of major monasteries in north China in the early 2000s.

{ PART II }

Religion, Culture, and Society

The Body: Health, Nation, and Transcendence
David A. Palmer

In the final scene of the 2006 film *Fearless*, the famous Chinese martial artist Huo Yuanjia, played by Jet Li, faces his Japanese challenger Anno Tanaka for a climactic kung fu combat. The place is Shanghai, and the year is 1910. The imperial Qing dynasty is on the verge of collapse. The Western powers and Japan have defeated China in several wars and carved up the Middle Kingdom into concessions and zones of influence. And to add insult to injury, muscular foreign bullies and ruffians, such as the American Hercules O'Brien, have come to beat Chinese in wrestling matches, knocking them off as "the sick men of the East." But Huo Yuanjia has stepped forth to meet the challenge and restore China's dignity. Using the secrets of Chinese fighting, he has defeated O'Brien and others, earning their admiration for his grace and chivalry. Now comes the final combat, against Anno Tanaka. The first round is a draw. During the intermission, the Japanese consul switches Huo's teacup with one laced with arsenic; within minutes Huo starts gasping and vomiting blood. Knowing that he will die anyway, he decides to continue the fight. Breathless and weakened, he is no match for Tanaka. He sees an opening to give a fatal blow to his Japanese adversary—but, in a show of mercy, delivers it without any force, and collapses to his own death. Tanaka, realizing Huo's skill and nobility, lifts him from the floor and declares him the victor.[1]

In this story, the body can be seen as a metaphor for the Chinese nation. Weak and sickly, the Chinese were humiliated and defeated by foreign aggressors. To defend the nation, the body needed to be restored and strengthened. How to do this was a subject of heated debate in China at the time of Huo Yuanjia. Many Chinese intellectuals and political leaders, exposed to Western ideas, ridiculed Huo's martial arts as circus tricks and superstitions: what China needed was rigorous Western-style military drills and sports. Physical education was taught in modern schools, and Chinese athletes were trained to participate in international competitions. They joined the Olympic movement and, by the early 2000s, were among the top medal-winning nations of the world. The crowning achievement was when Beijing itself hosted the Olympic Games in 2008 (see box 4.1).

But others prefer traditional martial arts as the true path for nurturing and strengthening the Chinese body. In the foregoing scene, the secrets of Chinese martial arts are the key to Huo's victories, giving him the nimbleness, virtuosity, and power to defeat adversaries far taller and more muscular than himself. But it is his moral integrity, his mercy, and his benevolence—also essential dimensions of Chinese martial arts—that give him the ultimate victory, in which Tanaka voluntarily concedes defeat, giving a spiritual significance to the contest.

What *is* the secret of Chinese martial arts? A related question is, why are we talking about martial arts in a book about religion? So Huo Yuanjia had a better fighting technique. So he was a man of integrity. Is there anything religious about that? To be sure, in the film *Fearless*, as in many martial arts courses and academies today, there are no visible signs of religion. Indeed, Huo Yuanjia himself was a founder of the first modern martial arts association, the Chin Woo Athletic Association, that gave itself the mission of erasing any trace of religion or superstition from kung fu. But if we look at other kung fu films, such as *Crouching Tiger, Hidden Dragon*, we see plenty of scenes of fighters flying through forests, running on the surface of lakes, using all sorts of magic, and encountering old wise men, Daoist wizards and Buddhist masters, who hold the secrets of defying the laws of gravity. Indeed, the two most famous centers for martial arts training in China, Shaolin and Wudang, are respectively a Buddhist and a Daoist monastery. In these traditions, martial arts are a form of spiritual discipline. "Soft" methods like *taijiquan* (known in the West as tai chi) are now practiced by millions around the world,

FIGURE 5.1 *Shaolin flying martial arts. (Hua Qing/FOTOE)*

not really for fighting but for health benefits. It's hard to draw the line between exercises that are practiced for fighting, for health, and for spiritual training. *Taijiquan*, for instance, merges the three goals together.

If you go to a park at dawn in a Chinese city, you will see groups of people practicing *taijiquan*, and others practicing other types of exercises: elderly men and women standing still, facing clumps of bushes, eyes closed, their hands in a circle below the abdomen. Others drawing arcs in the air with their stretched arms, following the rhythm of taped traditional Chinese music. Others may be stretching and contracting their bodies. These exercises are called *qigong*, "breath training." Here too, it is hard to imagine what connection that has to religion; it simply looks like a gentle type of physical fitness exercise. Some people prefer jogging, others weight training, and others, especially seniors, prefer the slow movements of *qigong* or *taijiquan*. But let's look at another type of *qigong* event, which was popular in mainland China in the 1980s and '90s. There are 5000 people assembled in a sports stadium, and a *qigong* master is giving a lecture while they sit in meditation. The master talks about how meditation can induce relaxation and good health—but he also talks about how, to really benefit from *qigong* exercises, you need to live a moral life, to be considerate to others, and to be concerned for the salvation of all sentient beings. His speech is peppered with stories about Buddhist and Daoist masters who have reached such high goals of accomplishment in *qigong* practice that they could travel into the past and into the future, could walk through walls, and could miraculously heal other peoples' illnesses. And while the master speaks, people in the audience start going into fits, some of them laughing and burping, others rolling on the ground. Some stand up and bob in the motions of Chinese dance or martial

FIGURE 5.2 *Taijiquan. (Zhang Tianlin/Photobase/FOTOE)*

arts. They are in a trance. And when it's over, they claim that their illnesses are cured: their back pains, their gallbladders, their ulcers, their diabetes, even their cancers. Paraplegics, who had come in their wheelchairs, stand up and walk. Excitement spreads throughout the stadium—the *qigong* master himself, right up there on the stage, has the miraculous powers of the wizards of old legends!

In another type of group practice session, called "spontaneous movements *qigong*" in mainland China and "spiritual mediumship" in Taiwan (see previous chapter), practitioners begin a set of gymnastic exercises or sitting meditation, get the cosmic energy (*qi*) flowing in their body, and then let themselves go. Their bodies might start rocking back and forth, they might begin tapping themselves as in a massage, bobbing up and down as if in a slow-motion dance, or doing rapid swings as if in kung fu combat, or even start running long distances. And then, some of them might find themselves possessed by a god—the Avalokitesvara Guanyin, or the Jade Emperor, or even Sun Wukong, the Monkey King.

In all of these examples, we see people practicing traditional disciplines for training the mind and body, with the hope of improving their health, increasing their mental and physical powers, and attaining higher spiritual states and levels of wisdom. Unlike in the West, where individual body disciplines such as workouts, weight training, swimming, or running are quite mechanical, and are not seen as organically connected to other aspects of life, what we see with these Chinese traditions is that these technologies—which all involve, in some way or another, harnessing the cosmic powers of *qi*—are quite readily connected with mystical experiences.

FIGURE 5.3 *Qigong practitioners in a Beijing park. (Photo David Palmer)*

religious visions, moral discipline, practices of combat (in the martial arts), and, as we will discuss later, even political resistance. How can this be?

The Body, Immortality, and Divinity

All of these practices, from martial arts to *taijiquan* and *qigong*, and even acupuncture and Chinese herbal therapies, are based on a common set of ideas about the cosmos and about the human body. Chinese cosmology sees no clear dichotomy between the mind and the body. Indeed, Chinese traditions have not objectified a physical body separate from mental functions or even the individual's social persona. The body is understood in a nondualistic sense that literally embodies all interconnected human functions, including thinking, feeling, moving, breathing, desiring, ingesting, digesting, and so on.

In contrast to the dualism common in the philosophical and religious traditions of India, ancient Greece, and Europe, which tend to sacralize the soul (or mind) while demeaning the body, in Chinese tradition the body itself (seen nondualistically as including mental and spiritual functions) is typically considered to be sacred. This view permeates popular culture and customs as much as it does Confucian and Daoist philosophy: as a sacred gift from our parents, the body must be protected in its integrity (in the past, cutting open the body for anatomical inspection was seen as a violation of the body's sacredness, a view reflected today in reluctance to donate organs); as the object of love and attention, a healthy body is the sign of and the repository of life, and so the body must be well fed and nurtured in order to attain good health and longevity. The care of the body is expressed through the great importance attached to food, to eating, and to the therapeutic qualities of different ingredients and dishes. It is also expressed through the rich and varied techniques of gymnastics, breath training, meditation, and other forms of "life cultivation," which aim to nurture and strengthen the vital energies and capacities of the body. Even the sexual act, or the "arts of the bedchamber," are seen as a form of life cultivation, which can be properly trained to minimize the loss of vital essence and to maximize the circulation and exchange of *yin* and *yang* energies (see next chapter).

While notions of nurturing, managing, and disciplining the powers of the human body are widespread in the popular culture, they are also the themes of specialized religious regimens. For a committed practitioner, the signs of accomplishment are typically considered to be vigorous health, longevity, and the ability to perform paranormal feats: so attuned are the powers of his body to those of the universe that he can accomplish anything effortlessly.

Indeed, in Daoist lore, such an adept would be able to escape death—not through the soul's liberation from his body, as in most religions, but through a process of meditational discipline, by refining his powers and bodily substance to such a degree that it becomes ethereal and immortal, no longer subject to the limitations of space and time. These visions of spiritual perfection draw heavily on alchemical metaphors: just as the alchemist attempts to forge the "philosopher's stone," known in Chinese as the elixir of immortality, by combining various mineral substances, refining them and inducing their transformation into a new substance, so the "inner alchemist" mentally collects the various energies and substances of the cosmos and of his body—notably breath, saliva, and semen—directs their circulation, and combines them in his body to produce the "golden elixir" of health and immortality. This process of spiritual refinement is said to go through three stages: the first stage involves techniques for ending seminal emissions (for men) and menstrual flows (for women), thereby preventing the dissipation of vital essence. Through meditation techniques, the essence is circulated and transformed into vital energy (qi). The next stage involves, through other procedures, turning qi into spirit, and from thence, from the realm of the spirit, to return to the void. The process is thus one of transmuting the essential substance of the body, turning it into something increasingly ethereal, until it can no longer be affected by processes of decay and death. Indeed, it is said to reverse the process of aging, returning to a state of infancy and even beyond, to a state of pure energy that has not yet condensed itself into the physical form of the human body. While in most cases, this immortal body is considered to exist in a rarefied and invisible form, in other cases, such as when a corpse does not decay after its death, this is also seen as evidence of the person's immortal accomplishment.

Those who have attained to immortality are said to have become a "perfected one," a "transcendent being." Connected with Dao, such beings aid the common people by curing the sick and the unfortunate. They do this either as living healers in this world, or, having become transcendent beings, they are worshipped as gods in temples, responding to prayers for health and protection.

BOX 5.1 Cremation and Burial

Cremation is the most widespread form of disposing corpses in Chinese cities today. But until the twentieth century, cremation was practiced only for Buddhist monks, as a sign of their liberation from cycles of death and rebirth. For most Chinese, however, the body was sacred, and it had to be properly buried. Families went to great lengths to find a geomantically suitable site for the tomb: well positioned according to fengshui principles, the tomb could bring powerful energies to the living patrilineal descendents; while a poorly placed tomb could bring misfortune. The countryside, particularly hillsides, was littered with tombs, where families would come to honor their ancestors during the "tomb sweeping" festival in April. By the 1930s, however, the Chinese state began to promote cremation, both to eliminate burial "superstitions" and to free up arable land. This policy was continued by the communist authorities after 1949, but met with great resistance in rural China, and even today is only partly followed in the villages. In the cities, however, cremation is now universal, even outside the mainland, such as in Hong Kong and Singapore, simply because land for burial plots is too scarce in dense metropolitan areas.

Explanatory Models for Illnesses

When people worship such gods and immortals in temples, they typically pray for divine blessings and protection, expressed through good health, longevity, having many sons, and material prosperity—the signs of a flourishing life. On the other hand, illness and disease traditionally call for a religious or cosmological explanation, which leads to specific types of religious/cosmological treatments. The disturbance in the body is seen as connected to a disturbance in the flow of cosmic forces, or it may be caused by a disturbance in the normal relationships between the sick person and invisible beings such as gods, ghosts, or ancestors.

When somebody falls ill—especially if it's a grave or unusual illness, and nowadays, if recourse to Western biomedicine seems to be of no avail—family members, friends, and neighbors, when they worry about the victim or gossip about the case, will speculate about some of those possible causes. And they might recall and talk about some local healer and the people he or she has healed, or about a nearby temple at which the god is said to be especially efficacious. And then they might go and see one of these healers or worship at that temple.

There are many types of healers and many types of explanations for illnesses. A few examples are included here. From these examples, we can see that several types of explanatory models exist in Chinese religious culture to explain and cure illness and misfortune. A specific set of therapeutic techniques, which is often the specialty of a specific type of healer, corresponds to each explanatory model.

ILLNESS CAUSED BY A GHOST

A woman repeatedly fell ill and remained barren after several years of marriage. The couple thought that the culprit was the ghost of the husband's brother, who had been beheaded by the Japanese during World War II. Those who die an unnatural death are said to have a huge unspent life force, while their soul cannot be properly worshipped as an ancestor. His soul was troubled and continued to hover around his surviving family members, causing the death of his mother from physical and mental illness. Now he was jealous of his brother, who was alive and married, and tried to stop him from having children. The couple burned offerings to the ghost at their doorstep, on the first and fifteenth day of each month, calling out, "We are giving you money and offerings; take them and be satisfied! Don't come back to bother our family!" The "money" they offered, on which the English words "hell bank notes" were printed, was burned as an offering for the soul of the dead, to cover its expenses in the netherworld; mandarin oranges were also offered to feed the soul. The couple also hired a Daoist priest to conduct rituals of exorcism to drive the ghost away. Now they planned to buy a silver plaque with the brother's name on it, place it in a funerary urn, and bury it in a permanent tomb for the soul to rest in peace. One night, the ghost spoke through a female spirit medium, saying, "It was not time for me to die. My head was severed by a Japanese sword. I am angry and lost because my bones are mixed with those of other people." But the ghost thanked the couple for all the offerings and money, and said that it would not be necessary to build a permanent tomb for him: it would be sufficient to write his name on a piece of silver paper, and hang it beside their ancestral altar. "If you do this," the ghost said, "I will try to help you, my brother, and your wife to have good luck and many children."[2]

ILLNESS CAUSED BY A GOD

During the Mao years, many people, caught up in the frenzy of political campaigns, vandalized temples and smashed the god statues to the ground. Years later, when these individuals died or suffered from illnesses, especially strange or debilitating ones, people would gossip that the illness was the god's revenge. In one case described by Adam Chau, during the Cultural Revolution, a young man used his hoe to smash the head off the statue of the Black Dragon King, the local god of a temple in Shaanxi province. Years later, his own head was blasted off by dynamite while he was working on building the runway at a military airport. His only son was a "half-witted village idiot." The villagers gossiped that these calamities were divine retribution.[3] In other cases, in order to "pay back" for his sins, the vandal would rebuild the temple and worship the god. Many temple cults were restored after the Cultural Revolution by such individuals.[4]

ILLNESS CAUSED BY BAD KARMA

A boy was born with a severe mental handicap, such that he would never be able to communicate or do anything on his own. Taking care of the boy was a heavy burden on his parents, who also had serious health problems of their own and what appeared to be a string of bad luck. They wondered why so many misfortunes were befalling them. One explanation they heard was that it was the result of bad karma: according to popular understandings of Buddhist notions of causality and cosmic recompense (see chapter 1), each deed has its consequences, either in this life or a future one; good and evil deeds will eventually come back to you. At some point in their past lives, they had committed some evil deed, and they were now reaping the bitter reward. Or perhaps the evil deeds had been committed in this life, because the parents recalled their own feelings of guilt over acts they had committed at a younger age. Among the ways to redress the karmic burden was to do meritorious deeds: to recite Buddhist scriptures or hire Buddhist monks to do so; to donate funds to a Buddhist temple; or to devote themselves to Buddhism, perhaps by entering a monastic order, in order to generate a great amount of karmic merit.

ILLNESS CAUSED BY DEMONS

Another explanation they considered was that the boy was possessed by a demon, based on the idea that the world is full of wild, unruly, hungry, or malicious ghosts and demons, who attack or attach themselves to human victims. In this case, the remedy would be an exorcism to exterminate the demons or to scare them away with an even stronger spiritual power. This involves both defensive and offensive measures—for example, to have the boy wear a talisman or an amulet on his body; or to protect the entrances to his home by pasting images of protective gods on the door (because the demons are afraid of the fierce expressions of the guards); or to affix a mirror over the door (because the demons would be frightened by their own hideous reflection in the mirror). Exorcistic rituals are often conducted by Daoist priests, or by spirit mediums (shamans), who enter into a trance and are said to enter the invisible world to personally do battle against the demons. Offensive acts often involve the healer (the priest or spirit medium) acting as the military commander of an army of spirits and gods—through ritual acts, he names the gods being summoned, blows a horn to array them in battle formation, and dispatches them against the demons. Or, acting as a celestial official, he issues written edicts that command the demons to disperse. These edicts take the form of talismans written in an esoteric script, which are pasted on the walls of the client's home. The talismans can also be burned, the ashes mixed with water, and then ingested by the sick person.

ILLNESS CAUSED BY BAD FENGSHUI

A boy suddenly went mad without reason. His parents called on a fengshui master to see if the problem had anything to do with the house or its environment. The role of the fengshui master is to identify where the problem lies in the geomantic

FIGURE 5.4 *Yin-yang figure with Eight Trigrams. (FOTOE)*

positioning of the client's home or ancestral grave. Using a special geomantic compass, and after making numerological calculations, the master would make suggestions for modifying the layout of the house, adding or removing a structure, in order to unblock the flow of *qi* or, on the contrary, to block the flow of negative energies toward the victim's home. At first, the master could find nothing wrong. Then he went to the family gravesite on a nearby hill. He noticed that the gate of the house and the front of the grave were directly facing each other. The master called this the "killing position," which has a morbid influence on the household. He instructed the family to reorient the grave. Then he went back with red paper and a brush. He cut out two pieces of paper and painted some Chinese characters on them. He placed one of them on the boy's forehead and rolled the other into a ball, which he asked the son to eat.[5]

ILLNESS CAUSED BY YIN-YANG IMBALANCE

A thirty-two-year-old woman went to see her doctor of Chinese traditional medicine, complaining of fatigue, hypochondrical pain, a feeling of oppression of the chest, migraines, and blurred vision. Her menstrual periods were always late and painful, and the discharge was dark with clots. She was restless in sleep, felt hot in the evenings, and had disturbing dreams. She felt aimless; her career and her relationship with her boyfriend were at a crossroads, but she felt that she "did not see the point of it all." The doctor examined her tongue, noting that it was red and without coating. Using the highly elaborate Chinese method, he checked her pulse, which he said was "floating," "empty," and "fine," but also "slightly wiry on the left side."

The doctor diagnosed her problem as a deficiency of the *yin* of her liver, in which the flow of *qi* and blood were stagnant, leading to the rootlessness of her soul, which caused the feeling of aimlessness and the disturbing dreams. The treatment he prescribed was a combination of herbs and acupuncture that would stimulate the circulation of *qi* and blood in the liver, nourish the *yin* in the liver, and root the soul.[6]

Cosmology and the Body

In the foregoing examples, several explanatory models have been evoked; these can be boiled down to two basic types: (1) illnesses or misfortunes caused by invisible personal agents—that is, gods, ghosts, or ancestors, and (2) those caused by impersonal cosmic forces. In the former case, health, long life, and prosperity can be assured by keeping ghosts and demons at bay, and by properly worshipping gods and ancestors. In the case of cosmic forces, health, long life, and prosperity derive from the circulation of such forces, both by properly positioning one's body or one's home in relation to flows of cosmic energy and by manipulating such flows to one's advantage. These cosmological methods are used in the many healing systems and body cultivation systems that are based on cosmic forces, such as fengshui, Chinese herbal medicine, acupuncture, martial arts, and *qigong*. In this section, we will briefly consider the common cosmology that is shared by all of these systems.

Central to any culture is its cosmology, that is, its view of the structure of the universe, of the different basic elements of the universe, how these elements are connected with one another, and the place of humanity in this universe. Associated with cosmology are systems of classification, which divide everything in the universe into separate categories.

In the basic cosmology of the Western scientific worldview, everything in the world is made of fundamental particles of matter. Higher level organisms are made of complex combinations of such particles. The questions most commonly asked are related to substance: "Does it exist?"; "What are its constituent parts?" And the most fundamental type of relationship is a binary one: yes/no, is/isn't, 1/0.

Chinese cosmology is more concerned with processes and patterns than with substances. The world as we experience it is the ephemeral expression of the ever-evolving unfolding of processes and the interrelation of forces and energy flows. The types of question this worldview gives rise to are of this type: What is the tendency? What type of process are we in? How are different processes interacting and how does this affect the overall pattern?

FIGURE 5.5 *Daoist talisman. (Photo David Palmer)*

This worldview is expressed through the symbols of *yin* and *yang*. *Yin* represents processes of inward contraction, tending toward receptivity, interiority, darkness, and rest, whereas yang represents processes of outward expansion, tending toward assertiveness, exteriority, brightness, and movement.

The notions of *yin* and *yang* appeared over 3000 years ago, when Chinese people observed the regularities of cycles of time and their association with aspects of geography and human life. These cycles were associated respectively with light and dark, hot and cold, south and north, going out and coming in, outside and inside, motion and stillness. These sets of opposites were symbolized by the characters *yang*, meaning "the sunny side of a hill," and *yin*, meaning "the shady side of a hill." *Yin* and *yang* were seen to be in a dynamic, complementary, copulative, and generative relationship: the alternation and union of *yin* and *yang* gives birth to all beings.

Yin-yang categories have been used in China to classify everything in the universe. For example, looking at social relations, the men went out into the fields during the day and came back into the home to their wives at night: masculinity was associated with *yang*; femininity, with *yin*. Looking at the body, certain conditions, such as cold and deficiency, are *yin,* whereas others, such as heat and excess, are *yang*. Looking at the landscape, certain features, such as mountains, are *yang,* whereas others, such as pools of water or graves, are *yin*. South is *yang,* and north is *yin*. Morning is *yang,* and evening is *yin*. Summer is *yang,* and winter is *yin*. The relative state of *yin* and *yang* can be compared to undulating waves: like the cycle of the seasons, at times *yang* is ascendant, and at other times *yin* is. Life is generated by this dynamic and harmonious interplay of *yin* and *yang*. But if the harmony is broken, if the processes are thrown out of balance, illness and possibly death will occur. In a case of *yang* deficiency, *yang* needs to be strengthened through appropriate exercises or herbs; and the converse is true for *yin* deficiency.

A more complex scheme of interrelated processes is called the Five Phases (also translated as Five Elements or Five Agents). Each component is symbolized by a natural element: wood, fire, earth, metal, and water. In the words of Ted Kaptchuk,

> each Phase is an emblem that denotes a category of related functions and qualities. The Phase called Wood is associated with active functions that are

TABLE 5.1 Yin-Yang Categories

Yin	Yang
Night	Day
Winter	Summer
Moon	Sun
Dark	Light
Cold	Hot
North	South
Coming in	Going out
Inside	Outside
Stillness	Motion
Feminine	Masculine

in a growing phase. Fire designates functions that have reached a maximal state of activity and are about to begin a decline or a resting period. Metal represents functions in a declining state. Water represents functions that have reached a maximal state of rest and are about to change the direction of their activity. Finally, Earth designates a balance or neutrality; in a sense, Earth is a buffer between the other Phases.[7]

Each of these processes is found in the human body, associated with one of the organs; each phase leads to the next phase according to what is called the "generative" cycle, while it overcomes another phase according to what is called the "restrictive" cycle. Excessive strength or weakness in one of the phases in the body thus affects the balance of all the phases and leads to illness. Diagnosis consists of determining the overall pattern of the body's processes and identifying where the imbalance is occurring. Treatment consists of taking herbal combinations, acupuncture sessions, or exercise regimens that are designed to reset the balance in the body's processes.

In Chinese cosmology, all phenomena in the universe are classified as either *yin* or *yang*, and as expressing one of the five cyclic phases symbolized as wood, fire, earth, metal, and water. The human body is conceived as a microcosm of the whole universe. *Yin-yang* and the Five Phases can be used to map movement in both space and time. Everything is seen as interconnected. Cosmic order is characterized by the cyclical alteration of *yin* and *yang* and the orderly succession of the Five Phases.

Underlying all of these ideas is the flow of *qi*, which literally means "breath," "gas," or "vapor," and, in discussions of cosmology, is often translated as "vital energy" or "cosmic energy." Sometimes understood as the essential matter of the universe, its nature is to flow and circulate; its expression is life. Blocked or disrupted *qi* circulation is a sure cause of illness or misfortune; the flow of *qi* needs to be restored through exercises, herbs, acupuncture, or modifications to one's house or environment.

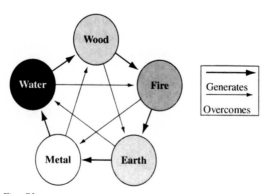

FIGURE 5.6 *The Five Phases.*

TABLE 5.2 Chinese Cosmology of Correspondences

Phase	Wood	Fire	Earth	Metal	Water
Time of day	Morning	Noon	Afternoon	Evening	Night
Time of year	Spring	Summer	End of summer	Autumn	Winter
Space	East	South	Center	West	North
Body	Liver	Heart	Spleen	Lung	Kidney
Color	Green	Red	Yellow	White	Black

Secularizing the Chinese Body

The cosmology I have just described, made up of impersonal energies and processes that follow an unchanging logic, sounds less "religious" than the often fickle gods, ghosts, and ancestors of the other explanatory models. In addition, body cultivation techniques based on Chinese cosmology—whether they be exercise regimens such as martial arts, *taijiquan*, or meditation, or therapeutic techniques such as acupuncture or herbal remedies—when practiced appropriately, are generally recognized as having beneficial health effects. Many people therefore claim that these practices have nothing to do with "religion" and that they are actually quite scientific.

This viewpoint has been widespread since the early twentieth century: as China came into intense contact with the West, and was defeated and humiliated in a series of wars against modern imperial powers, many Chinese intellectuals blamed China's weakness on its traditions and superstitions. Traditional medicine and religious therapies were, they claimed, responsible for the poor health of the Chinese people who could not defend themselves against the aggressors. Chinese armies were no match for Western soldiers and artillery, and Western medicine—which was being introduced by Christian missionaries who established China's first medical schools, in which many of the new intellectuals were trained—was seen as holding true and scientific remedies for illness. For these critics, the solution lay in modernizing China and replacing traditional martial arts, body cultivation, and herbal healing with biomedical science and modern military drills, sports, and physical education. One of the leading intellectuals of the time, Chen Duxiu (who was a founder of the Chinese Communist Party), wrote in his "Appeal to the Youth" in 1919:

> Our men of learning do not understand science; thus they make use of *yin-yang* signs and beliefs in the five elements to confuse the world....Our doctors do not understand science: they not only know nothing of human anatomy, but also know nothing of the analysis of medicines; as for bacterial poisoning and infections, they have not even heard of them.... The height of their wondrous illusions is the theory of *qi* which really applies to the professional acrobats and Daoist priests. We will never comprehend this *qi* even if we were to search everywhere in the universe. All of these fanciful

notions and irrational beliefs can be corrected at their roots by science, because to explain truth by science we must prove everything with fact.[8]

Others, however, came to the defense of Chinese body cultivation and healing traditions. They claimed that these were actually scientific systems of knowledge; and as such, they should be preserved, further developed, and even promoted internationally. But they acknowledged that the way these traditions were practiced was usually mired in superstition: it was not uncommon for an acupuncturist to also compose talismans for his clients, for martial artists to perform invincibility rites that involved trances and ingesting magic potions, or for meditators to worship Daoist immortals and gods. This was simply because traditional culture made no distinction between what modern people call "religious" and "secular" or nonreligious. The modern defenders of Chinese body traditions, however, were acutely conscious of such a distinction and did everything they could to modernize the traditions, to expurgate all their religious and "superstitious" elements and make them "scientific."

Through these projects, a new discourse emerged in defense of what became the new categories of "national medicine" and "national [martial] arts": both of these traditions were reformulated as part of China's "national essence," priceless gems that, along with calligraphy and art, should be proudly preserved by any self-respecting Chinese. This discourse fit squarely within the new nationalism; it vaunted Chinese medicine and martial arts as much for their Chineseness as for their intrinsic therapeutic or combat value. These projects of a Chinese medicine and martial arts, which could exist alongside with, and complement, Western medicine and sports, upheld the theoretical principles of the traditional cosmology while condemning most actual traditional doctors and fighters, who were blamed for the disrepute of the Chinese tradition. National medicine and martial arts were thus to be "scientized," with the goal of eliminating mystical and superstitious accretions, reformulating or reinterpreting classical theory in a manner compatible with science. In this system, occultism, mysticism, and magic were to be replaced by science—a science that would restore the original purity of the national essence, exemplifying the profound knowledge of physiology, mechanics, physics, and biology to be found in China's native wisdom.

The government of the People's Republic of China strongly supported these secularizing projects beginning in the early 1950s, which it applied both to Chinese medicine and martial arts and to the therapeutic traditions of minority nationalities, such as Tibetan medicine. It established large and prestigious hospitals and training academies for Chinese medicine, which could claim equal status with Western medicine. A nationwide system of training and tournaments was set up for martial arts. And meditation, breathing, and gymnastic traditions were promoted under the label of *qigong*. As a result of these secularizing projects, Chinese body traditions, including traditional Chinese medicine (TCM), *taijiquan*, and *qigong*, are usually seen as having nothing to do with religion, and are widely practiced both in socialist China and the West, by millions of people for whom the idea of a religious connection to these practices would never cross their minds.

It might appear, then, that these traditions have been successfully secularized. And yet, the religious connection can never be entirely cut out. These body practices often, and unexpectedly so, become gateways into worlds of mysticism and religiosity. In the 1980s and early 1990s, for example, *qigong* was actively promoted by the Chinese ministries of health and sports, and even by some of the country's top scientists and military leaders, as a cheap and efficient way to improve the health of the masses. But this led to a craze of trances and faith healing phenomena, as described at the beginning of this chapter. The passage to religiosity is facilitated by the dense Daoist and Buddhist symbolism associated with traditional body technologies. Attempts to secularize the techniques cannot obliterate a millennia-long history of their being embedded in religion. The lineages of which many masters are the inheritors, the religious symbolism of the classical texts describing the techniques, and the magical content of the kung fu films and novels that permeate Chinese pop culture, all conspire to make the religious roots of Chinese body traditions resurface. Many of the most popular *qigong* masters and meditation methods openly draw on religious symbols. Falun Gong, for example, claims to be a "Buddhist dharma," indeed to be the superior path of Buddhist discipline.

Furthermore, people who practice Chinese body techniques often have experiences that don't fit well with completely secularized worldviews. Indeed, it is not uncommon for *qigong* practice, for example, to trigger mental states and experiences that are difficult or even impossible to satisfactorily explain with materialist theories. These experiences include the sensation of flows of *qi* in the body, the sensation of receiving or emitting *qi* between persons, and visions and insights that can only be labeled "hallucinations" in biomedical terminology. The meaning of such experiences must thus be sought after elsewhere: either through concepts derived from religious traditions or through new theories that attempt to transcend the limitations of mechanical materialism. Either way, such practices draw the practitioner away from conventional secular worldviews. By exploring the inner universe of the body and directing the circulation of its energies, entering mystical realms through trances and visions, and connecting themselves, through a master, to ancient esoteric traditions, practitioners may enter an alternate world. Here, the body becomes a receptacle and a conduit of traditional wisdom and mystical symbols. Hitherto unknown forms of energy inside and outside the body can be experienced, monitored, directed, and emitted, leading to a feeling of better health and, often literally, of heightened power. Chinese body cultivation traditions offer ways of personally appropriating and embodying this new world of knowledge, power, and experience.

Even in Chinese medicine, debates constantly rage over where to draw the line between the "scientific," the "superstitious," and the "religious." At one extreme, there are those who want to look only at what can be observed and proven in the laboratory, and discard any trace of Chinese cosmology: study the chemical properties of Chinese herbs, for example, and isolate the active ingredients, extract those chemical elements, and manufacture them into pills that can be taken to treat diseases identified through biomedical diagnostic procedures. Others, however, claim that such an approach misses the entire point and efficacy of Chinese medicine: that it is the combination of different herbs according to carefully calibrated *yin* and *yang* properties as well as the Five Phases of water, wood, fire, earth, and metal; and that these calibrations are based on Chinese diagnostics, which look at how these properties are unbalanced in the patient. And still others go further, insisting that divination practices, exorcism, and deity worship continue to be important elements of Chinese medicine.

Part of the problem here is that although Chinese cosmology has a rational basis and need not include personified deities, it remains incompatible with the philosophical and ontological foundations of the Western scientific tradition, which cannot admit the existence of *yin* and *yang* or of the Five Phases, because they are neither observable physical substances, nor measurable physical forces. From such a perspective, they can only be considered to be metaphysical ideas or poetic metaphors. As a result, in spite of all the attempts to modernize and secularize Chinese body traditions, they have never been fully recognized or integrated into mainstream scientific thinking and practice.

A common response to their "rejection" by scientific institutions is a nationalist one: to claim that these practices are scientific, but that they are part of a Chinese science, one that is essentially different from, and even superior to, Western science. Advocates claim that this science has its roots in 5000 years of Chinese history and civilization, and that its advantage over Western science lies in its holistic worldview: whereas Western science looks only at the external appearances of things, these Chinese sciences look at the inner roots of phenomena. Another response to the rejection by Western science is for practitioners to reject materialism and to return to the spiritual dimensions of Chinese body practices.

Christians face a similar issue in relation to practices such as *qigong*: some consider it to be a secular form of physical exercise, or a form of spiritual cultivation that, either way, is compatible with Christian faith. Others, however, pointing to the powers felt by many practitioners, condemn them as demonic and warn Christians to stay away from them.

Holism and Virtue

The two responses—to advocate a Chinese (or Oriental) science, or to explore the spiritual dimensions of the tradition—are not incompatible: there are also attempts to create a new system of knowledge, one that would integrate both the scientific and the spiritual aspects of Chinese tradition into an all-encompassing, holistic wisdom. For example, one famous *qigong* master, Yan Xin, called for *qigong* to be seen as an ideal, all-encompassing form of erudition which includes multiple forms of knowledge, allows mankind to know himself and the universe, has an epistemology and a methodology, and contains a philosophy of life, of the world and of the cosmos. [. . .] It is a complete scientific discipline. [. . .] [As a science of the mind, *qigong* requires one] to stay in an enlightened, virtuous and moral state of mind, nourished by a high ideal. The ancient *qigong* masters of high antiquity had already recognized that man, if he wants true happiness, must have a luminous and infinite inner heart, and be benevolent to men and things. [. . .] The Ancients, in high antiquity, according to primary sources on *qigong* from 7000 years ago, [. . .] [emphasized the importance of] "being rooted in virtue." [. . .] Thus, the simultaneous training of both spirit and body is the most important characteristic of *qigong*. It is not merely mechanical gestures, nor the arduous but superficial training of ordinary martial arts, but a training of the inner spirit. It involves linking our thoughts to the great common aspiration of the whole world [. . .], to use our wisdom to harmonize all things in need of harmony. The greater our contribution, the greater our merit, and the higher our benefit; the bodily and spiritual benefit then becomes obvious. Thus, the concrete training of the body is of secondary importance.[9]

As this passage shows, Chinese body traditions reinforce the tendency, already strong in Chinese culture, to experience the corporal, the emotional, the social, and the spiritual as a single undifferentiated whole. The practitioner is thus led to seek a globalizing explanatory model, incompatible with the reductionist and analytical categories of medical science. From health technique, then, these practices lead relatively easily to mystical experience and religious belief. One passes easily from physical training to moral discipline and questioning on the meaning of life or the nature of the universe.

"Being rooted in virtue," more than any set of techniques, is always considered to be essential to any serious nurturing of the body. On the one hand, vital energy is strongly connected with the sexual urge and its sublimation into spiritual power; to avoid the dissipation of vital energy thus involves disciplining the basic instincts, harmonizing the emotions, and living a moral life. On the other hand, transcending the ego through conforming to Dao or Heaven leads to increased spiritual power, which is expressed through virtue and health. Moral behavior and Confucian propriety are thus integrated into Chinese cosmology. Man is seen as occupying a central position in the universe—between Heaven (*yang*) and Earth (*yin*), at the junction of *yin* and *yang*, containing within his body all the elements and powers of the cosmos. He must respect the *yin* and *yang* positions of authority and submission within the social hierarchy: the ruler is *yang* to the minister's *yin*, the father is *yang* to the son's *yin*, the husband is *yang* to the wife's *yin*. If man's behavior does not conform to the moral principles of the cosmic order, the disruptions can reverberate throughout the cosmos and come back to him in the form of illness or bad luck. This was all the more the case for the emperor in traditional China who, as the Supreme Man, was the fundamental pivot between Heaven and Earth. When the ruler's body was not disciplined, corruption would spread in government, cosmic harmony would be disrupted, and calamities, wars, epidemics, and natural disasters would be the result.

In Chinese cosmology, then, embodied virtue is power. It is key to obtaining, legitimizing, and maintaining political authority and social stability. In situations of chaos, however, or when political authority is weak or subverted, it is also the refuge of justice and righteousness. Thus, in the popular lore surrounding the martial arts tradition, wandering warriors hide in the marshlands, fight off gangs of bandits, and, when the ruling dynasty has become too corrupt and oppressive, they arise in rebellion. They owe their victories to the virtuosity of their bodies—a virtuosity that itself is rooted in virtue. Virtue is the source of their power and legitimizes their cause. Many of the martial arts forms popular today emerged during the Qing dynasty, among rebels and secret brotherhoods that hoped to overthrow the Manchu rulers. When the common folk of north China revolted against the Western powers and their churches in 1900, they were convinced, as "Fellows United in Righteousness" (known in the West as the "Boxers" or the "Righteous and Harmonious Fists"), that with their virtue, and the magic spells and martial arts techniques of "spirit fighting," their bodies could repel the evil foreigners' guns and bullets. And today, the most determined challenge to the rule of the Chinese Communist Party comes from the body cultivators of Falun Gong, who combine *qigong* exercises with the pursuit of a high level of moral virtue—which is said to purify the body of the "black matter" of accumulated karmic debts. As discussed in chapter 12, practitioners contrast the moral dimension of Falun Gong with the corruption of the Chinese regime, both to justify their campaign against the Communist Party and to strengthen the resolve of practitioners in the face of repression.

Conclusion

In the Chinese tradition, the body is a site for the battle against ghosts and demons, whose attacks are made manifest through illnesses; it is also a site for physical fights against "bad guys," national enemies or oppressive rulers, such as in the martial arts tradition. The priests, exorcists, immortals, emperors, and errant warriors mentioned in this chapter all have one thing in common: it is through their bodies, steeled through the discipline of virtue, that the battles against the forces of chaos and corruption are waged. At the same time, their bodies are sites for refinement toward ever-higher levels of spirituality, nurturing health through harmony with cosmic forces and processes, and even tending to transcendence. There are no clear lines in Chinese tradition between these functions of the body, which are combined in many of the body cultivation and medical practices that have evolved over the centuries in China. In modern times, attempts to secularize these practices have been promoted by the Chinese state and have facilitated their wide dissemination. But it is difficult, if not impossible, to completely eliminate their religious dimension; and they can become unexpected gateways for the emergence of popular religiosity.

Notes

1. Huo Yuanjia was a real historical figure, but many details in the film are fictionalized.

2. Case described in Jack M. Potter, "Cantonese Shamanism," in *Religion and Ritual in Chinese Society,* ed. Arthur P. Wolf (Stanford, Calif.: Stanford University Press, 1989), 208–209.

3. Adam Chau, *Miraculous Response: Doing Popular Religion in Contemporary China* (Stanford, Calif.: Stanford University Press, 2006), 70–71.

4. Stephen Feuchtwang and Wang Mingming, *Grassroots Charisma: Four Local Leaders in China* (London: Routledge, 2001), 63.

5. Case described in Ole Bruun, *Fengshui in China: Geomantic Divination between State Orthodoxy and Popular Religion* (Oslo: NIAS Press, 2003), 216.

6. Case abridged from Giovani Maciocia, *The Practice of Chinese Medicine: The Treatment of Diseases with Acupuncture and Chinese Herbs* (Edinburgh: Churchill Livingstone, 1994), 275.

7. Ted J. Kaptchuk, *Chinese Medicine: The Web That Has No Weaver* (London: Rider, 1983), 343–344.

8. Quoted in D. W. Y. Kwok, *Scientism in Chinese Thought: 1900–1950* (New Haven, Conn.: Yale University Press, 1965), 65.

9. Quoted in David A. Palmer, *Qigong Fever: Body, Science, and Utopia in China* (New York: Columbia University Press), 112.

Gender and Sexuality
C. Julia Huang, Elena Valussi, and David A. Palmer

The most popular deity in the Chinese world is probably Guanyin, the Bodhisattva of Compassion, or "Goddess of Mercy," whose porcelain statues can be seen everywhere. Even where other gods or ancestors are the main objects of worship, shrines to Guanyin can typically be found as well: in temples, in small domestic shrines in homes, even in open-air altars or at the foot of sacred rocks and trees.

Guanyin means "perceiver of sounds" and refers to the deity's ability to hear the cries of the suffering beings in this world. Guanyin is the Chinese name for Avalokitesvara, who is worshipped throughout the Buddhist world and has even been described as "the cult of half of Asia." However, Avalokitesvara has never been worshipped as a goddess in India, Sri Lanka, or Southeast Asia. In Tibet, the Dalai Lama (always a man) is considered to be the reincarnation of Avalokitesvara. Many tenth-century paintings from Dunhuang, on the Silk Road in west China, show him with a moustache. The sexual transformation from a masculine figure to a goddess seems to be a Chinese phenomenon, and has to do with the story of Princess Miaoshan (Wonderful Goodness).[1] The story appeared as early as the twelfth century, and it goes as follows:

> Miaoshan was the third daughter of King Miaozhuang (Wonderful Adornment). She was by nature drawn to Buddhism, keeping a vegetarian diet, reading scriptures by day, and meditating at night from an early age. The king had no sons and hoped to marry his daughters off, choosing an heir from among his sons-in-law. When Miaoshan reached the marriageable age, however, she refused to get married. The king was greatly angered by her refusal and harshly punished her. She was first confined to the back gardens and subjected to hard labor. But with the aid of gods, she completed her tasks. So she was allowed to go to the White Sparrow Nunnery to undergo further trials, in the hope of discouraging her from pursing the religious path.

FIGURE 6.1 *Miaoshan transformed into Guanyin with 1000 arms and eyes. (Nie Ming/ FOTOE)*

She persevered, however, and the king burned down the nunnery, killed the five hundred nuns, and had Miaoshan executed for her unfilial behavior.

Her body, however, was safeguarded by a mountain spirit, and Miaoshan's soul descended to hell, where she saved other souls by preaching the Buddhist Dharma to them. She returned to the world, went to the Mountain of Fragrances, meditated for nine years, and achieved enlightenment.

By this time, the king had become seriously ill with a mysterious disease that resisted all medical treatment. Miaoshan, disguised as a mendicant monk, came to the palace and told the dying king that there was only one remedy that could save him: a medicine concocted with the eyes and hands of someone who had never felt anger. She further told the astonished king where to find such a person, at the Mountain of Fragrances.

When the king's messengers arrived, Miaoshan willingly offered her own eyes and hands. The father recovered after taking the medicine and came to the mountain with a royal party on a pilgrimage to offer thanks to his savior. He recognized the eyeless and handless ascetic as none other than his own daughter. Overwhelmed with remorse, he and the rest of the royal family all converted to Buddhism. Miaoshan was transformed into her true form, that of the Thousand-Eyed and Thousand-Armed Guanyin. After the apotheosis, Miaoshan passed away and a pagoda was erected to house her relics.[2]

This story says much about the fluid possibilities in the gender construction of divinity in Chinese culture. A masculine god can be transformed into a feminine deity over hundreds of years. Much of the gender transformation parallels and overlaps the deity's relocation from India to China. Such transformation is done through the narrative of a female incarnation. Central to the narrative is the tension between filial piety and resistance to marriage. The dramatization of the conflict between familial duties and women's autonomy is a symbolic presentation of women's role in social reality. Religion—in this case, Buddhism—is the final resolution for a woman who could thus achieve autonomy while fulfilling filial piety.

Moving closer to the present, let us visit a township in southwestern Taiwan on a Sunday in 1997. Local lay followers of a Buddhist group, Tzu Chi (*Ciji*), are preparing for the arrival of more than fifty buses of visitors from different parts of Taiwan arriving to view the progress of a general hospital being built by their group. By 7:00 A.M., about thirty women and a few children have already shown up at the hospital construction site. Some have arrived as early as 5:00 A.M. and have been busy cooking sweet red bean soup and boiling fruit tea in the kitchen tent. Two of them frequently deliver trays filled with bowls of soup and cups of tea to the working women and warmly invite everyone present to enjoy them. About twenty women divide themselves around three round tables and start rolling dough by hand into rice cake balls.

By 8:00 A.M., several dozen men have arrived, taking on "heavy-duty" jobs, such as directing traffic and moving tables, although some just stand around chatting and admiring the hospital. A man in uniform joins one of the rice cake tables, and immediately the women start giggling and teasing him, the "single green among ten thousand reds." Later in the morning, most of the women move to the local branch of the Tzu Chi (*Ciji*) movement. On the sidewalk in front of the premises, some women wash and chop vegetables, while others stir professional-sized woks. Men occasionally stop by in different vehicles to drop off and pick up various items. Inside on the first floor, the space usually used for meditating has been converted to a lunch box packing floor, with columns of tables standing parallel to the two side walls. Each column is an assembly line that begins with a huge pot of white rice and piles of paper boxes, and ends in front of the altar to Guanyin, with bundles of chopsticks and rubber bands for the final wrapping of each lunch box. As more and more trays of food are moved to the tables, women begin to fill each lunch box with dishes in exactly the same pattern. By 11:00 A.M., about 300 lunch boxes for the visitors are ready for the men to pick up.

This vignette is a snapshot of how women and men participate voluntarily in an event that can be called a new genre of pilgrimage—followers come to a religious site not to worship a god but to view a hospital built with their religious donations. The scale and the pace of food preparation—and the festive atmosphere—resemble events at a community temple, such as a deity's birthday, in that all participants are local and can be mobilized on short notice based on existing networks. But it is also a new kind of festival mobilization because the religious group has no local origin—it is a nationwide organization, and even a global movement. The vignette tells us much about the division of labor along gender lines, and how a new kind of religious organization perpetuates traditional practices in public life.

The scene of the cooking team and the legend of Miaoshan illustrate the two sides of the main approaches to gender and sexuality in Chinese religions: the sociological and the symbolic. The former approaches religions in practice: the inspiration for and the regulation of social organizations, the division of labor in religious activities, and the religious source of morality, religious leadership, and religious movements. The latter focuses on religion as a symbolic construct and may look into the symbolism of rituals, deities, and myths, and the gender ideologies of different religious traditions.

This chapter considers some of the gender-specific dimensions of religious traditions in Chinese culture. It emphasizes the nuanced influences of religious ideas and practices on the roles that men and women play in public life and explains how those roles have evolved. Each major religious tradition is framed in gender-specific terms, through which the relationship between gender and religion should be understood as both symbolic constructs and social practices. We then discuss the important role of women in the revival of religions in contemporary China. The chapter concludes by considering the relationship between religion and masculinity in Chinese culture.

Symbolic Constructs and Social Practices of Gender and Sexuality

GODDESS ENIGMA: MOTHERHOOD VERSUS SEXUALITY

The pantheon of Chinese popular religion consists of territorial and hierarchical systems of masculine gods and nonterritorial exemplary popular deities. The celestial hierarchy very much resembles the ancient imperial administrative system: for example, from the top, the Jade Emperor rules over the city gods and the local earth gods, right down to the stove god, in the order of hierarchical levels from the state to the household. Just as higher level bureaucrats govern larger districts, the more exalted gods govern larger regions. Celestial bureaucrats and territorial deities—the gods worshipped in a community temple—tend to be masculine.[3]

Nonterritorial cults tend to focus on female and Buddhist deities. Among the popular exemplary goddesses are Guanyin, Mazu, and the Unborn Mother. These deities come from different religious traditions, but all are key figures in popular religion. We have introduced the legend of Miaoshan transforming into Guanyin at the beginning of this chapter. The leitmotif of Miaoshan's story is the resolution of the conflict between resistance to marriage and sacrificial filial piety. Similarly, the stories of Mazu and the Unborn Mother present images of femininity in which sexuality and the role of wifehood are absent. *Mazu*, literally the "mother ancestor" (also known as the Heavenly Empress [Tianhou] in Hong Kong and Guangdong), is a protector of fishermen. She is said to be the soul of Lin Moniang ("the silent lady"), who lived on Meizhou Island, off the coast of Fujian province. Lin Moniang's father and brothers were fishermen. One day when they were drowning in a typhoon, Lin Moniang went into a trance to save her father and brothers. She succumbed to an early death after this heroic act. Her spirit continues to protect seafarers and attracts a popular cult, which by now has spread far beyond the fishing villages on Taiwan and China's Southeastern coastal region and includes Vietnam and overseas Chinese in California. Her birthday festival during the third month of the Chinese lunar calendar (between late March and early April), attracts tens of thousands of pilgrims across Taiwan who walk in a ninety-mile procession, which has become an annual multimillion-dollar media extravaganza, as well as a much contested political arena on both sides of the Taiwan Strait.[4]

Another example is the cult of the Unborn Venerable Mother. The late imperial period witnessed the spread of many popular cults with one common feature: the cult of female goddesses, and most notably the Unborn Venerable Mother. The common feature that female goddesses present is their inclusivity.[5] Because these goddesses are symbolic mothers, they inherently have the capacity to bring their offspring together. The Unborn Venerable Mother is the ultimate mother, the first mother, mother of every other deity, including male deities. How could this better describe the concept of inclusivity? As described by the anthropologist Stephen Sangren, "female deities, unlike their male counterparts, do not favour the wealthy and influential over the poor, insiders over outsiders, or men over women."[6]

Moreover, the role of female goddesses as inclusive is implicit in the Chinese model of cosmology. If male deities are associated with hierarchy, authority, and legitimacy, it makes sense that, as Victor Turner puts it, "the sentiment of ultimate wholeness of the total community be assigned to female, especially maternal symbols."[7] At the same time as they acquire their status as all-encompassing mothers, these women lose their specific sexual and reproductive characteristics.

In some groups, members are said to be her adopted children.[8] She is another virginal mother to the world, carried to greater extremes than Guanyin holding a baby—the Unborn Venerable Mother literally is mother to us all, but without the pollution of actual procreation or birth. She is often portrayed as disappointed in her children, who have forgotten her and no longer follow the proper values. As one salvational text put it, "[Mother], thinking of her children with great pain and limitless sorrow, from the cool native land of utmost bliss has sent all the immortals and Buddhas to save the imperial [children] of origin. She sighs that they are lost in a 'yellow millet dream,' and in pity has descended in person to save the world, sending down from on high books written in [her] blood. . . ."[9] This idea has occasionally provided the seed for an ideology of cataclysmic world change in millenarian sects, but in most cases it has led instead to a call for moral renewal.

The general emphasis on motherhood alongside a downplaying of sexuality is a key to popular religion's gender construct. As Sangren writes,

> In sum, female purity as manifested in female deities involves the negation of woman as wife and affirmation of her role as mother (if not childbearer). In this way, Guanyin, Mazu, and the Eternal Mother each manage to embody

purely positive aspects of womanhood. Chinese conceptions of male deities, however, are more like their earthly counterparts—paternal and powerful figures to be sure, but susceptible to the foibles and foils of humanity. They may be bribed, manipulated, threatened, and cajoled. In contrast, Guanyin, Mazu, and the Eternal Mother are perfect in their generosity and purity; one need only ask with a pure heart, and all will be granted.[10]

However, studies of other female cults detail slightly different models of femininity from the all-inclusive nurturing mother, revealing that female deities were sometimes associated with the power of the sexual and reproductive capacities of daughters-in-law, a typical socially disruptive role.[11]

GENDERED BODY CULTIVATION IN DAOISM

The underlying tension between a nurturing and disruptive role is also at the basis of conceptions of the role of women and the female body and sexuality in Daoism—a tradition that is often seen as having a special relation with the feminine. This notion has a long history that starts with Laozi, considered the founder of Daoism and certainly one of its most revered patriarchs to this day, and the *Daodejing*, a book in eighty-one chapters attributed to him. In the *Daodejing*, Laozi refers to the Dao as "mother" in no less than five places, and the Dao itself is often equated to a "womb" from which everything ensues and to which everything returns. Concepts like "embracing the feminine" and the preeminence of metaphors like "water," "the valley," and "the mysterious feminine" are found throughout the text. These notions have been used by later scholars, Chinese and Western, to explain gender relations in a Daoist context, often indicating that Daoist philosophy preferred a more feminine approach to life, practice, and conduct. However, often, the reality of gender relations in a Daoist context has differed greatly from the ideal proposed in Laozi, and scholars are too quick to equate "the feminine" with "women." For male practitioners "embracing the feminine" meant more an exercise in balancing their inner worlds than balancing gender relations in society. Although it is certainly true that Chinese religion, and Daoism with it, is populated by a large number of female goddesses, and that these goddesses have a large number of female followers, often these goddesses, as has been explained earlier, circumvented the need for expected duties as wives and mothers by performing exceptional filial deeds in exchange for their unwillingness to marry. They are viewed and accepted as "exceptional." The women who worship them, however, are still expected to act according to the tenets of a highly patriarchal Confucian society; thus, neither the concept of "the feminine" in Daoism nor the exceptionality of the female goddesses has an impact on the balancing of gender power in society. Therefore, when we look at the reality of Daoist women's lives, in historical as well as contemporary terms, we need to recognize that it is influenced much more by social, political, and cultural concerns than by Daoist ideology.

The Tang dynasty was the heyday of religious activity for Daoist women. Their religiosity is described in Daoist texts as characterized by faith and reverence, usually already shown during childhood, good work, and Daoist religious observances. In terms of actual practices, we know little, but they certainly included sexual abstinence and fasting, as preliminaries to study and meditation. Meditation would in turn lead to "magical travel, visits from deities, the abilities to teach and transmit texts and liturgies, the power to perform miracles, gifts of the elixir of immortality, and the ultimate reward of eternal life and divine office."[12]

These women's choice to devote their life to religious pursuits, rejecting sexual activities and performing ritual fasting, can be seen as a rejection and transcendence of their female role. This leads to tensions between religious vocation and social and familial duties. Historian Suzanne Cahill describes these women as "outside the normal world and work of the Chinese woman":[13] most of them did not marry; others were widowed before their religious vocation manifested itself; others again, if married, managed to avoid reproduction. How, then, could they be models for female behavior? Why were their lives honored? Because they were not women any more, but symbols. By the very fact of being outside the norm, these women gave up their womanliness and became pure symbols—to be revered, but not necessarily emulated. The process of manipulation of a woman's life story into a symbol made her example socially and morally acceptable.

A Daoist practice that several scholars have described as empowering for women is female alchemy. Female alchemy is a Daoist self-cultivation practice that developed first in the seventeenth century, flourished in the nineteenth century, and is still used widely today in China, Taiwan, and Hong Kong. Female alchemy is similar to other kinds of Daoist self-cultivation techniques popular in China before the seventeenth century, whereby the adept undergoes a series of bodily practices in order to reach transcendence, but its peculiarity is that it is directed only at women. The tradition encompasses meditation, breathing, and massage exercises, as well as moral and ethical guidelines solely for women, taking into account the specificity of the female body, its psychological makeup, and its physiological peculiarities—first and foremost, blood. The first aim is to transform female blood into the more ethereal substance, *qi*, and then into spirit and nothingness, while at the same time the female body transforms into a less gendered, more androgynous body. The fact that this practice entails the loss of menstruation immediately reveals again the dichotomy analyzed previously between the idealized female goddess and the real woman. In this case, in order to become a transcendent, a woman has to give up her sexuality and her ability to procreate; her body loses her female characteristics, and she transcends gender. Thus, although this is a tradition for women, it does not really diverge from the notions of *yin/yang*, pure/impure, female/male that subtend Chinese cosmology and that view the female as less able to achieve transcendence. The impurity of the female body stands out from the beginning, and the difficulty in getting rid of that impurity, embodied by blood, is the center of discussion of the practice. Eventually, the aim of the practice is to "change into a male body" or, cosmologically, to create a "pure *yang*" body. Thus, for women, the meta-order is not a better balance of *yin* and *yang* elements, or a pure *yin* that would compare and contrast the "pure *yang*" meta-order of men. Female alchemy also comes with a set of moral guidelines that are very restrictive of female behavior, first and foremost the need to be practicing in the home, without contact with male teachers. Also, women of marriageable age were often discouraged from using this technique because it would create insurmountable strife within the family, since it would make the woman incapable of producing offspring. Even though these strictures have been relaxed in the present day, as we will see in the example that follows, the ideology that emerges from them tells us that this practice is steeped in the ideology current at the time of its development.[14]

Weng Taiming is the abbess of the Daodeyuan, a very active Daoist temple in Kaohsiung, on the southern tip of Taiwan. Weng lives there with four other adepts, and she holds regular courses for an audience of over 100 adepts. Weng was born in 1951 in a large family with three sisters and four brothers. Her father was very active in the religious community and brought her with him every time he went to a temple. Her religious interest began then and never diminished. She started meditating when she was twenty-three, and she became a vegetarian at twenty-four. She was never interested in romantic love, and she devoted her life to the practice of Daoism and internal alchemy. She studied different inner alchemical techniques with a series of Daoist male teachers. Her last teacher, also a man, taught her the principles of female alchemy. The path has been hard and long, but she has now achieved the first step of any practitioner of female alchemy: halting the menses. At the same time, she has also achieved a place of great honor and power within the Daoist religious structure, as the abbess of a very influential Daoist temple in Taiwan.

One evening, inspired by a discussion of the practice of female alchemy, she launched into a long exploration of the relationship between religious devotion and practice, and the social and familial duties of a woman. She said that a woman has first and foremost to follow her duties as daughter, wife, and mother, accommodating her desire to practice, however sincere, with the needs and expectations of her family.

Weng Taiming was using the same kind of rhetorical tools as many women had used before her, and that is very common in Chinese religious books for women. Although she herself had avoided sexual relations, marriage, and childbirth, and like the Unborn Venerable Mother was acting as an almost divine mother to her flock of adepts, she was urging the women in her audience not to upset the Confucian orthodoxy.

ANCESTOR WORSHIP AND CONFUCIAN GENDER ROLES

Confucian ideals define gender in familial and kinship terms. These roles and relationships are ritualized through and mutually strengthened with the patrilineal and patrilocal system, and crystallized in ancestor worship. The hierarchical dictates of patrilineal ancestor worship mean that only sons are valued because they continue the family line and, thus, fulfill ancestral obligations. A daughter is expected to become a wife and mother of a male heir to her husband's line. When she dies, she will be worshipped as a part of her husband's ancestral line. Yet women are also viewed as the transmitters of knowledge for domestic religious practices.

It can hardly be said that Confucian patriarchy still holds sway in every aspect of social life in contemporary Chinese societies. But the primacy of the male manifests itself in many typical decisions made by families: children are more likely to take their father's surname than their mother's, even though both choices are legal; though parents may leave an inheritance to both sons and daughters, one hardly hears of cases in which all assets are left to the daughter with nothing for the son; it is common to see women who keep having children until a son is born, but it is unusual to see the opposite situation; in cases of infanticide, a baby girl is far more likely to be killed than a baby boy. The link between these choices and the patrilineal system seems rather clear. In other words, one of the most important influences Confucian ideology has on gender and sexuality has to do with patrilineality, the influences of which persist to the present day.

Ancestor worship is part and parcel of patrilineal gender ideology. When a woman dies unmarried, her soul creates a problem because it should belong to her husband's lineage; her soul should be worshipped on the same altar as her husband. Without a husband, how can her soul be taken care of? Many practices have thus come into being to provide solutions. One anthropologist found an unmarried daughter's tablet dangling, literally, below a shrine in a dark corner of her family kitchen.[15] This example might be extreme, but the most common practice would be to put her ancestral tablet in a community temple or a Buddhist temple. In Jiayi (southern Taiwan), there are many unmarried daughters' tablets—crowded together with those of the unclaimed dead and the childless dead, in a side room where the Bodhisattva Dizang Wang is worshipped. The room was covered with dirt and cobwebs, and the altar for the all-too-many tablets was unkempt. Some new Buddhist temples nowadays have a bright and well-maintained worship room for this function. There are also ways to think outside the box. Anthropologists have found that things can be altered with money. An unmarried woman can leave her assets to nonkin, under the obligation of worshipping her tablet as an ancestor when she dies. A more dramatic solution is to "marry out" the unmarried woman in a so-called ghost marriage or afterlife marriage: she is "married" to the soul of a dead bachelor. Her family finds her a (deceased) fiancé and holds a wedding in which she is married to the dead man. She is then formally transferred to her husband's line.

AVENUES FOR WOMEN'S PARTICIPATION IN MONASTIC AND LAY BUDDHISM

There is a clearly gendered division of labor in popular Chinese religious worship. Women conduct most of the daily worship of household gods and ancestors. The man's role prevails at only the most formal and important ritual occasions—funerals,

BOX 6.1 *Abortion and Fetus Ghosts in Taiwan*

It is not an uncommon practice for Taiwanese, especially women, to appease the spirits of aborted fetuses in the hope that they will cease to trouble living adults who may or may not be related to the spirit. The idea of fetus ghosts is often used by religious entrepreneurs to convince women to spend large sums of money by worshipping in temples and shrines dedicated to this purpose. And yet, it provides psychological comfort to women who have had abortions, and an avenue for dealing with grievances and family conflicts associated with the abortion.

Fetus-ghost appeasement, especially its significant rise around the 1990s, is closely tied to the reality of rapid social change under modernization. Abortion was fully legalized in Taiwan in 1985, although it was already commonly available long before the legal change. Some statistics are astonishing: for example, one-third of all pregnancies in modern Taiwan end in abortion, and perhaps half of Taiwanese women have terminated a pregnancy at least once in their lives. This is a result, argues anthropologist Marc L. Moskowitz, of "increased sexual freedom, the easy availability of abortion, and the inadequacy of sex education in at least some schools" (*The Haunting Fetus* [Honolulu: University of Hawaii Press, 2001]). The propitiation of fetus ghosts, far from being ancient, is in large part something that has come to Taiwan from Japan within the past thirty years. Given the influence of Japan on popular culture in Taiwan, the transnational link is not surprising. At the same time, however, the concept of fetus ghosts resonates with a long tradition of beliefs in the personification of ghosts, the mother-son relation in Chinese Buddhism, the demonization of excessive sex, and notions of orphan souls.

jiao ceremonies of community and temple renewal (where women are usually forbidden to enter the temple), core functions of large lineages, and similar occasions. Women, however, care for the daily needs of ancestors and for most larger household rituals. Yet these are also her husband's ancestors, and in worshipping them on her wedding day she marked the putative end of her membership in her own natal family.

This kind of daily household worship offers little more to women than house-work does—perhaps the pleasure of a job well done, or the knowledge that they have contributed to the well-being of their families. Chinese popular worship has very few opportunities for roles in larger social organizations. Men dominate the local temple management committees, as well as the organizing roles in large community rituals. None of these roles offer opportunities beyond the local community. Thus, popular worship offers little to women dissatisfied with their role at home.

Buddhism, on the other hand, gives women a number of options. Women have always had the option of leaving the family to become nuns, striving for perfection by leaving the secular world and leading a life of shaved head, vegetarian diet, and celibacy. Yet this also poses problems for women. Even the phrase *leaving the family* implies its fundamental breach of filial piety: the celibate nun will neither bear sons nor care for her parents. This has historically been the greatest criticism of monastic Buddhism in China. Duty to family discouraged most women from this path at least as much as the rigorous disciplines of the nunnery. In modern times, criticism leveled at this option is that it implies fleeing from real problems and is irrelevant to the world.

Becoming a nun was never an important option for the majority of Chinese women, but they could more plausibly consider joining lay Buddhist groups that centered around the singing of sutras. Many of these groups meet in community temples or in their own "vegetarian halls."[16] They offer women a world of their own, where they can take organizing roles, and where they can develop a Buddhist religiosity without leaving the family. They sing together, even if they do not understand the words of the sutras. Some make themselves available for hire to people who want sutras recited, especially for funeral services.

These groups offer women room for self-cultivation without the moral and personal dilemmas of becoming a nun. Their role in funerals and other services also generates a small, independent income. More important for most women, they also create a sense of accomplishment in a more public sphere to which they normally have little access. Still, such organizations exist only on a very modest scale. Furthermore, in contrast to the modern Buddhist movements described in the following section, their ties to local temples and the lack of any centralized organization leave them inherently parochial.

Women in the Revival of Religions

Since the 1980s, there has been a significant religious revival in Chinese societies. Part and parcel of the revivals is the increasing visibility of women's participation, and, in many cases, the rise of women's leadership and activism. This trend has been visible in Christian churches, in reformed Buddhist movements, and in traditional cults. For instance, the central role of women in the resurfacing of the Catholic Church in post-Mao China was reported in China's national Catholic journal:

> With the Lord's grace, the embattled church [in China] again rose up. Churches everywhere were open. Priests returned to churches they had long been separated from to resume their familiar yet unfamiliar pastoral care. When religious activities first resumed, many Catholic men furtively watched from the sidelines, while the Catholic women rushed into the churches without reservation to participate heartily in the renewed services, and also encouraged other Catholics to worship in public.[17]

Women form the backbone of the Catholic Church; the situation is similar to that for other Chinese religions. The vast majority of worshippers in temples tend to be women. But the motives for religious participation seem to differ for men and women. For example, men also go to temples to worship, but they do so only when there are important rituals and public issues such as feuds. Women worship to pray for the recovery of sick children and for the health and tranquillity of their families.

The therapeutic dimension of women's religiosity can further be seen in the fact that most clients of spirit mediums are women. Many spirit mediums themselves are women. However, it is often issues stemming from patrilineal ideology, such as anxiety over bearing sons, that drive women to consult spirit mediums. The anthropologist Pui-an Law therefore argues that there is a reciprocal relation between the revival of folk religion and the patrilineal gender ideology.[18]

On the other hand, powerful female abbesses now head many Daoist temples. In a monastery on Laojunshan (Sichuan), in the mid-morning sun, two older laywomen (one the wife of a ritual master) were knitting away, very much part of the background. The abbess Zhang Zhirong, on the other hand, was discussing which talismans to use for an upcoming ritual with the ritual master. She was completely in charge. The monks and nuns at the temple watched her every move, gathering around her like a flock of chicks around their mother. As she said in an interview later, she had achieved this position of power and respect by concentrating her attention on herself, on refining her own position in the world, not by concentrating on a husband or on a family. Thus, the others now concentrated their attention on her. Negating her role as wife and mother, and the pollution inherent in the acts of sexual procreation, she became a higher mother. "In the logic of Chinese culture, escape from female pollution requires that a woman's connection with procreation be denied."[19]

Lately, these female abbesses, more than their male counterparts, have also been instrumental in the reconstruction of the Daoist heritage in China, which was damaged during and after the Cultural Revolution. They have been actively fund-raising and directing the restoration and expansion of Daoist temples. However, as a younger nun said in an interview, "The restoration and rebuilding of a new body of Daoist temples in the region has taken us away from refining ourselves, . . . we are putting our time into the restoration of the Daoist body in China that was so badly wounded; restoring it now means that the next generation will be able to practice."[20] In this case, the female body is being used to restore the nation's body. How these capable and strong-willed women at the head of Daoist temples will affect the place of women in the Daoist institutions of mainland China remains to be seen.

Traditional barriers to women pursuing the celibate path of a nun are eroding. In Taiwan, Buddhism is now characterized by the markedly increased significance and influence of nuns vis-à-vis monks. As Karma Lekshe Tsomo writes,

> Although still underrepresented in male-dominated bastions of ecclesiastical power, Buddhist women in Taiwan exert their influence through material generosity and sheer numbers. A significant number have rejected marriage in favor of ordination as Buddhist nuns. Women entering monastic life outnumber men more than five to one; on the whole they are better educated, more active, and younger than male candidates, entering the order as a first option, rather than after another career.[21]

However, not all the women in the recent religious revival have confined themselves to the role of worshippers or nuns. In many areas, local Buddhist women actively mobilize to pursue social welfare projects, such as building nursing homes.[22] Perhaps the most impressive example is that of modern Buddhist organizations expanding transnationally in the global arena. The Buddhist Tzu Chi (*Ciji*) (Compassion Relief) Foundation is one of the most prominent new religious movements among Chinese-speaking people around the globe today.[23] It was founded in Taiwan in the late 1960s as a small grassroots charitable women's group, and since the late twentieth century has expanded into an international humanitarian nongovernmental organization, with branches around the world, especially where Chinese communities are concentrated, such as North America. It is a lay movement under monastic leadership in the Mahayana Buddhist tradition. Its core practice is "doing good" as a modern nonprofit—or to use a term more familiar to readers in North America, a *faith-based organization*—by delivering disaster relief locally in Taiwan and internationally regardless of religious and ethnic boundaries. Among the distinctive features of Tzu Chi, the most conspicuous is the charismatic leadership of its founder and leader, the Venerable Cheng Yen (or, in the group's English writings, the Dharma Master Cheng Yen).

The Tzu Chi movement is part of the broader Buddhist revival that has followed the lifting of martial law in Taiwan in 1987. Beginning in 1966 as a small community of less than forty women in the backwaters of eastern Taiwan, Tzu Chi survived its initial difficulties, growing slowly during its first decade and then rapidly across Taiwan during the late 1980s—during a period when Taiwan was moving toward a wealthier economy and a more democratic polity. Three decades after its founding, Tzu Chi had become the largest formal voluntary association in Taiwan and a growing transnational organization among overseas Chinese. In today's Taiwan, it runs three state-of-the-art, 900-bed hospitals, a television channel, and a secular university with a respected medical school. Over the past decade, Tzu Chi has delivered relief to over thirty countries around the world. Such accomplishments have won its leader Cheng Yen several international honors.[24]

By the year 2000, Tzu Chi claimed roughly five million followers in 117 countries. It was women who took the initiative for localizing Tzu Chi transnationally. Until recently, women have been underrepresented in most overseas Chinese organizations,[25] except for some vegetarian associations and salvational societies in Singapore, which had therefore been characterized and looked down upon as "women's religions."[26] As with its growth in Taiwan, women continue to play a pivotal role in Tzu Chi's overseas development. The four branches studied by Julia Huang—New York, Boston, Malacca, and Tokyo—began with women's efforts; and their original image as a women's group did not hinder the organization from developing either locally or globally. The significance of this gender aspect lies in its confirmation that Chinese women are not socially inept, but endowed with the informal ties needed to mobilize civic associations.[27]

BOX 6.2 Homosexuality and Buddhism

Gays and lesbians are called *tongzhi*, "comrade," in Taiwan and mainland China.
The term became popular in the 1980s, when Taiwan was moving from the Cold
War to democratization. Similar to the gay and lesbian movements in the United
Kingdom and the United States, the gay rights movement in Taiwan has political
roots. But unlike its Western counterparts, the gay movement in Taiwan associated
itself not with civil rights, but with the political opposition party. Six years after the
founding of the first secular homosexual (lesbian) group, the first homosexual
church was founded in 1996 by a female Presbyterian pastor.

Six months later, the first gay Buddhist group, the Child-Brahman Abode, was
formed. Unlike the church and the global gay and lesbian movements, the
Child-Brahman Abode is not politicized, if not depoliticized. Yang Huinan argues
that the two leaders of the gay Buddhists represent two stages of the gay and
lesbian movements: one is to assure dignity and self-respect for the members, and
the other is to actively pursue rights and make waves in the larger society.
According to Yang's online survey, the two core issues deemed relevant by the
members concerned are as follows: all beings are equal for attaining enlightenment,
and the question of whether homosexual practice violates Buddhist precepts
(Huinan Yang, *Ai yu xinyang: taiwan tongzhi fojiaotu zhi pingquan yundong yu
shenceng shengtaixue* [Love and Faith: The Taiwan Gay Buddhist Rights
Movement and Deep Ecology] [Taipei: Shangzhou Press, 2005]).

Conclusion: Chinese Religion and Masculinity

As discussed in the previous chapter, the Chinese *yin/yang* cosmology ascribes a
gendered symbolism to all the beings, forces, and tendencies in the universe. It is an
ambiguous cosmology that, on the one hand, gives an equally fundamental and
interdependent role to both the masculine and feminine dimensions of being, but,
on the other hand, tends to ascribe primacy to one of the two—usually the masculine *yang*, but, as we have seen, in Daoist texts the feminine *yin* is often symbolically
privileged. Chinese religious practices combine this ambivalent cosmological symbolism with a social structure that was unabashedly patriarchal until the modern
era, and continues to be so in many aspects of social life.

This chapter has shown how, in Chinese religious culture, goddesses and women
have symbolically transcended the tensions inherent in their social roles, exploring
and transforming aspects of their gendered identity while respecting, and even
reproducing, the patriarchal social structure. Our discussion has focused on women
and femininity; however, the converse can also be said of men and masculinity.

The Confucian affirmation of a patriarchal and patrilineal social structure
appears to need little elaboration. However, the ethical teachings of Confucius and
Mencius on the proper attitudes and dispositions of the "sage" or "gentleman"
offer an alternative model of masculinity to many of the fierce gods and guardians
often encountered in Chinese temples. As a result, modern interpretations of

Confucianism often downplay the patriarchal ideology, and China's most popular contemporary proponent of Confucianism, the best-selling author Yu Dan, is a woman—to the dismay of the (mostly male) academic experts on Confucianism!

Indeed, a conceptual distinction is often made between the "civility" of the Confucian scholar and the "martiality" of the warrior—the priest of exorcistic battles against demons, and the martial artist of the rivers and lakes, described in the previous chapter. The martial arts tradition, which is based on Daoist body cultivation techniques, provides a model of masculine strength, virtuosity, loyalty, and chivalrous morality through the cultivation and control of *yin* and *yang* energies. In this tradition, the ideal image of masculinity combines the heroic power and virtue of the warrior with the cultured civility and wisdom of the sage. (In modern times, the image of the female martial artist has become more widespread, as exemplified in the recent films *Hero* and *Crouching Tiger, Hidden Dragon*. This image is not new, however, and dates back to the centuries-old tale of Mulan, made into a Disney animated film in 1998.)

Just as feminine alchemy hinges on the use of meditative techniques to stop the loss of bodily fluid through menstruation, Daoist body cultivation for men (called "inner alchemy"), in its more advanced stages, requires controlling and ending seminal emission. Semen is considered to contain the essence of life, and its leakage depletes vitality and shortens the life span. Body cultivation techniques begin with enhancing potency while controlling ejaculation. The sexual energy is then supposed to be converted through meditation techniques into *qi* and then into spirit. A tradition of sexual practices, known as "dual cultivation," is designed to train men and women to jointly engage in alchemical meditation through sexual practice.

These techniques have spread both in the popular culture and in Daoist spiritual discipline, but with different goals. In Chinese erotic novels and manuals on the "arts of the bedchamber," "dual cultivation" is presented primarily as a form of exercise to benefit health and promote longevity through the proper cultivation of vital essence and energies.[28] But it also becomes a technology for enhancing masculine prowess: through his ability to control ejaculation, the male can engage in intercourse with a consecutive succession of partners, absorbing their *yin* energies while keeping his *yang* to himself.[29] The famous Daoist scholar Kristofer Schipper has commented that the obsession with avoiding depletion of vitality through emission of semen reveals a fear of feminine power in the sexual act.[30] In Daoist spiritual discipline, on the other hand, dual cultivation gradually became fully internalized—instead of practicing with a sexual partner, the adept was to become a celibate monk and conjoin the *yin* and *yang* energies within his own body. The state of "pure *yang*" to which he aspires is a purely spiritual one. In the process of transforming himself into an ethereal body and, like a pregnant mother, nurturing an "immortal embryo" in his abdominal area, not only does his seed stop "leaking," his "turtle head" shrinks, and he squats like a woman to urinate, until he becomes, like the woman practitioners of feminine alchemy, a purely androgynous being.[31]

Notes

1. Chün-fang Yü, *Kuan-yin: The Chinese Transformation of Avalokitesvara* (New York: Columbia University Press, 2001), 1–2, 293–351.

2. Chün-fang Yü, *Kuan-yin,* 293–294.

3. Arthur Wolf, "Gods, Ghosts, Ancestors," in *Religion and Ritual in Chinese Society,* ed. Arthur Wolf (Stanford, Calif.: Stanford University Press, 1974), 131–182.

4. Mayfair Mei-hui Yang, "Goddess across the Taiwan Strait: Matrifocal Ritual Space, Nation-State, and Satellite Television Footprints," *Public Culture* 16, no. 2 (Spring 2004): 209–238.

5. Steven Sangren, "Female Gender in Chinese Religious Symbols: Kuan Yin, Ma Tsu, and the 'Eternal Mother,'" *Signs* 9.1 (1983): 5–25.

6. Sangren, "Female Gender in Chinese Religious Symbols," 15–16.

7. Sangren, "Female Gender in Chinese Religious Symbols," 16–17.

8. Sangren, "Female Gender in Chinese Religious Symbols," 10.

9. David K. Jordan and Daniel Overmyer, *The Flying Phoenix: Aspects of Chinese Sectarianism in Taiwan* (Princeton, N.J.: Princeton University Press, 1986), 262–263.

10. Sangren, "Female Gender in Chinese Religious Symbols," 14.

11. Kenneth Pomeranz, "Power, Gender and Pluralism in the Cult of the Goddess of Taishan," in *Culture and State in Chinese History, Conventions, Accommodations and Critiques,* ed. Theodore Huters, R. Bin Wong, and Pauline Yu (Stanford, Calif.: Stanford University Press, 1997), 182–206.

12. Suzanne Cahill, "Practice Makes Perfect: Paths to Transcendence for Women in Medieval China," *Taoist Resources* 2, no. 2 (1998): 28.

13. Cahill, "Practice Makes Perfect," 38.

14. For a general introduction to female alchemy, see Elena Valussi, "Women's Alchemy: An Introduction," in *Internal Alchemy: Self, Society, and the Quest for Immortality,* ed. Livia Kohn and Robin Wang (Dunedin, Fla.: Three Pines Press, 2008). For a discussion of its historical development, see Valussi, "Female Alchemy and Paratext: How to Read Nüdan in a Historical Context," *Asia Major* 21, no. 2 (2008), 153–193.

15. Emily Martin Ahern, *The Cult of the Dead in a Chinese Village* (Stanford, Calif.: Stanford University Press, 1973).

16. Robert Weller, *Unities and Diversities in Chinese Religion* (Seattle: University of Washington Press, 1987), 45–46.

17. Eriberto P. Lozada, Jr., *God above Ground: Catholic Church, Postsocialist State, and Transnational Processes in a Chinese Village* (Stanford, Calif.: Stanford University Press, 2001), 102.

18. Pui-lan Law, "The Revival of Folk Religion and Gender Relationships in Rural China: A Preliminary Observation," *Asian Folklore Studies* 64 (2005): 94.

19. Sangren, "Female Gender in Chinese Religious Symbols," 10.

20. Karma Lekshe Tsomo, "Mahaprajapati's Legacy: The Buddhist Women's Movement: An Introduction," in *Buddhist Women across Cultures: Realizations,* ed. Karma Lekshe Tsomo (Albany: State University of New York Press, 1999), 20.

21. Keping Wu, "Grassroots Religious Mobilization and Social Change in Southeast China: The Strategies of Two Popular Buddhist Communities." Unpublished manuscript.

22. The formal name of the organization in English, Tzu Chi (*Ciji*), literally means "Compassion Relief." Names that appear on the organization's website are given in Wade-

Giles Romanization, and this is followed here: Tzu Chi (the organization) and Cheng Yen (leader of the organization).

23. David W. Chappell, "Introduction," in *Buddhist Peacework: Creating Cultures of Peace*, ed. David W. Chappell (Somerville, Mass.: Wisdom, 1999), 15–25.

24. Edgar Wickberg, "Overseas Chinese Organizations," in *The Encyclopedia of the Chinese Overseas*, ed. Lynn Pan (Richmond, England: Curzon, 1999), 83–91.

25. Maurice Freedman and Marjorie Topley, "Religion and Social Realignment among the Chinese in Singapore," Journal of Asian Studies 21, no. 1 (1961): 3–23, 22.

26. Robert P. Weller, *Alternate Civilities: Democracy and Culture in China and Taiwan* (Boulder, Colo.: Westview Press, 1999).

27. Daniel Reid. *The Tao of Health, Sex and Longevity: A Modern Practical Guide to the Ancient Way* (New York: Simon & Schuster, 1989).

28. See R. H. van Gulik, *Sexual Life in Ancient China: A Preliminary Survey of Chinese Sex and Society from ca. 1500 B.C. till 1644 A.D.*, Sinica Leidensia Series, Vol. LVII, updated ed. (Leiden, The Netherlands: Brill Academic, 2003).

29. Kristofer Schipper, *The Taoist Body* (Berkeley: University of California Press, 1993).

30. Adeline Herrou, "Daoist Monasticism at the Turn of the 21st Century: Ethnography of a Quanzhen Community in Shaanxi Province," in *Daoism in the Twentieth Century: Between Eternity and Modernity*, ed. David, David A. Palmer and Xun Liu, 2011 (Berkeley: University of California Press, 2011). See also Herrou, *La vie entre soi* (Nanterre, France: Société d'ethnologie, 2005).

7

Chinese Cosmology and the Environment
Robert P. Weller

A few years ago I was part of a group treated to a large feast, hosted by the Gansu provincial government. The group at my table immediately scanned through the list of dishes to see what we could look forward to. I was struck by something called "winter insect summer grass," which I took to be one of those strangely evocative metaphorical names that you sometimes see on a Chinese menu, like "ants climbing trees" for a dish of ground pork and noodles. My Chinese hosts, however, told me there was no metaphor at all. We would be eating something that really was an insect in winter and a grass in summer, and a rare and expensive delicacy as well. They knew little else about the biology of this oddity, but they knew a lot about its Chinese medical properties, which they said were powerfully fortifying. Indeed, they explained, the great success of the Chinese national swim team was due in large part to its special diet, which included this very dish.

As I later learned, we were eating a caterpillar that has been parasitized by a fungus, sometimes called *yartsa* (after the Tibetan name for it) in English, or just *caterpillar fungus*. The fungus devours the caterpillar during a winter hibernation period underground and then sends up a grass-like shoot in the spring. The dish I ate looked like a lonely caterpillar floating in a bowl of clear broth, and did not taste too much like medicine at all.

Gathered in the western highlands of China, especially Tibetan areas like the Qinghai Plateau, its huge market demand has made it a major source of income in some very poor regions. Like many of the most medically powerful foods, caterpillar fungus crosses both physical boundaries (from Tibetan mountains to a swim team in Beijing) and mental ones. Is it alive or dead, animal or vegetable? As I will discuss, caterpillar fungus is just one small example of the old Chinese idea of a universe built around the varied flow of energetic force—*qi*—that characterizes all of both the natural and human worlds. It shows just how much, even today, earlier Chinese understandings of nature with close ties to religion continue to influence life. Here it takes shape in the bizarre biology of the caterpillar fungus in a way that affects both human diet and the environment and economy of the harvesting areas.

Let me offer another example, quite different from the first, of how intertwined ideas about religion and nature continue to influence the environment today. It involves a common goddess rather than exotic food, and environmental protest rather than medical effects on the body, but it also shows the continuing role of earlier ideas about religion and nature. One of Taiwan's earliest large environmental protests was a three-year battle in the city of Kaohsiung to prevent construction of a new naphtha cracker (a kind of light oil refinery, typically very polluting). In 1990, toward the end of the struggle, the government—which supported construction and felt confident of victory—decided to hold a referendum in which neighborhood residents could choose whether to come to a compromise or to oppose the factory completely. The night before the vote, opponents gathered in a local temple, where they made offerings to the god. As incense piled up in the large burner in front of the temple, it burst into a huge spout of flames. A huge crowd gathered as people heard of this sign of divine presence. Eventually the goddess Guanyin possessed the body of a woman in the crowd. Shaking with the power of the possession, surrounded by the smoke and smell of the incense and the large crowd, the goddess announced that the neighborhood was doomed if the factory were to be built. The opponents carried the day in the referendum, and everyone credited the events of the previous night.

These stories illustrate two simple points. First, they indicate that Chinese understandings of both nature and religion can be quite different from what we see in Europe or North America. Second, those ideas continue to shape China's lived environment today, even after a century of globalization. In the pages that follow I will offer a brief overview of Chinese ideas about the relations between humans and their environment as seen through the various religious traditions. I will then move on to more recent times to show how those ideas have interacted with broadly influential and very different concepts coming in from the West.

The Heritage

All of China's varied religious heritages addressed the environment in one way or another.[1] Let me begin with the idea of an "anthropocosmic" world, which had its closest ties to Daoism but spread far beyond any specific religious realm into the broader culture.[2] Anthropocosmism refers to a complex set of ideas that we might sum up very simply and briefly through the common Chinese reference to the "unity of heaven and humanity." *Tian*, the word usually translated as "heaven" in that phrase, is now more often translated as "nature"—a combination that should remind us that we are dealing with a concept that has no exact equivalents in English and Chinese. *Tian* refers to all the forces that shape the cosmos, and it was treated with great respect. The phrase as a whole, however, reminds us that humans are a part of that great order, that we share in the unity of the world, and that we have a special place within it. All things in that anthropocosmos share at their most fundamental levels a flow of cosmic energy (*qi*) that shapes everything — from the physical landscape of mountains and streams to the biological one of plants, animals and humans. This *qi* energy itself comes in endless variants, often classified into *yin* and *yang* or into China's traditional Five Phases (wood, fire, earth, metal, and water). These concepts are discussed at greater length in Chapter 5.

Within this image of unity, however, most people felt that the system should be guided for human benefit. Nothing is wrong with using *qi* to create a better life, although disaster can come from going against the Way of the universe. This is exactly what happens when a fengshui expert adjusts a house or a grave to benefit a family by using his ability to discern the energetic qualities of individual clients, the physical and built environment, and the time (see chapter 2). We see it as well in other uses of space, like the typical location of important pilgrimage sites in high mountains (with a powerful energetic flow), the fascination with landscape paintings in which the sinuous flow of *qi* is clearly visible in the shape of a mountain range, or in the Chinese collection of "strange rocks," which make the flow of *qi* clearly visible on their surfaces.

The oddness of an object often indicates its unusual or powerful *qi* — this can be a person, like the legendary Daoist hermits who appear as grotesque beggars, or it can be an object, like a strange rock. The same is true of the foods that have the most powerful Chinese medicinal properties or that are most in demand. Like the caterpillar fungus with which I began this essay, they almost always come from the geographic periphery (Tibetan highlands, in this case) or the cognitive periphery (between living and dead, grass and insect). Think, for example, of the Chinese demand for rhinoceros horn or pangolin (a scaly, tree-climbing anteater from the

---

BOX 7.1 Sacred Mountains and Sacred Landscapes

An idea of empowered landscapes grows directly out of a view of the universe in which everything is charged with different qualities of *qi* energy. Powerful energies concentrate in certain spaces in ways that affect nearby humans. Fengshui deals with this on the small scale of buildings and graves, but no one needs a fengshui expert to tell them that some landscapes are particularly sacralized. The ultimate of this kind of thing in China appeared in the idea of sacred mountains. As most people count them, China has five Daoist and four Buddhist sacred mountains. There is something about these spaces that attracted China's great religions, and each of these peaks became home to temples and monasteries that were important pilgrimage sites, including world-renowned centers of martial arts like the temples of Mt. Wudang or the Shaolin Monastery on Mt. Song. Associations between mountains and spirits appear in some of the earliest Chinese texts, and many emperors made personal pilgrimages up some of them. The idea of sacred mountains was just as important in culturally Tibetan areas, where they are often associated with pre-Buddhist deities and people come to circumambulate the peaks.

southwestern mountains). Even the foods of everyday life, however, have medicinal properties, and eating is one of the areas in which it is still easy to see these ideas about nature in action every day.

It is important to recall that these ideas imply a great respect for the dynamics of the anthropocosmic universe but are not at all the same as a Western biocentric ideal of respecting nature over human wishes. The devouring of endangered species, for example, which has greatly increased as China grew wealthier, comes directly from the anthropocosmic understanding of what makes a food desirable. We should recall also that Chinese have tended to deforest their land, not just in the previous century (when the problem became especially severe), but for many centuries before that. More positively, however, these ideas have allowed Chinese to transform their lived environment for millennia while still achieving high levels of productivity. There is no more man-made landscape, for example, than a rice paddy, which flattens every slope and redirects every stream. Yet this new and "artificial" ecosystem has also proved to be robust and stable over long periods.

These ideas that I have briefly outlined were only one of the resources that Chinese culture offered for thinking about nature.[3] Both Buddhist and Confucian teachings also had important implications for human relations with the environment. Buddhism adapted itself to Chinese culture in many ways but still added important new ideas. For thinking about the relationship to the environment, three core Buddhist principles stand out in particular.

BOX 7.2 Chinese Gardens and Landscapes

By late imperial times elite gardens had become showcases for the flow of *qi*. Making a garden resembled painting a landscape: neither process just imitated nature, but instead created a new flow of *qi* in the world in an act as creative as the one that created a natural landscape. These gardens thus often favored gnarled trees whose growth patterns revealed their history of life energy. Most valued were strange rocks, pierced with holes and strongly textured after millennia of underwater erosion. The skeletal web of stone that remained was said to show the flow of *qi* in a way that a "fat" rock could not. In some cases, elite gardens constructed "fake mountains," with paths through piled boulders where friends could wander and imagine themselves as Daoist immortals on cloud-draped peaks. In some ways this represented an aesthetic and elite version of the anthropocosmic understanding of stones that we also see when people burn incense for unusual ones in temples. Many of these elite ideals have become much more widely available to the general public, and this kind of aesthetics of *qi* is no longer limited to a thin upper crust of society. Some of those old elite gardens are now public spaces, for instance, and can still be visited—Suzhou is especially famous for them. In other cases, middle-class families can afford many of the same kinds of objects, even if the scale is reduced to decorating the front room instead of constructing an elaborate garden.

FIGURE 7.1 *Terraced rice paddies (Huang Ping/Photobase/FOTOE)*

First, Buddhists valued life in all its forms, and this showed up most obviously in the prohibition against killing sentient creatures. Devout Buddhists thus ate a strictly vege-tarian diet. Second, this prohibition ties to broader ideas about karma and reincarna-tion. Buddhism aims to allow its followers to give up all attachments to this world, to cease producing the karma that leads to reincarnation, and thus to achieve nirvana. This can encourage both a respect for other beings—human or animal—because they could be people one had known or could be one's own future. Even more important in recent times, the idea of reducing desires and connections in this world encourages a general ideal of simplicity, a minimizing of consumption that adapts easily to environ-mental concerns. Third, the ideal of the bodhisattva, which became particularly influ-ential in China's Buddhist traditions, held up the model of a being who could achieve nirvana as a Buddha, but chose instead to remain attached to this world until all other sentient beings could achieve enlightenment. This ideal encourages broad goals of car-ing, which in modern times sometimes extend to the environment as a whole.

The Confucian tradition is long and complex, but it includes several aspects directly relevant to the environment. First, China's rulers from very early times recognized some basic environmental principles, and so we have texts telling people not to hunt juvenile animals or later laws against land reclamation where it could lead to flooding. Probably more important than these piecemeal recognitions of environmental consequences, however, was the general conviction that the Confucian state was responsible for the welfare of its people. Environmental disaster was one of the signs of misrule, and people blamed an emperor whose reign was filled with floods or droughts for having lost the "mandate of heaven" and thus the right to rule. The result was a long history of attempts at environmental control and regulation, although such attempts often achieved only very limited success. It is important to recognize that Chinese greatly altered their environment from the beginning, in some cases with clear negative long-term consequences, as with the deforestation that occurred in many areas, and that such Confucian principles could not always override short-term economic incentives.

There were many Chinese ways of thinking about nature by late imperial times, but none of these important themes I have mentioned was close to what had become the dominant paradigm in the West: the assumed contrast between nature and culture, between a nonhuman environment and a world of human artifice. Nor was it a view of humans humbly submitting themselves to a broader order of nature, a view that also separates the natural from the cultural. Instead, nearly every Chinese view included some aspect of understanding and working with the broad flow of the universe for the benefit of humanity. Like any view of the world, this had consequences for the environment. It led to ecologically quite stable but also completely man-made agricultural environments like rice paddies, with their careful terracing of the land and precise manipulation of water. The intimate connection in some parts of China among rice cultivation, fishponds, and silkworm production is another remarkable achievement in balanced resource use. However, we should not romanticize these views; they also encouraged consumption of endangered species and sometimes irresponsible exploitation of the land.

New Environmental Ideas and Globalization

Much changed as China came into increasing contact with Western thinking about nature from the late nineteenth century on. The modern Chinese word for nature (*ziran*) took on this meaning only around the very end of the nineteenth century. Like many new Western ideas, the Chinese borrowed a term that the Japanese had coined to translate Western texts. The term is actually an old Chinese term; Daoists particularly used it to refer to the intrinsic spontaneity of the Dao itself. Yet the term took on the idea of "nature" as the nonhuman world, the opposite of culture, only as part of this new exercise in global translation. By the early part of the twentieth century, this new view of how humans relate to the environment had come to dominate intellectual and policy circles in China.

The discourse of nature in Europe and North America by the end of the nineteenth century was already complex. Some voices championed a developmentalist emphasis on human control over the environment, celebrated through feats like railroads, canals, and dams. There was, however, also a complex reaction that tried to reclaim the value of nature in ways that varied from the Romantic movement to John Muir and the American origins of national parks. All of these views entered China, but the develomentalist paradigm dominated. Perhaps its greatest modern symbol in China, the enormous Three Gorges dam, originated in the developmental vision of Sun Yat-sen, even though its construction had to await the twenty-first century. Textbooks for modern education abandoned early Chinese categories for thinking about nature in favor of Western scientific ones. They also began to feature new kinds of slogans, like "Man Must Conquer Nature!" which appears in both Communist and Nationalist campaigns. At least at the level of the political elites who made policy and wrote textbooks, early anthropocosmic, Buddhist, and Confucian views of nature had been given up in favor of one particular Western view—the strong developmentalism without the voices for the embrace of nature that also existed in the West at the time.

This new, globalized understanding of nature became an important part of the antireligious attitudes that all Chinese governments showed throughout the twentieth century. Deeply committed to their own images of "modernity," both the Nationalist and Communist governments used environmental arguments to oppose much religion. They harangued against cemeteries as a waste of good land, against food offerings to gods or ancestors as a waste of money and a danger to health, and against burning paper spirit money as a source of pollution. Fengshui lost its standing in court as a legal argument (except, ironically, in the former British colony of Hong Kong). Even a word like *dili* ("the order of the earth"), which originally referred to the cosmic geomantic balances of fengshui, came to mean simply "geography" in the Western sense of an insensate physical world by the early twentieth century.

Only much later in the twentieth century do we begin to see the more pro-nature side of the Western nature/culture divide take on significance for Chinese intellectuals and policy makers. We see it first in Taiwan. The new valuation of nature extends back only to some tenuous beginnings in the late 1970s, like a bird-watching club or groups of college students who would hike in the mountains on weekends. As more political space opened up in the 1980s, however, Taiwan soon sprouted an active environmental movement, which boasted some impressive victories, like blocking construction of a DuPont titanium dioxide plant in Lukang in 1985. By the end of the decade, the island also saw its first national parks, along with more entrepreneurial nature appreciation like glossy nature magazines or private nature tourism sites.

Many of the same things occurred in the People's Republic about a decade later, when we also saw the development of bird-watching clubs, environmental NGOs, local environmental protests, and increased nature tourism. China, of course, had not shared Taiwan's move to democratic politics, which has given activities in the People's Republic of China a more careful and less politicized emphasis. Nevertheless, we can see some people in both Chinese societies embracing a more positive view of nature and moving away from the developmentalist paradigm toward the end of the twentieth century.[4]

There are several points worth noting about these twentieth-century changes. First, neither the developmentalist discourse nor the nature appreciation relies much on earlier Chinese understandings of how people relate to the environment. Instead, they form part of competing global discourses with roots in the post-Enlightenment Western sundering of nature from culture. They vary, however, in which side of the nature/culture divide they prefer. In this, they are very similar to people advancing related arguments in the West. Second, most of these recent changes in the view of the environment were insistently secular. Unlike earlier Chinese views of how humans relate to the world beyond them, which were tied closely to religious ideas, these new ideas claimed legitimacy in science and economics. Finally, we should recall that the most powerful voices promoting the new views were the educated, urban elite. When we look beyond the worlds of politicians and intellectuals, we see a much more complex embrace of both global visions and the legacy of Chinese thinking about the environment, as I will discuss next.

Current Trends in Religion and Environment

The history of China's thinking about the environment in the twentieth century and beyond looks different as soon as we move beyond official media such as policy pronouncements and school textbooks. The new global ideas about nature have had a widespread influence, but they have not replaced earlier ideas so much as added another layer of possibility for people thinking about how to relate to the broader world. When we examine general views in the population instead of just the strongly secular official discourse about nature, we again see the centrality of religious ideas.[5]

For example, the anthropocosmic understanding of the world—that largely rejects the opposition between nature and culture—continues unabated. We can see this first of all in the robust revival of fengshui in much of China. Recent studies have shown how widespread the practice continues to be in many rural areas.[6] In other Chinese societies in which fengshui did not suffer the same political repression, the practice has thrived continuously. Fengshui compasses are widely available, and bookstores are filled with manuals describing how to do it yourself. At least according to rumor, even top Chinese officials rely on fengshui to site important new buildings. The most famous case is the Bank of China building in Hong Kong, whose sharp angles were said to be designed to cut through the fengshui forces that had supported the British governor's mansion and its colonial rule. The idea that a flow of *qi* unites both the social and natural worlds thus remains widespread. In some cases, we still see fengshui ideas brought into local arguments about the built environment.

Nature and culture intertwine again in the sacralization of stones or trees that we see under some circumstances. In parts of China we can still see "fengshui groves," where trees are left in order to protect the fengshui of a site like a cemetery. Beyond that, parts of China are continuing an old tradition of worshipping remarkable bits of the natural world, like ancient or enormous trees or stones that may exhibit strange properties. I first saw this on the mainland in rural Guangxi province, where some local cadres had taken me to the local scenic mountain for a bit of nature tourism. To my surprise and their dismay, however, it turned out to be a festival day for a temple on top of the mountain, and there were worshippers everywhere. Most remarkable to me was the path up the mountain, where the ground everywhere sprouted sticks of burning incense, carefully placed at the base of nearly every large tree and boulder. Burning incense is an act of respect, typically done for an ancestor or deity. Here the respect was for the natural power of the mountain itself—not as pure nature but as a powerful force that shapes the human world, just like a deity.

Taiwan also has a similar tradition, and it is not unusual to find remarkable stones worshipped in their own temples, sometimes draped in robes like a more standard deity (most of whom are the spirits of dead humans). As a typical example, one such temple in northern Taiwan centered on a large stone that blocked a rural path. A farmwoman moved it to the side and went on about her business. Strangely, however, it was back again the next day, and again the day after that. Thinking that there might be some special power in the stone, the woman burned some incense and asked the stone for help in a dispute with her neighbor. This apparently worked out well, and word spread about the efficacy of the stone. More signs of efficacy eventually led to construction of the temple. As with fengshui, we can see the continuing power of ideas that see nature and culture together—here as a stone living in a building and wearing human clothing—without the separation between them that usually typifies global and Chinese official talk about the environment.

BOX 7.3 Pilgrimage and Nature Tourism

It is not a coincidence that many of China's most important traditional pilgrimage sites are now also nature tourism sites. Bird watching competes with incense burning in many places. In fact, it may be a mistake to think of pilgrimage and tourism as separate kinds of activities in the Chinese context. Descriptions of late imperial pilgrimage sites regularly include rhapsodies about natural beauties and strange atmospheric effects in addition to temples and worshippers. One pilgrimage I joined in Taiwan, for instance, visited all the important temples to the goddess Mazu on the island and ended up at a nature reserve (now a national park) at the end. Bus tour services in Taiwan today trace their roots to pilgrimages of several decades ago and say that people booking nature tourism now always also visit nearby temples. Why the connection? Because in both cases people seek to experience a kind of anthropocosmic power, where the same flows of energy that shape a landscape also nurture divine power. Nature and culture (or religion, in this case) have not been severed from each other, unlike the implied contrast in English between nature *tourism* and *pilgrimage*.

Perhaps the most obvious place to find these views, however, is at the dinner table. Food everywhere, of course, is one of the points where environment and society mesh most closely. In the Chinese context all food has qualities based on the particularities of its *qi*. In folk classifications of food, this usually takes the form of distinctions between "hot" and "cold" foods, which refers to their effects on the body, rather than their physical temperature or spiciness. In this sense, Chinese traditional medicines are just extreme foods, ones whose medical effects are especially concentrated and potent. Powerful foods like caterpillar fungus are an extreme, but every food has these qualities, and every informant can describe the health effects of a wide variety of foods. Most people are also aware of some basic herbal remedies and will go to a traditional Chinese pharmacist for certain kinds of illness. At the point where the environment strikes us most intimately, that is with the things we incorporate from outside our bodies like food and medicine, most people in Chinese societies continue to rely on modes of thinking about nature that long predate global influences.

We can also see more directly religious action on the environment that owes little to imported notions of culture versus nature. The most common religious activities in China center around local temples, which often have no larger institutional organization and are run directly by the people of the village or town, rather than by any religious hierarchy of priests. At the most local level, these temples are one of the only ties that bring villagers together socially for joint activities and to create a common identity. The only other major mechanism like that, in some villages, is the lineage (which also had a strong religious aspect), as described in chapter 2.

It should thus not be particularly surprising that when villagers perceive an environmental threat to their health or economy, temples often play an important organizing role. The most usual cases involve severe air pollution that is clearly causing discomfort, especially among children or near schools, or water pollution suspected of damaging agricultural production like fishponds or irrigated crops. In the case of the Taiwanese protest against construction of a naphtha cracker, which I described earlier, residents complained of existing refineries that left a visible and flammable oil scum on their water, as well as severe air and noise pollution. The temple was an obvious place to organize people, because it already had the means to bring people together through its own rituals.

We can see a different sort of Taiwanese example in the annual festival for the hungry ghosts. Traditionally held in the seventh lunar month, this elaborate ritual involves temples organizing their communities and hiring priests to appease all the hungry ghosts who invade the world of the living at that time (see chapter 2). Although it originally had no direct connection to the environment, some Taiwanese areas (led by Taipei County), beginning in the 1980s, borrowed the symbolism to raise environmental consciousness. Hungry ghosts are people with no one to worship their lost souls, whose anger can cause them to make us sick. It was not such a big step for the organizers of these new-style festivals to say that the environment had been neglected in just the same way, leading to the same sorts of negative consequences for those who had caused the death of the island's rivers and streams.

All communities still celebrate the festival in its traditional ways, but the new environmental message has also become common.

This sort of thing is not possible on the mainland for political reasons. Nevertheless, localized environmental protest has occurred frequently, and temples sometimes play an important symbolic or organizing role, just as in Taiwan. One village in the northwestern province of Gansu, for example, protested pollution of the Yellow River by a nearby fertilizer company.[7] The key organizing elements were the temple to Confucius (this was a lineage of people who traced their ancestry to him) and several temples dedicated to fertility goddesses. This was the 1980s, when the birth control campaign was at its harshest, and the ability to raise one healthy and filial child was a great concern for people. That was the symbolic link that united water pollution, fertility goddesses, and local villagers concerned with what they saw as a health threat to their irreplaceable children.

Land use disputes are another issue that sometimes leads people to organize through local religion. In many areas these take place around the displacements caused when the government builds highways or dams, or when cities raze residential areas to build more profitable developments. Religion itself can sometimes be the main issue of dispute, especially among those minority groups that consider some lands inviolable, like the Tibetan sacred mountains. These issues have sometimes put people at odds both with local governments that want to develop "under-utilized" land and sometimes with foreign tourists who want to climb the peaks without showing proper respect.

Some local temples have also begun to reexamine their own environmental practices. In particular, they have been trying to mitigate the effects of burning incense and paper spirit money. Each individual worshipper contributes only a little pollution by burning a few sticks of incense and a stack of the spirit money, but the cumulative effect can be enormous, sending massive quantities of heavy particulates into the air, along with smaller amounts of chemical pollutants. Large festival days send huge clouds of smoke wafting over towns, and the largest temple centers will burn several tons of spirit money in a day. In response, there has been a recent trend, especially in Taiwan and Hong Kong, to introduce more efficient incense burners and spirit money incinerators. By burning more efficiently and at higher temperatures, these methods can greatly reduce pollution.

The more institutionalized traditional religions, especially Buddhism, have also been actively rethinking their role in the environment. The most important line of thought has grown out of the "humanistic Buddhism" tradition. This was an early twentieth-century attempt to reconcile Buddhism and modernity by stressing the bodhisattva idea I mentioned earlier—the need to help all living beings in the world. The environment was not a high priority for Taixu or the other leading monks who first developed these ideas, but it became very important when this tradition found new life in Taiwan at the end of the century.

One of the most active and important of these new Buddhist organizations is the Compassion Relief Tzu Chi (*Ciji*) Foundation (see chapters 6 and 8). The original goal of the foundation was to support itself through productive work rather than performing rituals in exchange for donations. Instead, income would be used to make the world a better place. This began with medical care, and the group has now built a medical school and several state-of-the-art hospitals. They soon expanded into other areas, including the environment. Several other global-scale humanistic Buddhist movements arose at about the same time in Taiwan, and all of them also have an environmental aspect to their work.

None of these movements in Taiwan are politically radical, and this is consistent with their largely middle-class membership bases. Instead, they define their environmentalism in Buddhist terms, in part as an concrete example of the bodhisattva ideal, and in part as a way of reducing the grasping greed that locks us into the karmic cycle of suffering and rebirth. That is, simplicity and minimal consumption were already important goals in Buddhist cultivation. The innovation of these new Buddhist groups has been to connect simplicity directly to the environment.

One result is that these new Buddhist groups generally promote environmental reform at the personal and household levels, rather than helping in protest movements or lobbying against government environmental policies. They have been crucial in the success of grassroots recycling programs. Local Compassion Relief branches, for example, typically organize neighborhood recycling programs around the world. We can see this in the actions of one of their branch leaders in Malaysia, who turned his large yard in a wealthy neighborhood into a recycling station. They also urge people to waste fewer resources in their own lives. Thus the founder of Compassion Relief once told me that she uses each sheet of paper three times—first writing in pencil, then in pen, and finally with the heavy ink of a Chinese writing brush. Followers are urged to do things like carry around their own chopsticks to avoid the deforestation that results from disposable chopsticks in restaurants. Buddhists have also introduced flea markets, which had never before been popular in Chinese societies, in order to get more useful life out of objects.

None of the other institutional religions have been nearly as environmentally active as the Buddhists. So far at least, neither Daoists nor Confucians have an institutional base at all comparable to the Buddhists, although Confucianism is undergoing a surge of popularity in China right now, and this could change. They are thus not as well placed to affect environmental behavior, nor have they so far really put strong efforts into it beyond a few piecemeal efforts. Christians outside of China, of course, certainly have been giving serious thought to environmental issues, but it is so far difficult to see much impact from that in Chinese societies.

Conclusion

One of the most notable features that emerges from this brief overview is that we can see little overlap between official environmental policy and any of the older religious traditions. For almost the entire twentieth century, much of the environmental thinking of intellectuals and nearly all that showed up in government discourse reflected the powerful new influences coming from the West. The idea that human culture stood outside of and in opposition to nature infiltrated everything from development planning to geography textbooks. This was true under all governments: Republican, Communist, and even the Japanese colonial rule of Taiwan. It led to major economic transformations and to equally devastating environmental damage. It was only toward the end of the century that the more environmentalist side of Western thought on nature began to have more of an influence in either China or Taiwan.[8]

In spite of the power of these imported ideas, China's own array of approaches to the relationship between humanity and environment continued to thrive and to influence people's behavior. As I have discussed, ideas about the anthropocosmic world continue to influence diet (and therefore also the landscapes of agriculture), architecture (through fengshui), and broad ways of behaving in the environment. Lines of early conceptions of the environment, like the idea that the heavens (i.e., nature) and humanity are one, continue to offer important resources for thinking about the future. Buddhist ideas about karma, the need to save all beings, and the importance of renouncing greed also continue to evolve and to foster new kinds of environmentalism. These ideas may not dominate policy making, but they certainly influence daily life and the ways policies are actually implemented (or not).

None of China's earlier religious traditions, even in the very new forms some of them are evolving today, have yet had a visible influence on environmental policy in any Chinese society. This is largely because, with the partial exception of some Buddhists, none of them have pulled together a clearly articulated environmental philosophy that can compete directly with the dominant global (and originally Western) discourses of developmentalism on the one hand, and biocentric environmentalism on the other. Rather than developing theoretically coherent and explicit arguments with these dominant influences, the Chinese traditions for the most part have thrived by remaining embedded in the practical contexts of daily life. We see them not in textbooks on environmental thought, but every day at the dinner table and the doctor's office, and at the heart of environmental protest when the situation demands it.

I originally began working on these topics hoping to find an alternative Chinese environmentalism. Except for the beginnings of some new Buddhist thought on the issue, there really is not such an alternative, at least not yet. Instead, global views continue the hegemony they have had for over a century. Yet this is not necessarily unfortunate. In fact, as we have seen, Chinese religious culture offers a wealth of alternative views of nature if we only look beyond the level of abstract argument and examine real behavior in context. What appears to be a weakness in competing on the global intellectual stage is also a strength in maintaining a deep pool of diversity in how we can understand and interact with nature. Instead of reducing a complex and variable set of contextual possibilities to a "Chinese environmentalism," we retain a living pool of ideas. This is as crucial in human culture as it is in a gene pool or an ecological system, where diversity is the best tool for adapting to a changing world.

Notes

1. We are fortunate to have several recent edited collections dealing specifically with the environmental teachings and implications of China's traditional religions, as part of the Religions of the World and Ecology series (Cambridge, Mass.: Center for the Study of World Religions, 1998). The most relevant books for Chinese societies include John Berthrong and Mary Evelyn Tucker, eds., *Confucianism and Ecology: The Interrelation of Heaven, Earth, and Humans* (Cambridge, Mass.: Center for the Study of World Religions, 1998); Norman J. Girardot, James Miller, and Xiaogan Liu, eds., *Daoism and Ecology: Ways Within a Cosmic Landscape* (Cambridge, Mass.: Center for the Study of World Religions, 2001); and Mary Evelyn Tucker and Duncan Ryukan Williams, editors, *Buddhism and Ecology: The Interconnection of Dharma and Deeds* (Cambridge, Mass.: Center for the Study of World Religions, 1998).

2. The term *anthropocosmic* comes from Wei-ming Tu, "The Continuity of Being: Chinese Visions of Nature," in *On Nature*, ed. Leroy S. Rouner (Notre Dame, Ind.: University of Notre Dame Press, 1984), 113–129.

3. Much more could be pulled out of the Daoist tradition, of course. See, for example, the essays in Norman J. Girardot, James Miller, and Xiaogan Liu, eds., *Daoism and Ecology: Ways within a Cosmic Landscape* (Cambridge, Mass.: Center for the Study of World Religions, 2001).

4. The depth of China's current environmental problems has led to a number of very useful studies of environmental conditions and policies in China, although they tend to downplay cultural and religious factors. For policy in general, see the collection of articles published in Richard Louis Edmonds, ed., *Managing the Chinese Environment* (New York: Oxford University Press, 2000), or the recent study by Elizabeth C. Economy, *The River Runs Black: The Environmental Challenge to China's Future* (Ithaca, N.Y.: Cornell University Press, 2005). Judith Shapiro has written a very useful history of environmental policy in the People's Republic, *Mao's War against Nature: Politics and the Environment in Revolutionary China* (New York: Cambridge University Press, 2001). Vaclav Smil was a pioneer in studies of China's environment and wrote many useful books, including, for example, *China's Environmental Crisis: An Inquiry into the Limits of National Development* (Armonk, N.Y.: M. E. Sharpe, 1993). It is worth remembering, of course, that the situation in China changes so fast that almost anything is out of date by the time it is published.

5. There are fewer studies so far on culture and the environment at the most local levels, but more should be coming out. The most useful recent work on fengshui in China is Ole Bruun, *Fengshui in China: Geomantic Divination Between State Orthodoxy and Popular Religion* (Honolulu: University of Hawaii Press, 2003). A good grassroots view of local protest appears in Jun Jing, "Environmental Protests in Rural China," in *Chinese Society: Change, Conflict and Resistance*, ed. Mark Selden and Elizabeth J. Perry (New York: Routledge, 2000), pp. 197–214. Broader analyses of Chinese culture, religion, and economy can be found in Chris Coggins, *The Tiger and the Pangolin: Nature, Culture, and Conservation in China* (Honolulu: University of Hawaii Press, 2003), and in Robert Weller, *Discovering Nature: Globalization and Environmental Culture in China and Taiwan* (Cambridge: Cambridge University Press, 2006).

6. Ole Bruun, *Fengshui in China.*

7. See Jun Jing, "Environmental Protests in Rural China."

8. Much more work on Chinese environmental attitudes has begun to appear in the last few years. Environmental history has been an especially lively field in Chinese studies as

well in many other parts of the world. Some of the earlier studies in English include Robert B. Marks, *Tigers, Rice, Silk, and Silt: Environment and Economy in Late Imperial South China* (Cambridge: Cambridge University Press, 1998), Peter C. Perdue, *Exhausting the Earth: State and Peasant in Hunan, 1500–1850* (Cambridge, Mass.: Council on East Asian Studies, Harvard University, 1987), and R. Keith Schoppa, *Xiang Lake—Nine Centuries of Chinese Life* (New Haven, Conn.: Yale University Press, 1989). Each of these books provides a fine-grained historical case study of interactions between humanity and nature during the late imperial period. Kenneth Pomeranz offers a rather different kind of environmental history in his book *The Great Divergence: Europe, China, and the Making of the Modern World Economy* (Princeton, N.J.: Princeton University Press, 2000). This book is a broad consideration of how natural resources related to the development of a modern economy, including a general reconsideration of the relationships between economy and environmental resources in China. Mark Elvin has also published a broad-ranging consideration of imperial Chinese ideas about nature: *The Retreat of the Elephants: An Environmental History of China* (New Haven, Conn.: Yale University Press, 2004).

8

Religious Philanthropy and Chinese Civil Society
André Laliberté, David A. Palmer, and Wu Keping

With the extraordinary growth of China's economy over the past decades, a new generation of successful business entrepreneurs and billionaires has appeared, most of whom are incarnations of dreams of "rags to riches." At the same time, the gap between the rich and poor has widened, and, far (and sometimes not so far) from the booming cities of the coasts, China's impoverished rural hinterlands often suffer from declining public investment in health and education. Many of the new barons of business have established charitable foundations to help alleviate poverty—a growing trend that is promoted by the Chinese state. In a bid to publicize generosity and encourage charity, many magazines and government bodies regularly publish honor rolls and lists of China's "top philanthropists." Most of them are wealthy real estate developers and pop stars—but one name that sometimes appears is that of an illiterate, eighty-year-old former beggar, Lin Dong, a charismatic Buddhist healer who has donated tens of millions of dollars to build schools in poor villages all over China.

Born in 1930, Lin Dong became an orphan as a child and began a life of errant mendicancy. He married another beggar and, after the People's Republic was established in 1949, was assigned a job as a manual laborer, helping to ship loads of goods along the waterways of Guangdong province. In the 1970s he lost his right hand in an accident, and a few years later he suffered from a stroke. In a state of near death, he had a vision of the Chinese god Jigong, who assured him that he would recover and entrusted him with the mission of rescuing those who suffer in the world.

Jigong (1130–1207) was a monk who had been kicked out of his monastery for eccentric behavior and his love of meat and alcohol; he then roamed the streets and acquired a reputation as a crazy trickster with a benevolent heart, who had magical powers and could always be counted on to help ordinary people. Over the centuries he was worshipped as a popular god and as a character in Chinese literature and folk legends; by the late nineteenth and early twentieth centuries, a wave of spirit-writing societies—in which a medium enters a trance and traces characters in a box of sand—produced texts and morality books that claimed Jigong as the author, and that exhorted their followers to live moral lives, to do good deeds, and to engage in philanthropy to save the world.

After his vision of Jigong and his seemingly miraculous recovery from his stroke, Lin Dong established an altar to him and worshipped him in his home, and discovered that he had uncanny healing powers. The sick flocked to him from all quarters. He prescribed Chinese herbs for them and exhorted them to do good deeds, to accumulate good karma and attain cosmic recompense. Many were cured and became his followers. Full of gratitude to him for saving their lives, they are willing to do anything for him. Lin Dong encourages them to donate money, and they gladly respond; living a simple life and wearing cheap clothes, he offers all the funds collected to build schools and homes for the aged. As a result, although he has no wealth of his own, Lin Dong has raised and donated sums comparable to those given by China's richest business tycoons. And he encourages his followers who have little money to offer their time as volunteers, visiting the poor and the elderly.

Lin Dong's experience and philanthropic actions are deeply rooted in China's religious culture of cosmic recompense, as mentioned in chapter 1. "To become a Buddhist," he says, "is like opening a bank account: we should try our best to make credits through good deeds, instead of continuous debits; if we continuously draw from the account we will have a deficit, and if we do not make repayment to the overdrawn account, nobody will help us to settle it. The more industriously we foster charitable deeds, the more our recompense will increase."[1]

Most people assume that philanthropy, or the voluntary association among people for the public good, is a Western concept, even a Christian tradition. However, there exists a rich tradition of philanthropy in Chinese culture and religion as well. This chapter moves beyond an exploration of philanthropy as it is understood in the West, and introduces readers to the different ways in which Chinese people through their history have understood philanthropy and have tried to achieve an idea of "the good" by giving and serving others.

Philanthropy, Charity, and Social Services in the Chinese Context

Is there a specifically Chinese way of doing philanthropy, and is it different from what we understand in the West as charity and volunteerism? To answer this question, it will help to recall that etymologically speaking, the English word *philanthropy* is the "love (*philos*) of humans (*anthropos*)," and the *philanthropist*, the "one who loves fellow human beings." In relation to this, *charity* is from the Latin word *caritas*, which is about love, but also, is the origin of the verb "to care."

Volunteerism suggests that individuals, of their own volition, decide to give or help other people, because they feel it is their moral duty to do so. It cannot be coerced, that is, it cannot be mandated by a government, no matter how benevolent the intention may be. This does not mean that people who are members of a religious association, which says in its *credo* that helping others is part of their religious duty, cannot be considered volunteers, or that they are coerced by their religion to help other people. Individuals have the choice, ultimately, in the way they interpret the scripture of their religious beliefs. The concept of compassion in Buddhism, for example, can be interpreted differently by adherents of that religion, to mean simply not to harm others, or to sacrifice one's own interest to help others first. In the People's Republic of China, many NGOs (nongovernmental organizations) that claim to be based on volunteerism are actually sponsored by the state, and participation in their activities can be compulsory. To work in such a government-organized NGO (GONGO) in such conditions cannot be seen as volunteerism. Recent events such as the grassroots mobilization of volunteers in the aftermath of the 2008 earthquake in Sichuan, however, suggest that genuine volunteerism is gaining ground.

It may help to use Chinese terminology to understand the Chinese approach to philanthropy. The word *cishan*, which is the usual translation for "philanthropy," "charity," and "benevolence," is formed of two characters with a larger meaning than their Western equivalent. The first character, *ci*, stands for "kind, benevolent, benign, charitable, loving, fond, merciful," and is also used for words associated with "maternal." Buddhist associations involved in philanthropy such as Tzu Chi (*Ciji*) from Taiwan (see chapter 6) or *Cihui* from Hong Kong, use this same character. The second character, *shan*, stands for "good, virtuous, goodness, good deed, benevolent action," and it is also a verb, as in "to remedy," and "to relieve." The name of Miaoshan, the goddess described in chapter 6, which means "sublime goodness" is another Chinese rendition for Guanyin, the Bodhisattva of Compassion. This suggests that in the Chinese context, the word for *philanthropy* also points to an action that is imbued with a profound ethical and religious significance. However, if one wants to find evidence for religious philanthropy in the long history of China, we find little mention of *cishan*, which suggests that the concept is modern, like *zongjiao*, the concept for religion itself. This does not mean that there was nothing comparable to this form of philanthropy, however, because there is ample evidence in Chinese traditions of a long history of benevolence and compassion, and dedication to the common good, from a purely religious perspective. Since the Ming dynasty, *shantang* (benevolent halls) and *shanhui* (benevolent associations) have been founded in almost all parts of China. Many of them are of religious nature. In recent years there has been a revival of *shantangs* in southern China.

Traditional Chinese Religious Philanthropy

Chinese religious associations had been conducting philanthropic or other social services before the modern notion of philanthropy emerged in China. This is not only because traditional Chinese religions already have a universalistic notion of compassion and benevolence that is compatible with philanthropic ideals, but also because religions in China had pervasive influence on Chinese lives at all levels—state officials, intellectuals, social elites, and peasants alike. Moreover, they were often the center of public life at the state level as well as the grassroots level. As a result, they could mobilize enormous amounts of the social and economic capital that is essential for philanthropy. In the nineteenth century, Christian missionary organizations introduced modern forms of philanthropy that became the model for social services, which were later taken over by the state or emulated by other religious communities.

One could start with Confucianism to find an expression of philanthropy that is embedded within an ethical and religious perspective. The concept of *ren* (benevolence) is central to the Confucian view of social and political life. Used extensively in Confucian thinking, *ren* has acquired many meanings, ranging from "benevolence" to "humanity," but it is generally accepted to mean an attitude of love and respect for others. In this view, benevolent conduct must extend according to the limits of one's ability. This starts with the cultivation of the benevolent mind in an individual, and then proceeds outward. It begins with filial piety and fraternal obligation, and extends to an ethics of responsibility. A good example is Guangren Tang (the Hall for Spreading Benevolence), which was established by the social elites in Tianjin in 1878 to offer shelter for orphans and chaste widows.[2] These moral prescriptions have exercised a profound influence on social practices. For example, Joanna Handlin-Smith found that during the Ming dynasty (1368–1644), the neo-Confucian orientations of the ruling classes and the newly emerging merchant classes, had imposed on them expectations about good behavior that encouraged philanthropy. As a result of these changes, new categories of temples were devoted to cater to the welfare of the common people. In her study of famine relief during the last decade of the Ming dynasty, she found that philanthropy was undertaken on a large scale and benefactors went to great length to show their good deeds. In other words, charity was seen as a socially positive trend to be encouraged.[3]

Daoism, which benefited from state patronage during the Three Kingdom period (220–280) and the Sui dynasty (581–618), approached philanthropy from a different angle. Daoist masters contributed to the development of Chinese medicine and medical ethics. Daoist priests were expected to provide protection against diseases and demons through rituals, exorcism, and healing. The most common form of Daoist charity was to provide free medicine and medical care to the needy.

The third tradition that influences the practice of philanthropy in China is Buddhism. Compassion is a major element of its teachings. The alleviation of human suffering that is central to its doctrine has appealed to a great number of people through Chinese history. It attracted many people affected by the social and economic dislocation of a divided China between the fifth and ninth centuries, and after a long eclipse following persecutions from the state that culminated in 845, it experienced a revival thanks to state patronage during the late Qing dynasty

(1644–1911). Lay Buddhists could benefit from that climate and created associations to support the development of their religion and set up philanthropic associations. By the twentieth century, this had inspired a major movement, known as "humanistic Buddhism," which puts philanthropy at the center of the practice, and which remains influential all over the Chinese world today.[4]

The most common form of religious practice and religious-based philanthropy, arguably, is through popular religion, which incorporates references to all three traditions. For instance, one of the prominent popular religious deities, the Great Lord for Protecting Life (Baosheng Dadi) commonly found in southern Fujian and Taiwan, was canonized during the Ming dynasty as a Daoist immortal. In his lifetime, his name was Wu Tao, and he was an adept Chinese doctor of the Song dynasty. Like many practitioners of Chinese medicine of his time, he was also good at Daoist rituals and magical arts. After he died collecting herbs in the hills, people established a temple to commemorate him, and with migration such temples were constructed in all parts of southern Fujian and Taiwan. Not only can worshippers pray for good health in the temples, but they can also access basic medical help for free. Today these temples still serve as free medical clinics for the local poor, although their services include Western medicine as well.

"Spirit-writing" associations, which were widespread in China prior to 1949 and continue to operate in Hong Kong, Taiwan, and Southeast Asia, practice a mixture of Confucianism, Daoism, and Buddhism in their rituals, which consist of mediums writing divine texts while they are in trance. Such activities, which offer devotees blessings and advice on health and other matters of concern, are often performed in a *shantang*, or "hall of charity." The syncretic *Dejiao* associations among Chinese in Malaysia and Singapore (often known in English as the "Moral Uplifting Societies") incorporate the "five teachings"—Confucianism, Buddhism, Daoism, Christianity, and Islam—into one. Jigong, mentioned at the beginning of this chapter, is one of the main gods worshipped by these groups. Besides spirit-writing, *Dejiao* associations provide free Chinese medicine and spaces for ancestor tablets and have become the largest charities among the Chinese communities in Thailand and parts of Malaysia.[5] That is another example of the flexible and creative channels through which popular Chinese religion provides philanthropy. Groups similar to *Dejiao*, which some scholars call "redemptive societies," were once common all over China,[6] but they were often repressed by state officials as "heterodox teachings" during the Qing dynasty or as "reactionary sects and secret societies" in the early years of the People's Republic. Many of them were simply mutual help societies and, as such, acted as philanthropic associations. Most of these associations would appeal to the same concepts as those of more traditional Chinese religious associations, such as benevolence or compassion.

Popular religion in China is traditionally territorialized, which means that it is usually based on "community temples" that provide services to the local residents. However, with the intensification of globalization, even popular religion is increasingly deterritorialized. For example, the Ghost Festival among the Chinese in

Malaysia in 2008 caught media attention because the local religious leaders assembled two large paper condo high-rises to be burned for the victims of the Sichuan earthquake that had happened earlier that year. Spirit mediums in Jiangsu province competed with Buddhist temples in hosting services to appease the ghosts of the Sichuan earthquake. The clients of those spirit mediums volunteered to mobilize the local community to donate money, paper money, incense, vegetarian meals, and so on. While spirit mediums performed the ritual for the victims for free, popular sutra chanting groups gathered and chanted for free.

Protestant and Catholic missionaries started providing social services in China in the late nineteenth century. Supported by the wealth of the Western powers—and sometimes by their armies—they were able to offer succor to victims of natural disaster and economic deprivation, and by the middle of the nineteenth century, they had established hospitals in Guangzhou, Ningbo, and Shanghai. In part as a consequence of this philanthropic activity, they were able to convert increasing numbers of people.

The unprecedented success of Christian missions in China in the nineteenth century paralleled the trend in Europe in which the modern notion of philanthropy came to the top of the agenda for Christian organizations. As shown in chapter 3 of this book, Christian missionaries were enormously successful among ethnic minorities such as the Miao, Yi, Jingpo, and Lisu. One of the earliest things the missionaries did was to establish schools, teach literacy skills, and build hospitals. Many of the schools and hospitals the early missionaries built are still in use today. Although Christian philanthropy is based on the idea of universal love, a concept that might seem foreign to Chinese minds, it resonates well conceptually with the notion of compassion found in all major Chinese religious traditions.

Contemporary Forms of Religious Philanthropy

In contrast to the popular notion and state rhetoric that claims that Christian philanthropy in China always means Western infiltration, many Christian organizations mainly rely on domestic resources to provide social services and philanthropy. The YMCA in Hangzhou is a good example. YMCA (Young Men's Christian Association) is a Christian organization that originated in England in response to deteriorating social conditions in the mid-nineteenth century. It soon developed into an international movement. The Chinese YMCA received help from its North American chapter at its establishment in 1914, but now it receives minimal aid from other international YMCAs or Christian organizations. It generates most of its income from property rentals, fees for classes, hotels, and other private donations. Financially the YMCA is independent of any churches as well. Instead it relies on local volunteers, who are mostly nonreligious university students, to carry out its main social service programs. The only international "aid" they receive are native-English speakers who volunteer to teach English in its various career training programs. They are able to establish community service centers in which they provide free medical and entertainment services to the elderly, education programs to laid-off workers, and a clinic for children with autism, an increasingly common disease among children in China. None of the services are directly modeled after Western Christian practices. Rather, their major inspiration and ideas of philanthropy come from the social services section in the China Christian Council and the Three-Self Patriotic Movement. Churches and Christian organizations all over China are represented in the council. The social services section is especially important in providing a platform on which different organizations exchange ideas to improve their operation. The two official national Christian organizations have been active in assisting the development of Christian philanthropy. Their aims are partly political in nature, but the result is a more robust Christian social services program in China. Under the current banner of harmonious society they can achieve more with the resources to which they have access.

BOX 8.1 The Amity Foundation

Philip L. Wickeri

The Amity Foundation is an excellent example of a Christian-initiated organization that has contributed to social development and poverty alleviation in order to encourage a "new kind of Christian involvement" in Chinese society. Founded in Nanjing in 1985, it was among the first NGOs of its kind in mainland China. Amity's purpose was threefold: to contribute to social development and openness to the outside world; to make Christian participation in society more widely known; and to serve as a channel for people-to-people exchange and the ecumenical sharing of resources.

Amity's approach has been to emphasize cooperation, not confrontation, with the state. Early projects included the recruitment of church-sponsored language teachers from overseas to teach in colleges and universities, support for blindness prevention and special education, and the encouragement of new initiatives in medical training. Gradually, Amity's work expanded to include integrated rural development; grassroots medical work; education in HIV/AIDS; relief and rehabilitation in response to natural disasters; and child-centered social welfare. The foundation did pioneering work in many of these fields. Amity has also sought to develop church-run social service projects that serve as a bridge between Christians and the broader society. Like church-related development organizations in other parts of the world, Amity does not proselytize.

Initially, a large percentage of Amity's funding and support came from overseas partner organizations, most of them Christian, as well as from church groups in Hong Kong. In recent years, support has increasingly come from Chinese businesspeople and young professionals, many of whom also serve as Amity volunteers. The Amity Foundation is close to the China Christian Council and the Three-Self Patriotic Movement, and Bishop K. H. Ting was the leading spirit behind the Amity Foundation in the 1980s and 1990s. Amity has come a long way since its beginning.

continued

BOX 8.1 (continued)

By 2010, it had a budget of more than 100 million *yuan* and a staff of over fifty, making it one of the thirteen largest charities in mainland China. Amity has tried to develop a professionalized staff as a means to put faith into practice. It emphasizes sustainable development in all its projects, draws on a participatory model for project management, and emphasizes cooperation with local governments and beneficiaries.

The Amity Printing Company was established as a subsidiary of the Amity Foundation in 1986. A joint venture with the United Bible Societies, the printing company was designed to "give priority to the printing of the Bible" as well as print other materials in service to society. Over the last two decades, the Amity Printing Company has printed more than eighty million Bibles and New Testaments. The overwhelming majority of these are for distribution to Protestant churches in China (including Bibles in eight minority languages), but in the last few years, Bibles have also been produced for export. By 2010, the Amity Printing Company had become the largest printer of Bibles in the world.

In China there has emerged a new model of Buddhist charity in recent years. Often a charity center affiliated with the temple is set up. The Hanshan Temple in Suzhou, Jiangsu province, for instance, established a charity center, which operates several nonprofit *cishan chaoshi*, or charity supermarkets. It provides the urban poor (such as laid-off workers and the physically and mentally handicapped) with a minimum monthly allowance that can be used to purchase basic merchandise, such as oil, rice, detergent, shampoo, and so on, for well below the market price. Even though the abbot of the temple is the head of this charity center and temple volunteers also volunteer in the center, the finances of the charity center and the temple are separate. A visitor to the temple will see two donation boxes at the main halls of the temple—one for the temple itself and other for the charity center. The city government plays an important role in the project. The charity center obtains a list of "those who live under the poverty line" from the city government and distributes vouchers to families whose names appear on that list.

The tourist destination and Buddhist site of Lingshan in Wuxi, also in Jiangsu province, also set up a charitable foundation as its own vehicle for philanthropy. This foundation has been successful in areas of education (it established schools and scholarships for students who cannot afford tuition), poverty relief, disaster relief, environmental protection, and moral education. Many a poor patient has obtained generous help from the foundation to cover medical bills. After the 2008 Sichuan earthquake, the foundation was among the first groups of NGOs to arrive at the front line with all sorts of goods such as clothes, medicine, tents, and food and personnel such as doctors and other volunteers. The honorary head of the foundation is Master Wuxiang, the abbot of the Xiangfu Temple that is located inside the Lingshan estate. The secretary general is the CEO of the Lingshan Company, a business that includes tourism, real estate, vegetarian food industry, and an incense and candle company. It was said that the CEO converted to Buddhism after he took up the Lingshan project. If Master

Wuxiang is the spiritual teacher of universalistic ideas of compassion and benevolence, the CEO of the Lingshan Company is the executor of those ideas. The sources of income, however, mainly come from public donations. The company shoulders the operating cost of the full-time employees, whereas specific projects are often conducted by volunteers who gather through personal connections and online recruitment. The "Lingshan model" is highly successful in molding religion, business, and NGOs together to most efficiently provide social services.

BOX 8.2 The Rise of Transnational Chinese Charity: The *Tzu Chi* and *Cihui* Foundations

---

Tzu Chi, the Compassionate Merit Society (*Ciji Gongdehui*) like, to a lesser degree, Foguangshan's lay affiliate, the Buddha Light International Association (*Guoji foguanghui*), has been active in providing disaster relief outside Taiwan since 1991. The relief operations of Tzu Chi have been launched in countries with which Taiwan has no diplomatic relations, at the same time as similar operations were initiated in the PRC. Tzu Chi performs eight different categories of activities in Taiwan: charity, medical help, education, cultural services, bone marrow donation, international relief, environmental protection, and community work. Since 1992, its volunteers have been sent from Taiwan, but also from overseas Taiwanese communities, to offer relief to victims of natural disaster, pandemics, or warfare, in all continents, and also in most provinces and autonomous regions of China. These activities have continued over the years despite important changes in Chinese and Taiwanese domestic politics, and despite dramatic tensions in cross-strait relations.

Its missions each last about a week or two, and its volunteers provide disaster relief by personally delivering clothes, food, and sometimes cash to victims of flood, drought, or earthquake. Some of the operations have deployed considerable logistics in cooperation with other NGOs, such as *Médecins sans frontières*, or the People's Liberation Army (PLA). In China alone, Tzu Chi has contributed to building homes in Anhui, Jiangsu, and Guangxi. In Hebei, even new villages have been built. It has also supported local health care by supporting financially the construction of ten nursing homes in Anhui, children's hospitals in nine provinces, and a rehabilitation center in Wuhan. It has also supported education by helping to rebuild schools in all regions of the country, and by offering scholarships.

Lay Buddhist organizations from Hong Kong are also involved in the PRC. Since 2000, a Buddhist charity led by a layperson, the Gracious Glory Buddhist Foundation (*Cihui fojiao jijinhui*, or simply Cihui), has sponsored projects for schools in twenty provinces. Cihui's founder, Yang Hong, who was born in Huizhou, Guangdong, suffered from persecution during the Cultural Revolution but decided to give back to society after becoming a phenomenally wealthy businessman. Although Yang is a layperson, he has developed very close affinities with monks in Hebei and Jiangsu, and his lectures on Buddhism generate the kind of fervor that is usually found among the audience of American televangelists. Besides providing material help, Cihui also sponsors lecture series on Buddhism in major universities in mainland China. This is a good example of how philanthropy can in turn promote the status and influence of religion in China.

The Revival of Communal Religion and Local Welfare

Community temples are still the major provider of services, networks, and economic opportunities at the local level. Adam Chau's work on a popular religious temple of the Black Dragon King in Northern Shaanxi Province demonstrates how the temple association was able to accumulate enough funds from donations to build better roads, irrigation systems, and schools, and to undertake tree planting programs. Those philanthropic activities, in turn, help the temple to gain legitimacy in its negotiations with the local state and village community. Moreover, although hiring dance troupes and folk music bands for festivals does not seem to be directly related to philanthropy, those festivals with free performances not only bring the villagers together to celebrate, socialize, and relax but the money they spend to purchase incense and candles, and the funds they leave in donation boxes, bring a significant income to temples, part of which is then channeled into philanthropic projects. The Dragon King temple, for example, used the surplus funds raised through incense donation boxes to launch a reforestation project, which won international acclaim as the only nongovernmental arboretum in China, and built a primary school that, with generous funding from the temple and excellent facilities, quickly became the best primary school in the entire district.[7]

In a comparative study of villages in Jiangxi and Fujian, Lily Lee Tsai concludes that single-lineage villages that practice village-wide rituals or with an active temple association "provide broad community networks that village officials can draw on for public services."[8] She notes that the committees formed to rebuild temples and lineage halls often evolved into "community councils" that organized religious, social, and philanthropic activities. Although villagers do not contribute to appeals for funds by village cadres, they "willingly and universally" contribute to public projects when solicited by temple boards. In one village, the temple committee's revenue was four times higher than that of the village government and had taken over all of the road building in the community. Local cadres often sought the support of temple boards for their projects and delegated responsibility for social services to them.[9] Thus, one scholar has claimed that communal religion has become a "second tier of local government" in many parts of rural China.[10]

Indeed, throughout the 1980s and '90s, the Chinese state increasingly disengaged itself from the village level, providing few resources to cash-strapped village governments and Communist Party branches whose main function often came to be limited to the unpopular activities of tax collection and enforcing the one-child policy. Often seen as corrupt, local cadres had little moral authority to convince villagers to contribute to public projects. Temples have frequently emerged as alternative centers of resource collection and allocation, to which villagers willingly contribute funds, which in many cases are spent by the temple board on local infrastructure such as the construction and repair of roads, bridges, schools, and even basketball courts.

Although these examples show how temples could become the direct providers of public services offloaded by the state, other research has shown that temples could reinforce the accountability of village officials and their ability to provide public investments and services. A quantitative survey of 316 villages in North and South China, led by Lily Lee Tsai, concluded that village-encompassing temples and lineages are informal institutions of accountability that, more than any other variable, ensure governmental performance and the provision of public services by village state agents. Compared with villages lacking temple groups, villages with temples had higher levels of government investment in public services, a higher probability of paved roads and paths, a higher percentage of classrooms usable in rain, and a higher probability of running water.[11] Using several statistical instruments to determine whether these higher levels of public services were caused by other factors, or whether the temples were a consequence (and not a cause) of the better public services, Tsai concludes that "even when we control for level of economic development and industrialization, variation in bureaucratic and democratic institutions, and differences in the demand for particular goods or the cost of particular goods due to the variation in location, geography, and size, village temple groups have a significant positive effect on village governmental provision of public goods."[12] Indeed, she even notes that the introduction in many regions of village-level democratic reforms since the late 1990s, in which village leaders could be elected in openly contested elections, was a less significant variable than the existence of an active temple in ensuring the village leaders' accountability and efficient provision of public goods.[13]

Tsai defines *temples* as "solidary groups" in which members are "engaged in mutually oriented activities who share a set of ethical standards and moral obligations."[14] When solidary groups encompass all the members of the administrative village, and embed local state officials as members, the village officials will be bound by the moral obligations of the solidary group, which can reward those who serve the group well with high moral standing, or punish corrupt officials by giving them a bad moral reputation. This constitutes a system of informal accountability, in a context in which formal (democratic) systems of accountability are weak or nonexistent and higher levels of government are uninterested or unable to force accountability on village officials. Such village leaders have an added incentive to make an effort to provide public services, while leaders of the solidary group are willing to mobilize the villagers to cooperate with the officials, complying with regulations and voluntarily contributing funds for public projects. On the other hand, village officials who are not embedded in a solidary group have little incentive to perform, not being bound to a solidary group's mutual obligations and moral standards (and being provided with few incentives from higher levels of government to perform). Temples are solidary groups that encompass all villagers and embed local officials within them, providing the common moral obligations and incentives to perform, cooperate, and comply.

Women and the elderly have always played active roles in Chinese popular religion. As socially marginalized groups, they benefit a great deal from participating in popular religious activities. Popular sutra chanting groups (*nianfo hui*) in southern Jiangsu, for instance, often consist of older women from the villages. Sutra chanting groups are often hired for ritual occasions such as funerals for a small fee (often cash is wrapped in red paper, called red pockets). By participating in those occasions, not only can the women who have otherwise no source of income get a small allowance that is at their own disposal, but they also gain an opportunity to socialize with other women from different villages and travel outside of the house where they are tied to arduous labor, day in and day out. Moreover, sometimes those sutra chanting groups organize pilgrimages to sacred Buddhist sites. This gives the women more mobility and provides moral encouragement to the family, since those trips are considered to generate karmic merit. Even though this function of popular religion may not be regarded as philanthropy in the modern sense, on a small scale and at the local level, it contributes to an important aspect of social welfare.

These examples show how religious values not only encourage charitable giving per se, but that this giving occurs in social situations that create shared moral norms and communal bonds. These bonds form networks and organizations that are distinct from the bureaucratic hierarchies of the socialist state and from the commercial transactions of the market economy. Religious groups thus constitute an important component of China's emerging "civil society" or "third sector," which, in spite of the restrictions imposed by an authoritarian political regime, manage to create a social space that is distinct from those of the state and of the market. Religious groups can create an autonomous social space precisely because their ethic of compassionate merit and philanthropic giving creates and reinforces new social bonds based neither on political coercion nor on economic gain.

The connection between civil society and Chinese spiritual values is emphasized by Pang Fei, a former philosophy student at Beijing University who founded the Yidan Academy, a grassroots NGO with thousands of student volunteers around China. These students gather on campus at dawn to recite the Confucian classics together, visit the elderly in their homes, and go out to schools in poor neighborhoods or villages to offer free instruction in the Chinese classics and history. They organize trips to the countryside to interview old people about their customs and traditions, and help them to set up rural academies to teach their traditional knowledge to the younger generations. According to Pang Fei, China sorely needs to develop a culture of public service and volunteering, and Chinese tradition, with its emphasis on ethics and duty to others, is the best resource to draw upon in promoting such a culture. Thus, he mobilizes youth volunteers to promote traditional culture, which in turn stimulates the volunteer spirit. Any type of action for the public good, he argues, must rest on a process of transforming people through moral instruction and example.

Notes

1. Quoted from the DVD *A Paradise on Earth—Tung Cheng Yuen founded by Mr. Lam Tong* (Hong Kong: Tai Tak Production, 2008).

2. Vivienne Shue, "The Quality of Mercy: Confucian Charity and the Mixed Metaphors of Modernity in Tianjin," *Modern China* 34, no. 4 (2006): 411–452.

3. Joanna Handlin-Smith, "Chinese Philanthropy as Seen through a Case of Famine Relief in the 1640s," in *Philanthropy in the World's Traditions* (Bloomington: Indiana University Press, 1998), 133–168.

4. Don A Pittman, *Toward a Modern Chinese Buddhism: Taixu's Reforms* (Honolulu: University of Hawaii Press, 2001).

5. Bernard Formoso, *De Jiao, a Religious Movement in Contemporary China and Overseas: Purple Qi from the East* (Singapore: NUS Press, 2010).

6. Prasenjit Duara, *Sovereignity and Authenticity: Manchukuo and the East Asian Modern* (Lanham, Md.: Rowman & Littlefield, 2003), 103–104.

7. Adam Yuet Chau, *Miraculous Response: Doing Popular Religion in Contemporary China* (Stanford, Calif.: Stanford University Press, 2005).

8. Lily L. Tsai, "Cadres, Temple and Lineage Institutions, and Governance in Rural China," *China Journal* 48 (2002): 1–27, 9.

9. Tsai, "Cadres, Temples," 21–23.

10. Kenneth Dean, "Local Communal Religion in Contemporary South-East China," *China Quarterly* 174 (2003): 338–358.

11. Lily L. Tsai, *Accountability without Democracy; Solidary Groups and Public Goods Provision in Rural China* (Cambridge: Cambridge University Press, 2007).

12. Tsai, *Accountability*, 130.

13. Ibid., 187–228.

14. Ibid., 12.

PART III

Religion, Politics, and the Economy

9

Religion in Chinese Social and Political History
David A. Palmer

In the previous chapters of this book, we presented general portraits of religious life in contemporary cities, rural areas, and ethnic minority regions, and then we explored how Chinese religious culture relates to the themes of the body, gender, environment, and civil society. In this and the next two chapters, we will see how the many ideas, practices, and communities fit together within a broader and evolving sociopolitical system, which can be understood only if we take a long-range historical perspective. Indeed, religious life today can be seen as made up of several layers of tradition, in which the social and political features of each era have left their mark, and in which each new element has interacted with previous layers. The aggregate result is the great diversity of religious beliefs and practices that exist in the Chinese world today—a diversity that, although it is not unified into a single structure, presents several common themes.

In this historical presentation, we will trace the appearance and recurrence of several of these themes, many of which were presented in previous chapters of this book. These themes include *divination*; the *veneration of ancestors*; the *ruler's relationship with Heaven or a supreme divinity* as a source of political legitimacy; the notion of the *mandate of Heaven* and the importance of *virtue and ritual propriety* in social relations and government; a *holistic cosmological system* of *yin-yang* powers and cycles; the search for longevity and immortality through practices of *body cultivation*; *millenarian movements* sometimes associated with rebellions; interference by the Chinese state in the *authority of religious institutions*; a *commercial ethic* associating morality and material prosperity; and the tensions and mutual interactions between the teachings of *Confucianism, Daoism,* and *Buddhism,* as well as with the later additions of *Islam* and *Christianity.* In spite of over one century of reform movements, revolutions, and modernizing campaigns from the nineteenth century until today, these themes continue to influence much of the religious life and sociopolitical relationships in the Chinese world today. They are also elements of the general religious and spiritual culture that, through processes of globalization, is now spreading to other parts of the world.

Ancestor Worship and the Religious Foundations of Political Legitimacy: The Shang (1766–1027 BCE)

THE EMPEROR'S TOOTHACHE

Five turtle shells lie on the rammed-earth altar. The plastrons have been polished like jade, but are scarred on their inner side with rows of oval hollows, some already blackened by fire. Into one of the unburned hollows, on the right side of the shell, the diviner Chui is thrusting a brand of flaming thorn. Fanned by an assistant to keep the glowing tip intensely hot, the stick flames against the surface of the shell. Smoke rises. The seconds slowly pass. The stench of scorched bone mingles with the aroma of millet wine scattered in libation. And then, with a sharp, clear, "*puk*"-like sound, the turtle, most silent of creatures, speaks. A crack has formed in the hollow where the plastron was scorched. Once again the brand is thrust, now into a matching hollow on the left side of the shell. The diviner cries out: "It is due to Father Jia!" [the king's uncle, a deceased former king].[1]

The first historical dynasty of China was called the Shang, which ruled around 3000–3700 years ago. This was a kingdom of warriors and conquerors, the first to unify the many tribes around the middle course of the Yellow River, in the North China Plain. Most of the people were peasants who lived in Stone Age conditions; they were ruled by noble clans that owned horses and war chariots and lived in walled towns that served as the capital of their domains.

The largest structures in these towns were the tombs of the dead kings and noblemen, and the temples in which these ancestors were worshipped. Kingship rotated between ten branches of the royal clan—but the supreme lord and arbiter of human fortune and misfortune was a deity named Di. This god was inaccessible to humans, but the ancestors of the royal clan could intercede on behalf of living rulers. The ancestors, on the other hand, needed honor, food, and provisions from humans. The art of ruling, then, involved managing a mutually beneficial relationship with the ancestors, through reverential veneration and generous sacrificial offerings of grain and wine, presented in exquisite bronze vessels, as well as animals, and even humans.

Victories in battle and good harvests—political power and economic prosperity were seen as signs of the ancestors' satisfaction and of Di's favor, which could be repaid through more sumptuous and costly sacrificial offerings. The awesome scale and cost of these rituals impressed on the hearts of ministers, subjects, and rivals that the king was favored by the Lord, that his domination was legitimate and beneficial.

Defeat in war, mutual calamities, and illness, on the other hand, signified that the ancestors were unhappy. They were not lobbying the Lord Di on the king's behalf, and were even sending down curses: they needed to be placated with more worship and offerings.

In such cases, the king wanted to know which ancestors were unhappy, and for what reasons, for example: "Is there a curse? Does the deceased Chin-wu desire

BOX 9.1 Oracle Bones and Chinese Writing

The questions and answers of oracle bone divination were recorded on the turtle plastrons, using China's most ancient pictographic script. Over 200,000 such inscriptions have been uncovered by archaeologists, providing us with a precious record of the life and culture of ancient China. Over the centuries, the oracle bone characters evolved into modern Chinese characters, in which it is possible to uncover the original religious meanings. For example, the original form of the character *zun* (see figure 9.1, *right*) shows a bottle of liquor being held up by two hands, as a sacrificial offering to the spirits; the modern form (*left*) means, more broadly, "to honor, to respect."

FIGURE 9.1 *Etymology of the Chinese character* zun *(to honor, to respect): oracle bone form* (right) *and modern form* (left).

---

something of the king?" He also wanted to know if they would support him in his plans, for example, for a military attack on an enemy army. The king and his priests tried to find answers to these questions through a process called "oracle bone divination." A priest would stab a burning stick into a hole drilled in the dried plastron of a turtle or a cow's bone, making it crack. The fissures were then interpreted by the priests as the ancestors' answers to the questions, usually formulated as *yes* or *no*, *auspicious* or *inauspicious*. Though many diviners assisted him, the king himself was the supreme priest and mediator with the ancestors.

The Shang kings' relationship with their ancestors thus followed the same pattern as their relations with their subjects: a relationship of reciprocity and mutual obligation, in which subjects accorded honor, reverence, and gifts of tribute to their ruler, and in exchange, the ruler provided the protection, peace, and security that were the foundation of prosperity. This type of exchange took place in ritualized ceremonies. Through the gestures they made, the clothes they wore, and the types of gifts they gave, the respective ranks of all the actors were made visible and performed in one harmonious order.

Many elements of the Shang sacred regime continued to exist in Chinese culture, politics, and religion until modern times: filial reverence expressed through the veneration of ancestors; techniques of divination used as aids to decide on courses of action; the combined roles of the king as warrior and priest.

Rule by Virtue and the Mandate of Heaven: The Zhou (1122–771 BCE)

Invaders from northwest China, the Zhou overthrew the Shang kings. Although they had successfully defeated the Shang, their ancestors were not among the clans considered to be able to intercede with Di. How could they legitimize their new power over the realm? Their answer was that the supreme Lord—whom they called *Tian* (meaning "Heaven")—was so angry with the immoral conduct of the Shang kings, who were oppressing the people, that he had revoked their right to rule (called the "Mandate of Heaven") and transferred it to the Zhou. *Tian* was a universal god who ruled over the world—"all under heaven"—and who, rather than being surrounded by the ancestors of the different noble clans, could be directly approached and sacrificed to, but by one person only: the king, who styled himself "Son of Heaven." Ritual worship and sacrifice were necessary but not sufficient, however: to obtain heavenly favor, the king had to conduct himself as a paragon of virtue—otherwise, floods, famines, and earthquakes would occur, the people would become restless, the Mandate of Heaven would be lost, and the dynasty would collapse.

In contrast to the Shang, whose divine legitimacy came from being descendants of a select lineage of privileged ancestors, in the Zhou conception of political legitimacy anyone could theoretically become king, provided he earned the Mandate of Heaven through exemplary virtue; falling into corruption, however, he could also lose the mandate as well. Virtue became fundamental to political legitimacy, bringing heavenly blessings and earthly order and prosperity. Zhou legends extolled the lives of civilizing heroes: Fuxi and his sister/wife Nüwa, for example, were said to have been the only humans to survive a great flood, and introduced the use of fishing nets, the taming of wild animals, and the use of writing. The Yellow Emperor (*Huangdi*), later considered be the ancestor of the Chinese people, was said to have established civilization after an epic battle with the beastly warrior Chiyou. These ancient sage kings were depicted as bringing morality, order, and civilization to a chaotic and savage world.[2]

Whereas the central principle of political and religious authority among the Shang had been kinship and ancestor worship—which carried with it a logic of fragmentation, since each clan could access spiritual power through worshipping its own ancestors—the Zhou introduced the notion of a universal polity, "all under Heaven," under the centralized rule of a single emperor who enjoyed exclusive access to Heaven on the basis of his own virtue.

Each locality had its own altar of the soil, for worshipping the earth spirit of that particular spot. This spirit symbolized local power. The Zhou king sent clods of earth from his royal altar of the soil at the capital, and enshrined them in the soil altars of his vassal's towns. In this way, he acknowledged the local powers symbolized by the soil altars, but also subordinated them to his own power by having his own soil worshipped at each locality's altar. At the same time, through rituals of investiture, the King delegated rights and responsibilities to his vassals.

The Zhou system thus tried to use ritual means to unify the many localities of China into a single polity. But this principle carried with it a logic of potential revolution and dynastic change, and of disintegration into smaller units: when the emperor's virtue was contested, he could no longer unify the realm, his dynasty would be deposed, and the forces of localism would break up the empire into feuding regional units.

Kinship-based reverence to ancestors and territorial-based loyalty to virtuous kings and officials would remain in creative tension as alternative idioms of community building and political loyalty throughout much of Chinese history.

Ghosts, Immortality, and *Yin-Yang* Cosmology: The Warring States (771–256 BCE)

In 771 BCE, invasions and unrest led to the collapse of the Zhou social order. For the next 500 years, although the Zhou royal clan continued to be honored, its authority remained merely symbolic, as the realm broke down into hundreds of warring states. Feudal honor, authority through virtue, and solidarity through ritual order were replaced by shifting alliances, blood oaths, treachery, and massacres. Trust broke down, and people assumed that others had evil intentions. They feared not only the living, but the dead as well. The souls of the dead were considered to be bitter and malevolent: if they were not properly taken care of by their living descendants through ancestor veneration, they would become ghosts and return to haunt the living, bringing illness and bad luck. With so many people being killed and displaced in incessant wars, crowds of the hungry ghosts of these forgotten souls were believed to be wandering around the world, seeking revenge. The people called on priests to use exorcistic techniques to frighten the ghosts away.[3]

Many, particularly among the aristocracy, dreamed of finding a way to avoid dying at all. Legends circulated about extraordinary individuals who had become "immortals" by turning their bodies into a sublime, ethereal substance, purged of all impurities that could lead to rotting and death. Immortals were able to ride on the clouds and were said to live in earthly paradises beyond the oceans of the east, or deep in the Kunlun Mountains to the west. It was said that this bodily transformation could be achieved through secret techniques of diet, meditation, and ascetic techniques, as well as through preparing and ingesting a magical elixir, the pill of immortality (see chapter 5).

With the pervasive uncertainty under the Western Zhou, and much of life subject to unpredictable chance, people were more anxious than ever to discover their fate and know the future through magical divination techniques. Reading the stars (astrology), the forms of the earth (geomancy), the features of the body (physiognomy), and numerological computations became popular forms of prognostication. During these observations, they paid close attention to cycles of time and their association with aspects of geography and human life: day and night, summer and winter, sun and moon. These cycles were associated respectively with light and dark, hot and cold, south and north, going out and coming in, outside and inside, motion and stillness. These sets of opposites were symbolized by the characters *yang*, meaning "the sunny side of a hill," and *yin*, meaning "the shady side of a hill."

BOX 9.2 How to Use the *Book of Changes*

Take forty-nine milfoil stalks. After a complicated procedure of repeatedly dividing the stalks and placing them between the fingers of your left and right hand, you get a numerical value of six or nine.

If it is nine, then draw a solid line ——, representing *yang*, firmness, movement.
If it is six, then draw a broken line — —, representing *yin*, softness, stillness.

Repeat the operation six times, drawing each additional line on top of the previous one. There are sixty-four possible combinations of solid and broken lines: each is called a *hexagram*. Look up your hexagram in the *Book of Changes*: you will find a symbol representing a direction of change in the universe and a set of cryptic riddles, proverbs, and "judgments" to be used in interpreting the meaning of the hexagram in relation to your situation and question.

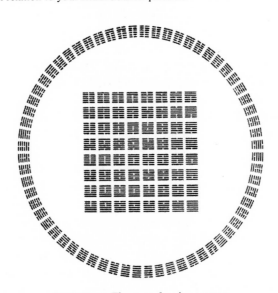

FIGURE 9.2 *The sixty-four hexagrams.*

Yin-yang cosmology was systematized in the *Book of Changes* (also known as the *I Ching*), a divination manual that remains popular until today as one of China's main classics of cosmology and philosophy, and is also one of the best-known Chinese religious texts in the West.

Harmony, Spontaneity, and Ritual Propriety: Laozi and Confucius

The late Zhou period (403–221 BCE), called the Spring and Autumn Warring States, saw the flourishing of hundreds of schools of thought, as kings, lords, and aristocrats employed all kinds of experts to give them advice in the arts of governance, military strategy, ritual, medicine, divination, magic, immortality, and so on—perhaps comparable to the professional consultants, management gurus, and spiritual entrepreneurs of today. Thousands of masters competed against one another, traveling from one kingdom to another to provide their services to the rulers, and teaching their knowledge to bands of disciples. Each promoted a specific "way," or *dao*, as the best path to success in government, warfare, health, or longevity. Although the vast majority of these masters have been forgotten by posterity, two figures would have a profound influence on the religious, social, and political life of future generations of Chinese: Laozi and Confucius.

Little is known about Laozi—his existence is even doubted by some scholars. Legend has it that he was once employed as a court archivist, and one day, riding on the back of a buffalo, set off to disappear in the mountains of the west. On reaching the border post of Louguantai (in present-day Shaanxi), the guard Yin Xi asked him to teach his wisdom. Laozi taught him a collection of 5000 verses, which Yin Xi transcribed onto bamboo slips. These came to be known as the *Daodejing*, the "Book of the Way and Its Virtue," which would later become a key scripture of the Daoist religion. The book taught that the universe and all creatures and phenomena are generated by an invisible, unnamable, and mysterious power called *Dao* (often rendered in English as *Tao*), the Way. For the ruler, true power could come only from aligning himself with Dao, spontaneously following its operation, and not interfering with its movements as expressed through the workings of nature. Rather than imposing rigid laws and moral codes, the ruler, through his natural spontaneity, could induce the free obedience and harmony of the people. The *Daodejing* (Tao Te Ching) stressed following the path of water, which flows to its goal without taking fixed form, and nurturing the generative powers of the feminine. Ostensibly written as a manual for rulers, the *Daodejing* could also be read as a guide for the individual cultivation of Dao through practices of the mind and body. Its philosophy of mystic spontaneity and detachment could be invoked to quit the political struggles and the competition for name and fame in this world, and to retreat into the mountains to seek spiritual enlightenment and immortality. But the book's philosophy could also be understood to mean that the power of a ruler came from his being in tune with Dao—and, conversely, that a person truly in tune with Dao could be more powerful than the king and could aspire to occupy the throne himself.

Around the same time, Confucius (552–479 BCE) looked with despair at the breakdown of social order around him and yearned for a return to the peace and harmony of the early Zhou. By studying the rites and ceremonies of bygone centuries, he derived a system of principles for the appropriate conduct of human relations. This system was based on the notion of *li*, a term that has many layers of meaning: the ritual offerings given to ancestors and gods; social ceremonies; the respect for proper conventions and norms of hierarchy, and the inner attitude of sincere deference that should accompany the outward expression of respect to other people, to ancestors, or to Heaven. For Confucius, the proper observance of *li* was the foundation of social life: without *li*, as Confucius and his contemporaries could observe around them, social chaos and corruption would set in.

Although Confucius referred to the sacrificial rites of the early Zhou kings which were no longer practiced in his own day—Confucius advocated a universal set of moral and social principles, which could be applied by anyone in any situation. The goal was to act with the noble motives and benevolence of a gentleman, rather than following the selfish inclinations of a petty man. Each person should diligently and sincerely play his role in a sacralized social hierarchy: the prince acting with princely virtues, his ministers with appropriate submissiveness, the father with paternal love, his sons with filial reverence, the husband with manly responsibility, his wife with womanly discretion. In such a society, order would spontaneously arise, without the need for harsh impositions of authority.

For Confucius, it was in the family that all of these relationships were grounded, that the proper feelings could be nurtured and the norms of behavior inculcated. It was through filial piety that one gained the experience and practice of *li*—by obeying one's parents when young, by taking care of them when they grew old, by holding a proper funeral for them when they died, and by properly nurturing their souls through ancestor worship.

Confucius stressed the importance of study, and he and his disciples learned and commented on the classics of his day: the *Book of Changes*, the *Rites of the Zhou*, the *Book of Songs*, and other records of history and music. As experts in ritual, they could officiate at religious ceremonies. Their bookishness and deferential manners earned them the title of the "gentle ones." They would give birth to the Chinese tradition of education and schooling.[4]

Religion and the Political Unification of China:
The Qin and Han (221 BC–220 CE)

Confucius wandered from one kingdom to another but found no ruler willing to seriously consider his teachings. In the dog-eat-dog environment of constant warfare among kingdoms, rulers preferred another school of thought—the legalist. This school considered that morality, virtues, and ceremonies were of little import. One should not rule through virtuous example; aristocratic *noblesse oblige* should be replaced by an impersonal, bureaucratic structure of government. The ruler's decrees, and his codes of law, should be enforced through harsh punishments. Respect for ancestors, the Heavenly Lord, or ethics had little place in the legalist scheme.

The state of Qin fully applied the legalist approach and, one by one, ruthlessly conquered all the other kingdoms: China was united, for the first time, into a single empire in 221 BCE. The first emperor, Qin Shihuang, brutally eliminated any source of opposition, unified the Chinese script, and launched the construction of the Great Wall to defend China against tribal invaders from the north. He was also a deep believer in immortality: he sent magicians to the fabled fairyland of the eastern seas to search for the drug of immortality and, hoping to continue his conquests in the afterlife, had an entire army of life-sized terracotta warriors buried around his tomb, which can be visited today near the city of Xi'an.

But the cruelty of the first emperor's legalist rule could not win over the hearts of the Chinese people. Shortly after his death, revolts erupted, which toppled his short-lived dynasty. A rebel leader, Liu Bang, crowned himself emperor of the new Han dynasty, which lasted for 400 years in relative peace. Although legalism was not abandoned, Han rule was softened and legitimated by the adoption of Confucian and Daoist approaches to government and social organization. The Han synthesis became the paradigm for a unified Chinese civilization for the next 2000 years.

The Han integrated Chinese religion and cosmology into a single system, in which the emperor occupied the central position and pivotal role. All phenomena were classified as either *yin* or *yang* and as expressing one of five cyclic phases symbolized by five elements: wood, fire, earth, metal, and water. The human body was conceived as a microcosm of the whole universe. *Yin-yang* and the Five Phases could be used to map movement in both space and time.

In the Han cosmology, everything is seen as interconnected. Cosmic order is characterized by the cyclical alternation of *yin* and *yang* and the orderly succession of the Five Phases, as described in chapter 5. Calamities, wars, epidemics, and natural disasters occur when the cyclical harmony is disrupted. Moral behavior and Confucian propriety were an integral part of the system of correspondences. Man was seen as occupying a central position in the universe—between Heaven (*yang*) and Earth (*yin*), at the junction of *yin* and *yang*, containing within his body all the elements and powers of the cosmos. He also had to respect the *yin* and *yang* positions of authority and submission within the social hierarchy: the ruler is *yang* to the minister's *yin*, the father is *yang* to the son's *yin*, the husband is *yang* to the wife's *yin*. If man's behavior did not conform to the moral principles of the cosmic order, the disruptions could reverberate throughout the cosmos and come back to him in the form of illnesses or bad luck. This was all the more the case for the emperor who, as the supreme man, was the fundamental pivot between Heaven and Earth. As described in one Han text,

> [The monarch] holds the position of life and death over men; together with Heaven he holds the power of change and transformation....Therefore the great concern of the ruler lies in diligently watching over and guarding his heart, that his loves and hates, his anger and joy may be displayed in accordance with right, as the mild and cool, the cold and hot weather come forth in proper season....Then may he form a Trinity with Heaven and Earth....Thus may he be called the Equal of Heaven.[5]

This theory legitimized the absolute power of the emperor, who was seen as higher than even most of the gods. But it also required the emperor to act with virtue and benevolence. When calamities and famines occurred, this could mean that the emperor's corruption was disrupting the cosmic harmony, and that he had lost the Mandate of Heaven—in such circumstances, it was thus legitimate to arise in rebellion. Furthermore, the Five Phases theory assigned each dynasty to a corresponding phase. The Han were Fire and Red. This meant that eventually the cycle would move to the next phase of Earth and Yellow, which would be incarnated by a new dynasty. When would such a change occur? Natural events, such as eclipses, weather patterns, or movements of the stars were often interpreted as omens of imminent changes.

Millenarian Rebellion and the Daoist Heavenly Masters

Such speculations reached a climax in the years approaching 184 CE, which, according to the Chinese calendar, would mark the beginning of a new sixty-year cycle. Intrigues and corruption at the court were rampant, and costly wars against invaders severely taxed the people. Millenarian scriptures and prophecies circulated widely, predicting calamities, famines, pestilence, and floods. Most people would be annihilated. Only a small group would be saved: those who followed the teachings of a "divine man of the great Dao" and his scripture, the *Book of the Great Peace*. This book spelled out a vision of an egalitarian society based on the Dao, in which leaders would live modestly, care for the poor and the elderly, and reduce the taxes of the common people. These ideas inspired an uprising, known as the Yellow Turban Rebellion, led by the charismatic healer Zhang Jue, who conducted mass healing rituals for those who confessed their sins. He quickly attracted a following of hundreds of thousands of rebels in northern China, who were organized in regiments and planned to overthrow the ruling dynasty in 184. After a series of bloody massacres in which thousands were killed, the revolt was crushed. But the insurrection further weakened the Han dynasty, which collapsed a few decades later. Although the Yellow Turban Rebellion failed, it would become the paradigm, always feared by Chinese dynasties and governments, of charismatic millenarian movements turning into armed uprisings, creating social chaos, aiming to topple the ruling house and establish a new dynasty.

At around the same time, another movement arose in western China (in what is now Sichuan and Southern Shaanxi provinces), in which several charismatic healers spread the teachings of the magician Zhang Daoling, who was said to have received revelations from Laozi, ushering in a new cosmic cycle. The movement organized the people into dioceses led by priests, the Heavenly Masters, who held written contracts from the divine hierarchy, empowering them to cast away the demons and protect the people. A bureaucracy of priest-administrators, modeled on the Han civil service, was established and integrated into a wider system of cosmic administration run by a bureaucratic pantheon of gods. Prayers and communications from these gods were presented as written petitions, reports, and standardized forms to fill out. The work of a priest involved, like a clerk, being able to compose such forms and reports on behalf of the people, and transmit them to the relevant officials in heaven by following the appropriate ritual procedures.

The Heavenly Masters movement only lasted some thirty years, until it was crushed by Han troops. But the Heavenly Masters continued to transmit their tradition: they would become the main religious functionaries of Chinese local temples and community cults—one of the main priestly orders of what came to be known as the Daoist religion.

The Spread of Buddhism

After the collapse of the Han dynasty in 220 BCE, for 400 years China was divided into small kingdoms and short-lived dynasties, several of which were ruled by non-Chinese tribes. Some of these made Daoism into their state religion, whereas others favored Buddhism, which was penetrating China through the Silk Road, from India, by way of Afghanistan, to the desert oases of Central Asia, and from there to western China. In the absence of political unity, the Chinese elites turned away from the this-worldly social concerns of Confucianism, and were drawn to a spiritual concern with the self, whether through Daoist techniques for cultivating long life or immortality, or accumulating Buddhist merits for a better afterlife.

The rapid spread of Buddhism was met with resistance and controversy. Daoists were spurred to strengthen their organization, systematize their teachings, and to claim that Buddha was but a barbarian student of Laozi. The idea of monasticism—in which monks break their ties with their family to devote themselves exclusively to spiritual salvation—was seen as an affront to the sacred notions of filial reverence: if a son broke ties with his parents, he would not worship them after their death, and they would become hungry ghosts; by remaining celibate, he would not have sons to care for his own soul, and he would suffer the same ignominious fate.

This tension was expressed and solved through mythical narratives, such as the story of Miaoshan recounted in chapter 6. There was also the story of Mulian, a disciple of Buddha, who travels through the underworld in search of his mother, meeting countless ghosts and masters along the way. Finally, in the most frightening of all hells, he finds his mother impaled on a bed of nails, as punishment for not giving alms to a mendicant monk. By conducting rituals of salvation, calling on the merit of the faithful, and appealing to the Buddha himself, Mulian rescues his mother from hell and leads her to rebirth in paradise. This story showed how, by accumulating Buddhist merit, a monk could do more to save the souls of his parents than worshipping them as ancestors. Indeed, Buddhist monks came to be seen as specialists in the salvation of the souls of the dead—capable of saving not only their own ancestors, but the souls of all sentient beings. They thus became the main providers of funeral rites. Mulian's story was often ritually performed during the midsummer Ghost Festival (during the seventh lunar month) dedicated to the collective salvation of all wandering souls and hungry ghosts who, because they had no sons to worship them, or had died an unnatural death, were not taken care of through the ancestor cult.

In contrast to the vertical ethics of the Confucians, which stressed reverence of one's parents and loyalty to one's ruler, Buddhism advocated a more horizontal, universal ethics: good deeds would lead to a better rebirth in the next life; such merit-accumulating good deeds could be carried out for the benefit of others besides one's own kin or ruler. Popular forms of meritorious deeds included giving alms to monks, making donations to build or repair a temple, contributing funds to print religious literature to be distributed for free, and doing charitable works for the poor and destitute. Enjoying the generous donations of their wealthy patrons, many Buddhist monasteries became powerful institutions, their leaders going so far as refusing to bow down in submission to the emperor, on the grounds that they were not subject to his this-worldly authority.

Religion, Commerce, and Markets in the Tang and Song Dynasties (618–1279)

In 618, China was once again reunited under the Tang, whose emperors claimed to be descendants of Laozi, thus fulfilling millenarian prophecies about the advent of a Daoist messiah. The Tang dynasty is typically considered to represent the apex of Chinese civilization, a time when arts, literature, and the economy flourished. Traders of many nationalities and religions, including Muslims and East Syrian Christians, came and went along the Silk Road, and even served the government as officials. The Tang empire's influence radiated into Tibet, Central Asia, Mongolia, Korea, Japan, and Vietnam. Both Daoism and Buddhism enjoyed unprecedented wealth, power, and influence under imperial patronage. But the emperor was displeased with the power of the Buddhist clergy and its immense tax-free landholdings. In 845, he decreed a severe repression of Buddhism—more than 4600 monasteries and 40,000 temples and shrines were destroyed. Buddhist institutions never fully recovered, remaining weak until today.

The preeminence of Buddhism was gradually eclipsed by a resurgent Confucianism, which had absorbed the metaphysical aspects of Daoist and Buddhist philosophy. In the Song dynasty (969–1279), the imperial state expanded its powers and implemented a meritocratic system for recruiting officials by requiring candidates to pass examinations based on the Confucian classics. The state bureaucracy was mirrored by a celestial administration: the emperor gave himself the prerogative to promote and demote gods in the heavenly hierarchy. Although the imperial state maintained a policy of the harmony of the Three Teachings (Confucianism, Buddhism, and Daoism), government administration was firmly in the hands of the Confucians, who succeeded in restricting the influence of Buddhist and Daoist institutions, and reinforced ancestor worship among the population. In

South China, clans of kinsmen organized themselves into large corporate groupings, which built grand lineage halls to worship their common ancestors, and established schools to educate their children in the Confucian classics in order to prepare them for the imperial examinations.

This was a period of rapid commercial expansion, technological innovation, and proto-industrial development. Market cities flourished along trade routes—deeply impressing Marco Polo, the traveler from Venice, who had never seen such large and prosperous cities in his native medieval Europe. Merchants and producers organized themselves into guilds, which worshipped a common patron saint, built temples, and sponsored festivals. The main shrine in each city, the city god temple, was also a central public square and marketplace, and a place where business deals were sealed by making oaths before the god. Buddhist and Daoist priests, as well as fortune-tellers and mediums, offered their services to clients for a fee, acting as independent consultants.

Money was ubiquitous, and the logic of cash transactions penetrated popular religious life. Offerings to ancestors included special paper money, sent to the otherworld by burning it, which they could use to bribe the officials of hell and purchase whatever they needed, as well as to repay debts to gods. Sins and good deeds were recorded in accounting books—the "ledgers of merits and demerits"—by pious individuals who hoped to maintain a "positive balance" each day. One of the most popular gods was the god of wealth, who was prayed to for material prosperity. Confucian morality and the market culture fused into an ethic that claimed that moral behavior would lead to all-around prosperity: happiness, talented and healthy (male) offspring, higher social rank, and material wealth (see chapter 12). Conversely, prosperity was seen as a sign of virtue: something that the wealthy could demonstrate through charitable deeds like building roads and bridges and, especially, by funding the building and expansion of temples where the people could pray for blessings.[6]

Literacy became more widespread, and more people sought personal spiritual growth by reading scriptures and morality books, and by practicing meditation and body cultivation regimens. Many groups engaged in charitable deeds, building the benevolent halls described in chapter 8. Several lay religious movements emerged, which provided organized outlets for this popular spirituality: in Pure Land Buddhism, for example, one could attain salvation by repeatedly reciting the name of the Amitabha Buddha. Complete Perfection Daoism systematized the practice of inner alchemical meditation (it later adopted monastic forms derived from Buddhism, becoming the dominant institution of Daoism). The White Lotus movement gathered congregations of laypeople to recite Buddhist scriptures. Some groups, which worshipped a goddess called the Unborn Mother (see chapter 6), revived millenarian expectations with prophecies about the advent of the Maitreya Buddha. Some of these groups were associated with rebellions. The imperial state tried to stamp them out, but they continued to grow.

The Emperor as an Actor in Religious Conflicts: Tibetan Buddhism and Roman Catholicism in Late Imperial Times (1279–1911)

Indeed, the throne positioned itself as the ultimate authority and arbiter in religious issues—promoting and demoting gods in the pantheon, and supporting or banning religious sects and communities. Under constant state control and interference, indigenous religious institutions were permanently weakened. In the Yuan (1279–1368), the Ming (1368–1644), and the Qing (1644–1911) dynasties, the emperor became involved with the much more powerful and assertive religious institutions of Tibetan Buddhism and Roman Catholicism. Tibetan Buddhism was the religion of the borderland peoples of Tibet, Mongolia, and Manchuria, who were divided into several competing sects, often at war with one another, and under shifting relationships with the Chinese empire and its rulers. In order to secure the loyalty of those people, the emperor patronized Tibetan Buddhism and some of its religious leaders, often supporting one sect over another in order to advance imperial interests. During the Mongol Yuan dynasty, the emperor Kublai Khan, having been snubbed by the head of the Black Hat sect, established ties with the head of the Sakya sect, the Phagpa Lama, who recognized Kublai as the supreme sovereign in political affairs, while Kublai recognized the Lama as his master in spiritual affairs. In the early Ming, the Chinese emperors favored another line of lamas, the Karmapas, inviting them to officiate at solemn rites at the capital. By the mid-seventeenth century, the head of the Gelupka or Yellow Hat sect, the Dalai Lama, through an alliance with a Mongol prince, defeated the rival Red Hat sect and became the preeminent religious figure in Tibet and Mongolia, with supreme political authority as well in Tibet. The newly established Manchu rulers of the Qing dynasty, hoping to enhance their influence over Tibet and Mongolia, established alliances with the Dalai Lama. Lamas were believed to be reincarnated divinities; after they died, a search was conducted for a child who would be recognized as his reincarnation. Owing to the political and religious influence of the Dalai Lama, these searches were fraught with political intrigues in which the Qing empire and competing Tibetan cliques often had a hand. Rival factions assassinated several young reincarnate Dalai Lamas. By the eighteenth century, representatives of the Qing state, which was at the height of its power, played a direct role in the process of selecting reincarnations of Dalai Lamas.

In the late sixteenth century, when Roman Catholic Jesuit missionaries first came to China, they found a powerful, flourishing civilization that firmly saw itself as the center of the world, with nothing to learn from foreign barbarians. The Jesuits, led by Matteo Ricci, were quite impressed, and realized that if they were to make any inroads in China, they would need to fully understand Chinese culture. So they learned the Chinese classics, dressed as Confucian scholars, and engaged in philosophical debates with the Chinese literati. They tried to demonstrate their superiority by showing examples of the latest advances in Western science, in astronomy, optics, hydraulics, and perspective drawing. They enjoyed a measure of success, and by the seventeenth century, missionaries worked for the imperial court, as tutors for the young emperor, Kang Xi, as astronomers, and as landscape designers. They wrote many reports and books about China, which were widely read in Europe and had a deep influence on Enlightenment philosophers such as Leibniz and Voltaire. Their idealized descriptions of the Chinese civil service, made up of philosophers, chosen through impartial examinations, who administered the nation by implementing the rational teachings of Confucius, contrasted sharply with the prevailing European monarchies, where official positions were inherited by incompetent noblemen or purchased by ambitious businessmen. Impressed that Confucian virtues were so similar to Christian values, the Jesuits considered that Confucianism was an ethical philosophy, not a religion, and therefore, that one could join the Catholic Church and practice Confucian morality at the same time, and even continue to honor one's ancestors according to traditional Chinese rites. Others in the Catholic Church did not share this point of view. Heated debates, known as the "Chinese rites controversy," ensued in Europe. In the end, Pope Clement XI ruled in 1715 against the Jesuits and supported an exclusivist definition of Catholicism. This led to the Chinese emperor, Yongzheng, banning the Catholic Church in China, in 1721—for in his eyes, it was the Chinese emperor, as the Son of Heaven, who had the final authority in religious matters, and not a foreign pope.

Christianity and the Beginnings of Chinese Modernity: The Collapse of the Traditional Order (1839–1911)

By the first decades of the nineteenth century, corruption and incompetence were weakening the Chinese polity, while the Western powers, enjoying a newfound military and economic supremacy, did not hesitate to use guns to open the Chinese market. After the Opium War (1839–1842), in which Britain forced China to allow imports of opium from British India, China was obliged to sign a series of "unequal treaties" with the Western powers and Japan, which gave special rights to foreign nationals—rights which, notably, extended to Catholic and Protestant missionaries. Christian proselytism, in contrast to the Jesuit approach a few centuries earlier, was now more aggressive and far less accommodating to Chinese culture. And when conflicts occurred between Christians and nonbelievers, the Chinese authorities were required by the "unequal treaties" to protect Christian interests. Many Chinese, who came to view Christianity as a tool of Western imperialism, viewed this as a humiliation and as cultural aggression.

Two major rebellions in the second half of the nineteenth century, which can be seen as vastly diverging religious reactions to the introduction of Christianity and to the presence of the West, contributed to the weakening and eventual collapse of the Qing empire. The first was the Taiping movement, which caused what was probably the bloodiest civil war in the history of humanity, with an estimated thirty to fifty million casualties.[7] It is best understood as a confluence of the

Chinese tradition of millenarian rebellion and Christian messianism. The leader, an unaccomplished Hakka scholar, Hong Xiuquan (1812–1864), was exposed in 1836 to Protestant tracts, which led him to reinterpret earlier visions as a revelation that he was in fact Christ's younger brother. He then founded a "God-worshipping society" and smashed the deity statues in local temples. He organized disenfranchised Hakka laborers into a utopian society in the Guangxi highlands and, with the help of other visionaries acting as spirit mediums possessed by members of a wildly expanded holy family, directed the group as an army bent on toppling the Qing regime and establishing a puritan paradise on earth. Although it failed to conquer Beijing, the Taiping Heavenly Kingdom held on to its capital in Nanjing from 1851 to 1864, causing untold destruction. Although the Taiping were, in the end, thoroughly crushed, and completely disappeared as a religious movement, they can be said to represent the irruption of modernity into Chinese religious history, combining for the first time, and in a bloody blast, three elements that would, throughout the next century, never cease to interact with explosive consequences: apocalyptic revolution, Christian influence, and communistic utopianism. The latter aspect could be seen in Taiping doctrines advocating the abolition of private land property, the equitable distribution of land and surplus produce, the equality of men and women and a ban on foot binding, the use of vernacular language and punctuation, and the hierarchical organization of society in nested units of twenty-five families fully integrating religious, civil, and military functions. Prefiguring many elements of Chinese modernism, socialism, and Maoism, these ideals would inspire future generations of Chinese revolutionaries, including Sun Yat-sen, while the Chinese Communist Party would claim an explicit filiation to the movement.

A few decades later, at the turn of the twentieth century, another rebellion erupted, this time centered in north China, led by the "Righteous and Harmonious Society," labeled "Boxers" by contemporary Western observers. The Boxers were a type of self-defense village militia who practiced martial arts along with possession cults that were believed to provide magical invulnerability: they believed that, after practicing the appropriate rituals and using the right spells, they could repel the bullets of Western guns. Whereas such groups normally limited their activities to the village level, a chain of events in the years 1899 and 1900 caused them to spread and unite through northern China (particularly in Shandong and Hebei provinces), and attack Westerners and Christians, seen as the cause of all problems in a rapidly impoverishing and state-neglected countryside. They mobilized much of the unemployed population, obtained the support of a large part of the local elites, killed missionaries and Chinese Christians, and took control of the cities, including Beijing. The Empress Dowager Cixi officially sided with them and declared war on Western powers. This provoked a crushing military retaliation by the allied forces. The Boxer rebellion was a revolt, through local religious culture, against Western power and its churches, in which the rebels hoped to compensate for their material weakness through recourse to magic. In the end, the humiliating defeat, with its heavy human, political, and financial costs, convinced China's political elites that Chinese religion, out of which the Boxers had emerged, was a tangle of superstitions, a major hindrance to progress, and a threat to China's survival. If China wanted to be a strong and modern nation, they concluded, it would have to cleanse itself of her traditions and build a fully secular state on the foundations of Western science.

Paradoxically, the missionaries also introduced Western science through the schools and colleges they began to establish in the latter half of the nineteenth century.[8] The Taiping and Boxer movements notwithstanding, the missionaries established churches and church institutions during this period that were to have a significant impact on Chinese society and cultural exchange between China and the West. Protestant and Catholic missionaries built schools, colleges, and hospitals that were to endure through the middle of the next century. Protestant missionaries also became advocates for social reform, promoting causes such as the education of women, the end of the opium trade, and democratic change. The churches the missionaries established also attracted an increasing number of Chinese Christian converts, and their numbers would grow in the twentieth century. The missionary presence was maintained through the influence of the Western powers, but at the same time, Christianity began to establish indigenous roots in China.

Notes

1. David Keightley, *Sources of Shang History: The Oracle-Bone Inscriptions of Bronze Age China* (Berkeley: University of California Press, 1978), 1–2 (quotation simplified for readability).

2. See Anne Birrell, *Chinese Mythology: An Introduction* (Baltimore: Johns Hopkins University Press, 1993), and K. C. (Kwang-chih) Chang, *Art, Myth, and Ritual: The Path to Political Authority in Ancient China* (Cambridge, Mass.: Harvard University Press, 1983).

3. See Mu-chou Poo, *In Search of Personal Welfare: A View of Ancient Chinese Religion* (Albany: State University of New York Press, 1998).

4. See Benjamin I. Schwartz, *The World of Thought in Ancient China* (Cambridge, Mass.: Harvard University Press, 1985).

5. Dong, Zhongshu, *Chunqiu fanlü*, in *Sources of Chinese Tradition*, trans. Wm. Theodore de Bary (New York: Columbia University Press, 1960). Quoted in Julia Ching, *Mysticism and Kingship in China* (Cambridge: Cambridge University Press, 1997), 105.

6. Edward L. Davis, *Society and the Supernatural in Song China* (Honolulu: University of Hawaii Press, 2001); Richard John Lufrano, *Honorable Merchants: Commerce and Self-Cultivation in Late Imperial China* (Honolulu: University of Hawaii Press, 1997); Richard Von Glahn, *The Sinister Way: The Divine and the Demonic in Chinese Religious Culture* (Berkeley: University of California Press, 2004).

7. On the Taiping rebellion, see Jonathan Spence, *God's Chinese Son: The Taiping Heavenly Kingdom of Hong Xiuquan* (New York: Norton, 1996).

8. See Ryan Dunch, "Science, Religion and the Classics in Christian Higher Education to 1920," in *China's Christian Colleges: Cross-Cultural Connections, 1900–1950* (Stanford, Calif.: Stanford University Press, 2009) 57–82.

10

The Social Organization of Religious Communities in the Twentieth Century

Vincent Goossaert

By the turn of the twentieth century, as we saw in the previous chapter, China's intellectual elite had come to the conclusion that China needed to become a modern nation, and to seriously question the validity of its traditions. A discursive change took place that turned the relationship between state and religion on its head. Religion itself was not changed overnight, but the public discourse and the political management of religion did change quickly and deeply. New words began to appear, notably *zongjiao* ("religion") and *mixin* ("superstition"). All were adopted from Japanese neologisms crafted a few years before and were used to express Western notions that had not existed in the Chinese discourse until then. These neologisms were part of a larger set of imported categories used to reclassify the whole of knowledge and social and political practices, also including such words as "science" or "philosophy." *Zongjiao* and *mixin* seem to have been made popular in 1901 by Liang Qichao (1873–1929), an influential essayist. Religion was now understood in the Western post-Reformation sense as a system of doctrine organized as a church separated from society. The word *religion* was first equated with Christianity, and debate began (and is still going on to this day) regarding what, in the Chinese tradition, might be put under this category. Clearly, Christianity and Islam were immediately included; Buddhism, and, with more hesitation and reservations, Daoism, eventually were; Confucianism was and still is a matter of heated debate; and most of the religious communities in local society were excluded from this category. The result of these debates, which have been reflected in the policies of the Chinese state toward religion from the early twentieth century until today, is a hybrid system in which a "confessional" approach to religious affiliation, management, and academic discourse (in which people are labeled as either atheist or "believers" in one exclusive "religion" managed by a single institution) is superimposed on the Chinese religious culture in which cosmology, ritual, scriptures, practices of worship and spiritual cultivation, and temples and communities are pervasive but interconnected and organized in a very different way.

This chapter traces how this hybrid system came into being in the twentieth century. We begin with the broad contours of the traditional social organization of Chinese religion—clerical traditions and the various types of communities—first at the end of the imperial regime, around 1900, and then as it evolved under the influence of a Western-inspired normative model of "religion," from the beginning of the twentieth century to the present day. Although the top-down imposition of this model was successful in certain respects, such as making the national religious associations key public institutions, many types of communities have not adopted it. As a consequence, the official domain of *religions* does not cover the whole of lived religiousness, and the quantitative figures available for religious belonging and practice in the various Chinese societies are subject to much caution and debate.

Institutional Religions in 1900

THE THREE TEACHINGS IN THE LATE IMPERIAL POLITY

Up to the end of the Qing empire in 1911, China lived with an official religious doctrine that endorsed plurality, as there were three officially recognized and supported teachings (*jiao*), namely Confucianism, Buddhism, and Daoism, but not pluralism, as it did not value religious difference for its own sake, and did not welcome any new religion either. There was instead a plural orthodoxy, but everything else was defined as heterodoxy, and as such banned. The situation was thus different from much of the Western experience, which was predominantly predicated on the principle of one religion per polity, even though some countries, most notably the United States, did accommodate a large variety of Christian denominations. This dual heritage—acceptance of plurality but aversion to pluralism, that is, recognizing several religions but keeping a closed list of them—was maintained throughout the dramatic changes of the twentieth century, but definitions of what was acceptable religion and what was not changed considerably. To understand the history of these changes up to the present day, it is necessary to first sketch what the situation was around 1900, when the changes began.

The Three Teachings as supported by the imperial regime were defined quite differently from what we now call *religions*. They were precisely defined, each with a distinctive clergy, a canon of scriptures, a liturgy, and training centers. A *clergy* is a body of religious specialists observing a coherent set of rules and having gone through a fairly homogenous training and ordination process. Buddhist clerics, probably around a million persons by 1900, with a large minority of women among them, were mostly celibate and vegetarian monks and nuns, living in large elite monasteries or, for the majority of them, hired as priests in local temples. Daoist clerics were either celibate and vegetarian like the Buddhists or, much more often, married; in both cases, they offered ritual services to the population at large: running temples, officiating at community festivals, performing death rituals, expelling demons, and so on. They were probably as numerous as the Buddhists (although with a lower proportion of women) but were much less well tracked and accounted for by authorities. Confucians were defined (both legally and by themselves) as those who had passed at least the first of the three levels of civil service examinations (only the third level was a guarantee of civil service employment); most of them (around five million by 1900) worked as teachers; some also offered ritual services: Confucians performed sacrifices of animals (mostly pigs and poultry) to gods, and family rituals such as weddings, burials, and sacrifices to ancestors.

The three clergies each had their canon, a large collection of scriptures defining their doctrine, rules, and liturgy (that is, their way of doing rituals, including texts to be read, but also music and dance, and meditation); and training centers in which the canon was kept and clerics were trained and ordained: Buddhist monasteries, Daoist monasteries and large temples; and Confucian academies.[1]

Within Chinese religion, the Three Teachings did not function as separate institutions each with their own believers; rather, they all served the entire society, either through the teaching of individual spiritual techniques—such as Buddhist Chan meditation (known as Zen in the West), devotional Pure Land spiritual exercises (invoking the savior Amitabha), Daoist psychophysical techniques to transform the body and make it immortal, or Confucian moral self-cultivation (like counting one's good and bad deeds and keeping ledgers of merit)—or through the providing of ritual services to associations and communities. Buddhists, Daoists, and Confucians were all routinely invited by village and neighborhood communities to officiate at their festivals, offering sacrifices and submitting prayers to the gods on their behalf.

In late imperial times and well into the twentieth century, only clerics and a small number of devout laypersons would identify themselves as Buddhist, Confucian, or Daoist, but most people at least occasionally engaged in rituals officiated by priests of one or more of the Three Teachings. That is, the vast majority of the population did not call themselves Buddhist or Daoist but found it natural, if not necessary, to invite Buddhist or Daoist clerics to perform rituals at funerals, to oversee major junctures of community life (refurbishing of the village temple, New Year celebrations, etc.), or to respond to situations of crisis (epidemics, locust invasion) or when an unnatural disease, attributed to malevolent spirits, created the need for divine help. Similarly, only those engaged in learning for the imperial civil service examinations called themselves *Confucian*, but Confucian classics, ethics, and teachings were revered by much larger numbers of persons, indeed including Buddhists and Daoists. In all such cases, people invited the most competent and available religious specialist, or specialists; the Three Teachings were seen not as exclusive but as complementary. For instance, it was considered fitting that rich families would invite, at the same time, Buddhists, Daoists, and Confucians to celebrate a funeral, each doing their own ritual in parallel, side by side but usually not mixing or merging.

This form of plurality was therefore not equivalent to syncretism, in which a conscious attempt is made to integrate, synthesize, and supersede all existing teachings. The imperial state doctrine of the coexistence of the Three Teachings reinforced their cooperation (as well as occasional competitive tensions); at the same time, functional differences remained, with Confucians monopolizing statecraft and playing a privileged role in ancestor veneration; Daoist ritual structuring communal celebrations such as village temple festivals; and Buddhist priests usually being the preferred choice for funerals.

Some scholars have suggested that the Three Teachings correspond to an *elite religion* in contrast to *popular religion*. It is true that elites in imperial times tended to identify more readily than the rest of the population with one (or several) of the Three Teachings and their textual traditions; in each of the three, there are philosophical, speculative, and mystical explorations that can and do satisfy the most demanding intellects. Yet, most of China's population had access to and used Buddhist, Daoist, and Confucian intellectual and ritual resources, while at the same time declining to be subjected to these Three Teachings' clerics and authority. For instance, many village temples hired Buddhists or Daoists to perform services but did not allow them to take leadership roles and dictate to local people what they should or should not do. Therefore, the large majority of temple communities were not Confucian, Buddhist, or Daoist: they are often placed under the label of "Chinese popular religion," but this term does not necessarily imply a lower social class, lack of intellectual sophistication, or deviation from orthodoxy. On the other hand, while the Three Teachings had nationwide institutions, cult communities were fundamentally local in nature and they have been therefore aptly described as "vernacular," "communal," or "local religion."

FORMS OF RELIGIOUS COMMUNITIES

Until 1900, and long after that date in most of the countryside, people did not consider themselves members of such and such religion, or "teaching," but as members of one or several communities: households, clans, territorial communities, professional guilds, devotional associations. All of these communities had an altar where they worshipped their own ancestors and/or patron saints or gods. Most of them were organized around temples, but not all, as traditional temples (all made of wood, a highly expensive building material in a largely deforested country) were and are very expensive to build; newer and/or smaller communities could make do with just a consecrated statue of their god(s) and an incense burner (at its simplest, a clay pot) placed at a member's home.

A temple belonged either to the clerical, or more often, lay community that built and used it as its meeting place. It was devoted to one or several deities: local heroes (who had performed extraordinary feats for the community and became protective gods after their death), healing gods and goddesses, or ancestors, who all embodied local identity and history. Only temples built by and for clerical communities—that is, Buddhist monasteries, Daoist central temples, and Confucian academies—could be said to be specifically affiliated to one of the Three Teachings. For all other temples, community leaders were regularly chosen through a variety of methods,

BOX 10.1 Is Confucianism a Religion?

Ever since the notion of religion was introduced to China during the very early
years of the twentieth century, and up to the present, debates among Chinese
intellectuals have raged as to whether Confucianism is a religion. Of course, the
answer basically depends on what one understands by both *Confucianism* and
religion. Starting from a highly ecclesiastical definition of religion (a system of
thought, practice, rules, and ritual grounded in scriptures revealed by God and
followed by assemblies of believers), as most people in the West and China did in
the early twentieth century, would yield a negative answer, unless one reinvented
Confucianism. Starting from a more anthropological definition, more in use now
(religion defined as a system of symbols explaining and offering some leverage on
the universe, death, and human destiny), it is much easier to argue that in imperial
times self-avowed Confucians believed and practiced a religion (as well as an ethic
and a philosophy, like all religions), with deities, rituals, specialists, and scriptures.

  A large array of Chinese intellectuals, from 1900 to the present, have offered
their own solution to the conundrum of squaring a notion of Confucianism with a
notion of religion. Some have attempted to create a Confucian religion on the
Christian model (with Confucian churches, ministers, Sunday worship, etc.) but
with a very limited success, even though the idea lives on in some parts of the world
(Hong Kong, Korea, Indonesia). Most have rejected the idea of religion (and all
indigenous religious practices; indeed, a number of them converted to
Christianity), preferring to identify what they defined as their Confucianism with
another Western category, *philosophy*. Since the end of the twentieth century, it has
been increasingly popular to draw attention to the spiritual dimension of this kind
of narrowly defined Confucianism, but it is still devoid of any ritual or communal
dimension and therefore limited to small numbers of urban intellectuals.
Meanwhile, religious practices—moral self-cultivation, spirit writing (whereby a
medium is possessed by a god who writes with the medium's hand), and sacrifices
to Confucian gods and to Confucius himself—that were until 1900 part of
mainstream Confucianism have been carried on by other groups.

including bids (many leaders were wealthy locals who paid dearly for the symbolic
capital of religious leadership), rotation, heredity, and election by the god through
divination or by drawing lots. To the present day, and throughout the Chinese
world, it brings great honor and prestige, and possibly even electoral success, to be
a temple leader, and to be seen to devote time, energy, and money for the community's temple. These lay leaders preside over rituals, enforce temple regulations, hire
priests to conduct rituals and manage temple assets, including landed property—a
major resource for temples until 1900; after that date, the land assets were confiscated. In a minority of cases, the leaders also hired spirit mediums (who become
possessed by the gods and as such can offer healing or predictions) or clerics
(Buddhist or Daoist) to reside in the temple and run it on a day-to-day basis, but the
supervision and control of the leaders.

The types of communities that owned temples and organized religious activities varied in the different regions of the Chinese world, between rural and urban areas, and between China proper and Chinese communities in other countries (those with a high density of ethnic Chinese, notably in Southeast Asia, being closer to the models in mainland China than more distant, smaller communities in the West). Some of these communities, such as village temple communities and clans, were identical with the structures of local society, whereas others, such as devotional societies and self-cultivation networks, were more purely religious. Many socioeconomic groups such as clans, guilds, or village communities and alliances were officially sanctioned as cult communities by the imperial state, which granted titles to their gods and tried to regulate them. After the establishment of the republic in 1912, the formal relationship between these communities and the new secular state ended. The new secular state was utterly averse to recognizing and dealing with local gods. This changed the balance of power in local society. But predictions that the end of the imperial world order would spell the end of local cults that were tied to it proved false—indeed, many local cults have proved remarkably resilient to the present day; though they are no longer connected to an imperial authority, they still symbolize moral order within local society.

What best characterizes the social organization of religion in China is the autonomy of each community. Although they could, and often did, negotiate alliances and build networks for both religious and secular purposes: staging festivals, maintaining order (training and paying militias, for instance), building infrastructure (roads, bridges, dikes), or arbitrating local conflicts. All temples and religious groups were independent, not subjected to any external authority, be it secular or spiritual, until the dramatic expansion of the modern state into villages. Even then, these communities resisted state control as well as they could. Some scholars have described the networks of cult communities as China's civil society, or its "second government." One example among many is the irrigation systems in several parts of China, where very large and expensive systems of canals have to be maintained (the cost being borne largely by the locals) and the sharing of water rights has to be negotiated between villages. Such negotiations typically take place in the framework of temple alliances, gods being the warrants of the contractual agreements, and transactions taking place during temple festivals when local leaders meet, renew alliances and contracts and vow to respect common interests. This was commonplace until 1900, and, in some parts of China, it is still observed today.

A useful distinction of Chinese religious groups is among ascriptive communities in which adherence is compulsory for all concerned households, and congregations characterized by free and individual participation. Three main types of ascriptive communities are common: territorial communities, clans, and corporations. Territorial communities, such as villages and neighborhoods, unite for the cult of either an impersonal earth god or a local hero. Participation, primarily in the form of financial contributions toward temple upkeep and the organization of the yearly festival, was compulsory for all residents of the god's territory, almost like a parish.

Such territories were delineated from adjoining territories by a procession (carefully treading the boundary lines) in the course of the festival. Throughout the twentieth century, the territorial bond almost disappeared in most urban neighborhoods, but it has remained strong in many villages. Sharp differences in religious life were created between cities and countryside that rarely ever existed before 1900.

Clans and lineages—groups tracing descent from a common ancestor—were also found throughout China. While each household honored immediate forebears, families also allied on a large scale to maintain written genealogies and worshipped at the tombs of more distant ancestors. In some cases families worshipped in freestanding ancestor halls. In China, even humble peasant families could have very detailed genealogies extending over three of four centuries. Some parts of southern China were famous for their large-scale clans, which commanded huge corporate resources, including schools, or even companies.

The third type, corporations, included professional guilds and associations of sojourning merchants from the same locale, all of which were organized around cults to patron saints, either in the corporation's own temple or in a shrine within a large temple. Corporations were the most active religious communities in the cities, organizing the largest and liveliest celebrations. However, corporately active religious communities have declined more dramatically than descent groups or territorial communities, as they were gradually replaced over the course of the twentieth century by state-owned industrial bureaucracies, secular chambers of commerce, and professional associations.

The voluntary congregations were extremely varied. Buddhist and Daoist pious societies, typically under clerical leadership, financed rituals and mutual aid among members. Devotional groups organized festivals (with opera, procession, sacrifices, and banquets) to celebrate the birthday of their god or contribute to the upkeep of a temple. Pilgrimage associations to holy mountains or major temples trained all year long to be ready for the pilgrimage season and perform, for free, short theater shows, stilt walking, displays of martial arts prowess, and so on. Many congregations ran charitable programs that, for example, offered tea or food to pilgrims or beggars; provided medicine, clothes, or coffins to the needy; or saved animals from being butchered. Finally, many congregations were oriented toward individual salvation and spiritual practice. This category included spirit writing cults formed of laypersons, in which spirit mediums received direct revelations from gods, either as advice to individuals or as general exhortations; in the latter case, the revelations were often published in book form. In spirit writing, one or two mediums are said to be possessed by a god and hold a wooden fork or another instrument that, moved by seemingly involuntary movements, writes (in sand or ashes) messages that are immediately transcribed on paper by an assistant. Many such texts were morality books, exhorting people to do good, honor the gods, respect life, study the classics, and be thrifty and useful to society. These cults also engaged in charity, and often doubled as philanthropic foundations. Other groups were also geared toward revelation, the study of sacred texts, and meditation. A distinctive body of scriptures introduced a female deity, the Unborn Venerable

Mother (see chapter 6), who is said to have created the universe and to be aghast at her creatures' drifting away from moral ways; this hints toward an apocalyptic eschatology that expects the imminent end of the current cosmic cycle. Although their moral teachings were usually not much different from the other groups, their apocalyptic worldview gained them hostility from the imperial state, which tried, with limited success, to repress them.

In short, the relative weakness of central religious authorities (the imperial state and the clerical institutions) made possible until 1900 a blossoming of a very diverse religious landscape including huge numbers of autonomous religious communities of all kinds. The imperial state tried to manage this large variety of groups using various criteria to differentiate them; it supported clans, corporations, and territorial communities; it tolerated voluntary associations when led by members of the elite but banned, and sometimes violently repressed, the others. The attitude of the modern regimes (Nationalist, Communist) has often been similar to that of the imperial state—that is, attempting to control and limit such diversity and autonomy—but based on very different foundations. The imperial state regulated on a theological basis (the emperor, as Son of Heaven, was a religious authority and could decide what was orthodox or heterodox); the modern regimes regulate on a legalistic basis (they define legal, objective standards for accepted religion and repress groups or people who ignore them).

ISLAM AND CHRISTIANITY

The integration of two world religions, Islam and Christianity, into this densely woven religious system is a daunting enterprise that is still under way as of the early twenty-first century. Although there were both Christians and Muslims active in Tang (618–907) China, the modern presence of Islam antedates the presence of Christianity by several centuries. Muslims from Central Asia were an important part of the Mongol Yuan (1271–1368) regime's administrative and commercial elites, and many of them stayed on after the fall of the Mongol regime, creating small communities embedded in the larger Han society. Today Chinese-speaking Muslims claim that they are the direct heirs of these people, but it is actually likely that the early communities grew through conversions as much as natural reproduction. Throughout Ming (1368–1644) and Qing (1644–1911) times, the imperial regime let Muslims practice their religion, even though occasional bouts of official hostility and Muslim uprisings, which the Han claimed were caused by the Muslims' excessive sense of communal solidarity and self-defense, did create tensions and violence. Up to the present day, Muslim and Han villages might engage in feuds, often expressed as issues of ritual difference (the Han eating pork, the Muslims eating beef, both meats being abhorrent to the other), but the overwhelmingly dominant pattern is peaceful coexistence. Muslims typically have lived, and still live, in predominantly Muslim villages and neighborhoods with a strong occupational specialization. The Chinese Muslims have specialized in food, meat processing, and animal products (livestock, furs), and they are respected in this economic role.

Long considered a religious group, Chinese-speaking Muslims radically redefined their identity during the early twentieth century when, along with the spread of racial notions under Western influence, they were redefined (by both the state and their own leaders) as an ethnic group, called Hui, rather than a religious one, which guaranteed certain rights but also severely curtailed the possibility of converting outsiders. Thus the Hui were known after the 1910s as one of China's five constituent nationalities (following the Western concept of people or nation) along with the Han, the Manchus, the Mongolians, and the Tibetans; the PRC further elaborated this concept, and defined fifty-six nationalities, one of them being the Hui, made up of Chinese Muslims (who are linguistically and culturally similar to the Han), and several others being Turkic- or Persian-speaking Central Asian Muslim ethnic groups. The latter were integrated into the Chinese polity at a much later date (the Qing empire conquered what is now the province of Xinjiang, where most of them live, during the eighteenth century); whereas the Hui are remarkably well integrated into Chinese society, the other Muslim nationalities present a very different picture.[2] (See chapter 3.)

By contrast, Christian integration into Chinese society is a more recent and violent story. Catholics, at least those in villages converted in imperial times, tended, rather like Muslims, to live in villages that are identified as Catholic and thus form closely knit communities that can, thanks to strong solidarity and village identity, weather times of hostility or downright persecution. This was a strategy consciously pursued by missionaries during the early times of the Jesuit and other missions (from the late sixteenth century to the imperial ban on Christianity in 1724, when it was labeled as one of the "heretical teachings" to be crushed by officials), and again after the victorious gunships of the Western powers forced the Qing empire to legalize Christianity anew and allow missionaries to go into China, in a series of so-called unequal treaties from 1842 onward.

Whereas Catholics tried to build sustainable and cohesive Christian villages, Protestant missionaries, beginning in the early nineteenth century, aimed more at individuals, converting isolated persons who staffed or were affiliated with numerous but tiny mission posts throughout the huge swathes of the empire. In both cases, converts were assisted and protected by foreign missionaries who used, and in some cases abused, their consular protection—in particular, all Catholic missions were placed under the protection of the French consulate in Beijing. Beside the fact that some converts, dubbed "rice Christians," were mostly interested in the material benefits offered by the missionary institutions, consular protection that put pressure on local officials to safeguard the interests of the Christian converts were a topic of contention in local society. Non-Christians accused Christians of unduly using foreign protection to win lawsuits and escape customary duties, notably financial contributions to village institutions (including temples and festivals, which missionaries claimed were unacceptable to Christians, following a logic of exclusive religious affiliation that was very unfamiliar to the Chinese). The overall level of tension between Chinese Christians and non-Christians in local society is a matter of divergence among historians. Some claim that beyond resentment caused by the

BOX 10.2 Jews in China

China has always been a rather welcoming home for all of the world's religions. Small numbers of Jews settled in China, probably as traders, during the first millennium BCE; a community claims to have survived, isolated from other Jewish groups for centuries, in the northern city of Kaifeng. By the time they were discovered by Christian missionaries in the late nineteenth century, they had lost almost all of their religious and ethnic practices. However, during the first half of the twentieth century, several waves of Jewish migration reached Chinese cities, notably Shanghai, Harbin, and Hong Kong, some as traders and some as refugees from Russia.

occasional instrumentalization of missionary protection by unscrupulous individuals, Christianity was accepted at the village level as just one more religious option in an already very diverse religious landscape. Others point to the very numerous conflicts between converts and their fellow villagers that culminated in the Boxer rebellion, a movement of self-defense village militia in northern China that turned against foreigners and Christians and killed many between the fall of 1899 and the summer of 1900, when the intervention of the Eight Nation Alliance quelled the movement and killed even more in retaliation. Given this bloody history, the presence of Christianity in the Chinese countryside has been throughout the twentieth-century more tense and controversial than the Muslim presence.[3]

To further complicate the picture, there were some Protestant groups independent of the missionaries that began to emerge after the turn of the century. By the 1920s and 1930s, groups such as the "Little Flock" and the Jesus Family were well established in some parts of China. They could be categorized as voluntary congregations, using the terminology introduced above.

The Building of Modern Religions

THE NOTION OF *RELIGION*

At the same time, Christianity had a strong impact on the development of Chinese nationalism and modern religious and secular reform movements. Kang Youwei, a scholar who was called on by Emperor Guangxu (1875–1908) to enact a campaign of political reforms in 1898, hoped to turn China into a modern power by revitalizing Confucianism. A close friend of the missionary Timothy Richards, he sought to establish Confucianism as a national religion, with church-style congregations and Sunday mass. He also launched a campaign to seize local temples and convert them into modern public schools—a movement that, over the course of the twentieth century, would lead to the confiscation, and often destruction, of hundreds of thousands of temples.

The revolutionary movement led by Sun Yat-sen, considered to be the father of the Chinese nation, deposed the Qing emperor and established the Republic of China in 1912. Sun, who became China's first president, was baptized as a Methodist, and compared the idea of revolution to the notion of Christian rebirth. In his own words, it was "mostly from the church that I learned the truth of revolution. The establishment of the Republic today is due, not to my efforts, but to the service of the church."[4] Many of the political and financial backers of the Nationalist Party (KMT) were also Chinese Christians.

Religion—understood under the Christian model—was thus considered to be a strong, moralizing, and unifying force contributing to the power of the Western nation-states and was, in the early period (1900–1937), generally considered by Chinese intellectuals as something positive. Many believed that China needed its own religion if it wanted to gain moral strength and survive foreign aggression; they were divided between those who felt that the religion to be adopted should be Christianity and those who promoted modernized versions of Confucianism, Buddhism, Daoism, or a combination of the above. After years of Maoism and Marxist ideology that rejected religion per se, this view has resurfaced since the 1980s. But it is still common for intellectuals to have a positive appraisal of the role of religion in modern society while condemning practices that they do not consider as proper religion and vilify as "superstition." In other words, it was, and still is common among Chinese intellectual and political elites to be religious (notably Christian or Buddhist) and radically antisuperstitious (opposed to whatever is not grounded in and strictly limited to the spiritual and moral self-perfection delineated by the theological scriptures of a world religion: Christianity or Buddhism). This distinction is quite different from the traditional orthodox/heterodox divide of imperial times: many local cults and practices independent from national organizations and textual traditions that were once regarded as orthodox were now branded as superstitious. Notably, all temple cults, not being part of a "religion," were now categorized as superstition and therefore targeted for suppression. An important aspect of this process was the "turn temples into schools" movement, which first appeared in 1898, fully developed after 1904 and continued unabated through the Cultural Revolution (1966–1976). This movement turned hundreds of thousands of temples into modern schools (as well as government offices, barracks, granaries, factories, etc.), often through violence and the destruction of temple property and artifacts (statues, texts, art).[5]

By contrast to widespread antisuperstition, which found multiple expressions in popular media as early as 1905, the rejection of religion as such did not appear until the 1920s. This occurred at a time when many other societies in the West and in the colonial world were adopting militantly secular policies vis-à-vis religion. In France, the Law of 1905 had established the principle of laïcité, which forbade the interference of religion in public education. In Mexico, the Constitution of 1917 adopted anticlerical provisions that limited the influence of the Church. The same year, the Russian Communist Party sought to establish the first socialist state and set up policies that were predicated on the disappearance of religion. In Turkey, Kemal Ataturk abolished the Caliphate in 1924 and launched a series of reforms that were aimed at establishing a modern secular state.

The antireligious, or atheist, movement was formulated at that time under the direct influence of European Marxists and freethinkers and primarily aimed at Christianity in its relationship with imperialism. The most brilliant and famous advocate was Chen Duxiu (1879–1942), a professor at Peking University but also a founding member of the Communist Party. But Chen's position was, until the Communist takeover, marginal among the Chinese intellectual and political elites. Most of these espoused antisuperstition as part of a *pro-religious* discourse. For the political elites then, and still to this day (even in the People's Republic where radical antireligion still exists among officials but is declining), it is acceptable to believe in one religion but shameful to take part in local festivals, pilgrimages, and other communal activities.

The Republican regime's management of the religious scene was based on a thorough promulgation of the religion/superstition paradigm. The provisional constitution of the Republic of China, proclaimed on March 11, 1912, stipulated the "freedom of religious belief." This was carried over in all subsequent Chinese constitutions. This text did not guarantee protection against the destruction and nationalization of temples, but elites saw no contradiction between protecting the freedom of religious belief on the one hand, and eradicating superstition on the other. The early Republican government indeed elaborated a new official doctrine for religious policies as early as 1912, establishing quite clearly the modern Chinese state's fundamental positions in matters of religious policies, and these positions have more or less remained the same ever since: the state was ready to recognize "religions" as doctrinal, spiritual, and ethical systems with a social organization, but only if they got rid of "superstition," including most of their ritual. It at first left open the list of such religions, which were to be protected by the constitutional clause on religious freedom, but at the same time, it granted official recognition to associations representing Christianity, Islam, Buddhism, and Daoism. After passionate debates, it decided not to recognize Confucianism as a state religion. Thus, during the first months of the Republic, five religions (Catholicism, Protestantism, Islam, Buddhism, and Daoism) came to acquire state recognition, a situation that would remain in place for the following century. National associations were set up for each of them in order to define and negotiate the scope of their autonomous organizations. Some new religious movements, such as Zailijiao (Teaching of the Abiding Principle) or Daoyuan (School of the Dao), also gained official status during the 1920s and 1930s and have maintained their existence in Taiwan, Hong Kong, and abroad, but they have been and still are strictly forbidden in mainland China. So, the list of officially registered religions has not changed much in the mainland since it was first designed.[6]

The criteria by which the modern Chinese state decided whether or not to include a religious tradition within its list of recognized religions have mostly remained hazy, with few explicit guidelines. The Chinese state's attitude has been quite pragmatic: a religion was recognized if it could prove it was "pure" (spiritual and ethical in nature), well organized in national associations, as well as useful (patriotic and contributing to social welfare and progress). At the same time, any public ritual, devotional, or spiritual activity not integrated into these religions was not covered by any official protection. Within the field of Chinese religion, this amounted to dramatically redefining and reducing the extent of legally and intellectually legitimate religious practices, notably by excluding local temple cults. Temple communities have had to reinvent themselves as Buddhist or Daoist to obtain protection, or, more often, they live in a legal limbo, buying tacit tolerance.[7]

THE REINVENTION OF CHINESE RELIGIOUS TRADITIONS

The Chinese approach to the way religion is defined and regulated in the public realm has undergone a sea of change in the twentieth century. Whereas for centuries, religious specialists, groups, and practices had to conform to certain standards of orthodoxy, they now had to conform to a category of the "good" religion, the paradigm of which was imposed from the West and modeled on Protestant Christianity: an organization of individual converts/believers, separate from other social institutions, based on scriptures, theology, and ethics, and geared toward action in this world (charity, education, publications, proselytizing). Of course, a number of Chinese chose to be modern by just converting to Christianity. But if such converts were very influential in some quarters of society (professionals, intellectuals, entrepreneurs), they never became a majority in any part of the Chinese world.

More than the number of converts and the direct action of the Christian elite, the greatest impact of Christianity in modern China has been through its normative models, in their various Catholic and Protestant versions, of what a religion should be, which were adopted by the intelligentsia, the state, and even the leaders of other religions. Not only was Christianity the model for "religion" that informed the Republican state's policies, but this model forced activists of other religions to rethink their religious engagement and how they should live, think, and act as "Buddhists," "Confucians," "Daoists," and so on. The social engagement of Christians in famine relief (as early as the 1870s) and public health (notably through the building of hospitals) pushed many members of local elites to take part in charity as Buddhists or as Confucians, in both imitation and contradistinction to Christian initiatives (see chapter 8). The Red Cross was widely seen as a model of religious engagement, and was widely imitated within both Buddhism and new religions: China's largest charity, the Red Swastika Society, was founded in 1922 by a large new religious movement, the Daoyuan. Missionary dynamism, involvement with modern media (notably the confessional press), and so on were also practices that reformist Buddhists, Daoists, and Muslims undertook enthusiastically. The native reformists also heeded Christian calls to distance themselves from "superstition" and local cults (with which they had closely allied for centuries), and to advocate education, science, and social services.

Probably the largest and most successful reformist movement along this model was the Buddhist revival around Taixu (1890–1947). Taixu became a self-described "revolutionary monk" around 1908 after reading works by political thinkers, and he decided to save Chinese society through social reform and Buddhism. He developed plans to radically reform the Buddhist clergy through a complete overhaul of clerical training and management of monastic property, and a reorientation away from ritual and toward social service and teaching. Until his death in 1947, Taixu established countless associations, institutes, and seminars, currying favor with Nationalist politicians, traveling all over China and the world, and publishing books and tracts outlining ambitious ideas for reform. His vision of reformed Buddhism, which he called "this-worldly Buddhism," was influential, and he is now claimed as foundational by the leaders of all the major Buddhist organizations in the Chinese world.

Another widely influential movement to indigenize Western models of the good "religion" was the creation of hundreds of new religious movements that attempted to synthesize the whole of the Chinese religious heritage into one new, modern whole. Scholars now call these groups "redemptive societies" and identify the largest ones (with apparently tens of millions of members each) as Zailijiao, Daode xueshe (Moral Studies Society), Tongshanshe (Fellowship of Goodness), Wanguo daodehui (Universal Morality Society), Daoyuan, and Yiguandao (Unity Teaching). While all different, they shared a project of combining age-old Confucian ethics, Daoist self-cultivation, and Buddhist spirituality with modern science; they taught classical culture in a modern classroom setup. They published journals and were serious about converting the whole world. Although most of these societies have now declined (Yiguandao, extremely active worldwide, is the major exception), they did play a crucial role in transmitting classical culture in a context that was hostile to most things "traditional."

MODERN INSTITUTIONS

At the level of institutions, the most important vehicle for the adoption of reformist visions that attempted to create proper religions in China was the national religious association. This particular form of organization, as it appeared in 1912 and developed throughout the rest of the century, indigenized Christian models of clerical training, community organization, confessional identification, and social engagement. In the context in which a religion, to be recognized by the state and protected by law, had to create a national association capable of representing it, Buddhism, Daoism, Confucianism, and Islam attempted for the first time to organize themselves into unified national, hierarchical institutions. Such a reinvention was no easy enterprise, not only because it generated internal conflicts and confusion, but even more so because traditionally these religions did not operate as centralized organizations: clerics operated independently in the service of local cults, temples, and mosques. And with the exception of Islam and some new religions, they did not have a membership of declared adherents.[8]

Many such associations, with varying sizes, degree of representativity, and reformist zeal, appeared as early as 1912. The largest were recognized by the state, which cooperated with them for managing local religious affairs. The corporatist approach of the Nationalist regime (1928–1949, and after 1949 in Taiwan) implied that there should be only one association for each religion, that religionists should settle their differences among them, and that they should offer a unified stand to the outside world. Only after the lifting of the martial law and the adoption of more liberal laws on religious associations in Taiwan in 1987 did the institutional landscape there open up, and myriads of new institutions (notably among Buddhists) appeared and flourished. The Nationalist corporatist approach was continued in the People's Republic of China, which established anew an association for each of the five recognized religions, appointed strongly reformist, antisuperstitious leaders, and gave these associations absolute monopoly over religious institutions and activities. Whereas the religious associations during the Republican period had mostly failed to conduct radical reforms, under the People's Republic, they did go much further in centralizing and unifying practices. For instance, the Protestant association abolished the denominations in the late 1950s. Some people dismiss the five national associations as just extensions of a repressive government, but it is the only venue through which clerics can negotiate with local officials for the right to organize rituals, reclaim confiscated temples, churches, or mosques, and more generally try to increase their space for practicing religion. This has been, since 1978, a long and convoluted process, but one that has delivered tangible results. The five national associations are also engaged in training clerics according to modern seminar-style teaching and a uniform curriculum, trying to replace the traditional master-disciple apprenticeship, even though at grassroots levels, most clerics are still trained in the "traditional" model.

In exchange for such concessions from officials, religious associations have to carry out the religious policies of the government and participate in mobilization campaigns when asked to. They are also supposed to work toward building modern, ethical religions, but their success in this regard has been rather limited. Notably, their influence over laypersons is very limited, as they are seen as purely administrative entities, not endowed with any spiritual authority. As a matter of fact, throughout the twentieth century, the Buddhist and Daoist associations have remained, by and large, clerical associations. Some laypersons have played very important roles (for instance, the late president of the Buddhist Association, Zhao Puchu, 1907–2000), but most practitioners are not even members. The very notion of a unified China-wide Buddhist or Daoist community remained an elusive goal throughout the twentieth century, and the institutional leaders can be excused for being at a loss for ideas on how to conjure that modern dream. Their subsequent failure can be contrasted with the situation of the Muslim community, which, through its associations, managed as early as the 1930s, and even more so since 1978, to mobilize, notably through its print media, large numbers of militants to stage protests against perceived insults or threats.

Modes of Belonging, and Quantifying Religions in Contemporary China

The whole religious policy and public discourse on religion in modern China is predicated on a concept of religion in which people are considered to either (1) be atheist and without religion or (2) believe and belong to one religion. This, however, does not accurately describe the actual situation. As we have seen, in traditional society, and to this day in most of the rural world, the prime criterion for religious participation is not to believe, but to belong to a community, such as the village temple community, the clan, or a pilgrimage association. The notion of belief did and does exist but was conceived as a bond between a human and a god or ancestor rather than an exclusive faith. The communist authorities on the mainland have long encouraged citizens to declare themselves as atheists, so they usually do so when asked, even though they may well go to temples, pray, and so on. Some have even claimed to "believe in superstition," since superstition is the name the government gives to what they do, such as call a geomancer to chose the place of their grave or to ask spirit mediums to find out whether their illness is due to a malevolent ghost.

The modes of belonging have strongly diverged between city and countryside in the course of the twentieth century. In the villages, it remains a dominant mode to belong first and foremost to ascriptive communities (territory, clan, etc.), and one major aspect of village life, closely linked to growing prosperity since the 1980s, has been to rebuild or lavishly enlarge the communal temples. Even people who have recently migrated to urban centers still maintain and treasure this bond; for instance, in Taiwan, many urbanites go back for major festivals to the village where their family used to live (see chapter 2). By contrast, people who have lived in cities for a longer period tend either to have no communal religious practice (they may nonetheless go to temples individually to pray if the need arises) and to engage in very individual forms of spirituality, as described in chapter 1, or to join globally oriented communities, such as new Christian or Buddhist movements. It should be stressed that these two different developments do not stand in contrast to each other: both the numbers of local temples built or rebuilt and the numbers of converts to Buddhism and Christianity rise rapidly at the same time.

In such a context, no Chinese polity has reliable official figures on religious affiliation, even though social surveys in Taiwan, Hong Kong, and Singapore do provide rather detailed pictures of the situation there. One reason for the paucity of statistics is that most people would not claim affiliation with an officially identified religion; although social surveys try to use categories like *popular religion, ancestor worship,* or *Daoism* in ways that overlap and intersect, such categories are often not understood by people in the same way as those who draft, publish, and analyze the surveys. Religious institutions themselves most often cannot provide useful figures; confessional associations are usually limited to a membership of clerics and a core of activists. Furthermore, large numbers of believers or practitioners are members of illegal groups. A third reason is that figures, especially in the PRC, are devised and published for political goals. Figures released during the 1980s suggested that about 100 million Chinese were religious, thus accounting for a small proportion (less than 10%) of the population. With new policies since the early 2000s that very cautiously grant religions a larger role in building China's new "harmonious society," new figures, produced by social scientists, and published with the blessing of the government in February 2007, suggest that the figure is more like 30% of the population.[9] For all these reasons, charts giving numbers of religious adherents are highly unreliable and furthermore difficult to compare from one country to the next, as they use different categories. Data provided in table 10.1 gives an idea of the figures that scholars, politicians, and religious leaders use and debate, rather than an accurate counting.

In spite of the very unreliable nature of the figures, it is quite obvious that the number of people claiming a specific confessional affiliation is rising, notably among Buddhists and Christians. Although the number of Christians has not continued to grow since the 1980s in Hong Kong and Taiwan, in Singapore, it grew at a rate comparable to that of Buddhism: from 11% to 16.5% between 1980 and 2000, although the growth slowed in the '90s. In North America, after Christianity had been virtually shut out of the Chinese community for a century, conversions to Christianity, typically of the evangelical variety, rapidly increased from the 1960s, so that, by the end of the 1990s, Christianity was the main declared religion (one-third of Chinese Americans, compared with one-fifth who identified as Buddhists, and half claiming no religious identification).[10]

TABLE 10.1 Religious Adherents, as Percentage of the Population

	Mainland China	Taiwan (2005)	Hong Kong	Singapore (2000)
Buddhism		35%	13%	42%
Christianity	2–5%	4%	7%	15%
Catholicism	1%	1%	3%	
Protestantism	1–4%	3%	4%	
Islam	2%	<1%	1%	14% (mostly ethnic Malays)
Daoism and local cults		33%		9%
Yiguandao		4%		

Sources: PRC: author's estimate of the numbers of Christians and Muslims based on the current literature (counting Buddhists or Daoists or other groups just does not make sense in the current PRC context); Pang, Choong Chee. "Religious Composition of the Chinese in Singapore: Some Comments on the Census 2000." In Suryadinata, Leo, ed. *Ethnic Chinese in Singapore and Malaysia: A Dialogue Between Tradition and Modernity.* Singapore: Times Academic Press, 2002, pp. 325–336; Ng, Peter Tze Ming. "The Changing Market Shares of Christianity and Buddhism since the Return of Hong Kong's Sovereignty to China." *Quest* 3(1), 2004, pp. 109–124; http://www.gio.gov.tw/taiwan-website/5-gp/yearbook/2002/chpt25.htm (accessed May 23, 2009).

But it was in the mainland that Christianity underwent the most remarkable growth. Although observers in the 1990s described this growth as occurring primarily among older, poorly educated rural residents, and in large part due to the efforts of healing evangelical preachers, it was clear by the late 1990s that Christianity also had a strong appeal among educated urbanites. For large sections of the urban population, Christianity has a positive image as a world religion intimately linked with success in this world, moral values, and science. Building on this receptivity, Christian groups and networks are growing, and younger, well-educated believers account for an increasing proportion of new converts. The growth of Christianity in the cities was largely extra-institutional: while official churches were simply unable to respond to demand, McDonald's restaurants became as likely a place to conduct Bible study sessions as private apartments (see chapter 12).

The growth of Buddhism, which has been even stronger in many parts of the Chinese world, has fed on some of the same reasons. With globalized, missionary Buddhist movements—most notably the Tzu Chi (*Ciji*) Foundation, Foguangshan and Fagushan—based in Taiwan now reaching out through universities, language programs, and charity on five continents, it has become common for upwardly mobile persons to claim a Buddhist identity as part of both a bond to traditional Chinese culture and values and an attachment to modern progressive values such as care for the environment (see chapters 6, 7, and 8).

In brief, then, a century ago, the dominant religious institutions were local communities building and managing temples. Successive modern regimes have tried to disqualify if not suppress such communities, and reclassify people as either nonreligious or as belonging to one of the world religions institutionalized within China as a national association (Buddhism, Daoism, Islam, Protestantism, and Catholicism). Such top-down efforts to reorganize religious institutions and people's modes of religious belongings have had limited effect, however. Although a growing number of Chinese people identify themselves with one of these world religions, local religious communities have also resisted, adapted, and are thriving anew. Therefore, the religious field in the Chinese world is proving remarkably plural and able to accommodate not only different religions, but also different types of religious institutions and modes of belonging.

Notes

1. On Buddhists, see Holmes Welch, *The Practice of Chinese Buddhism* (Cambridge, Mass.: Harvard University Press, 1967); on Daoists, see Vincent Goossaert, *The Taoists of Peking, 1800–1949: A Social History of Urban Clerics* (Cambridge, Mass.: Harvard University Asia Center, 2007).

2. Dru C. Gladney, *Muslim Chinese: Ethnic Nationalism in the People's Republic* (Cambridge, Mass.: Council on East Asian Studies, Harvard University, 1996).

3. Daniel H. Bays, ed., *Christianity in China: From the Eighteenth Century to the Present* (Stanford, Calif.: Stanford University Press, 1996), 40–52.

4. Timothy Tseng, "Chinese Protestant Nationalism in the United States, 1880–1927," in *New Spiritual Homes: Religion and Asian Americans*, ed. David K. Yoo (Honolulu: University of Hawaii Press, 1999), 1999, 19–51; quotation on 20.

5. Vincent Goossaert, "1898: The Beginning of the End for Chinese Religion?" *Journal of Asian Studies* 65, no. 2 (2006): 307–336. On the ideological side, see Myron L. Cohen, "Being Chinese: The Peripheralization of Traditional Identity," in *Kinship, Contract, Community, and State. Anthropological Perspectives on China*, ed. Myron L. Cohen (Stanford, Calif.: Stanford University Press, 2005), 39–59. Anthropologist Cohen provides an analysis of how modernist inventions of the categories of *religion* and *culture* have stripped religious elements of Chinese identity as formulated by ideologues of Chinese nationalism.

6. A good general presentation of the situation of the five institutional religions in the PRC by the early twenty-first century, along with more articles, is found in Daniel Overmyer, ed., "Religion in China Today," special issue, *China Quarterly* 174 (2003).

7. Rebecca Allyn Nedostup, *Superstitious Regimes: Religion and the Politics of Chinese Modernity* (Cambridge, Mass.: Harvard University Press, 2009).

8. Vincent Goossaert, "Republican Church Engineering. The National Religious Associations in 1912 China," in *Chinese Religiosities: Afflictions of Modernity and State Formation*, ed. Mayfair Yang (Berkeley: University of California Press, 2008), 209–232.

9. Wu Jiao, "Religious Believers Thrice the Estimate," *China Daily*, http://www.chinadaily.com.cn/china/2007-02/07/content_802994.htm (accessed May 23, 2009). See also Paul Badham and Xinzhong Yao, *Religious Experiencing in China Today* (Cardiff: University of Wales Press, 2007).

10. Fenggang Yang, "Religious Diversity among the Chinese in America," in *Religions in Asian America: Building Faith Communities*, ed. Pyong Gap Min and Jung Ha Kim (Walnut Creek, Calif.: Alta Mira Press, 2002), 71–98.

11

Contemporary Issues in State-Religion Relations
André Laliberté

Introduction

In the run-up to the Beijing Olympic Games in the Spring of 2008, many people were shocked by riots in Tibet and the passionate response they elicited all over the world among overseas Chinese and Tibetans. The official Chinese media's denunciation of the Dalai Lama as an "evil personage" seemed to illustrate the atheist Chinese regime's lack of respect for the holiest man of the Tibetan people. Earlier, the passing of a law regulating how the lamas could be reincarnated appeared as the epitome of an authoritarian state that seeks to extend its control not only to this life, but even beyond. In this particular instance, the apparent absurdity was that a government and a ruling political party that profess to an ideology of militant atheism could claim any competence in deciding who, when, where, and how reincarnations could proceed. Every year, human rights organizations have criticized the Chinese government for its heavy-handed approach to religious groups: forced reeducation of the adherents of Falun Gong and other religious organizations, persecution of Christians, and harassment of Muslims in Xinjiang who are accused of separatist or terrorist activities. These instances of state persecution suggest that despite its constitutional protections offered to religious believers, the government of the People's Republic of China tries to control and limit the expression of religious fervor as much as possible.

But there is another side to the relation between the state and religion in China. Tourists are invited to visit superb Buddhist shrines that have been restored with the state's support. They are told that this is part of the glorious Chinese tradition. Scholars in China and abroad will confirm that China has a rich religious tradition that is multifaceted, and that both throughout history and today, there are episodes of peaceful coexistence or symbiosis, if not outright state sponsorship of religion. When local authorities are not promoting the economic benefits of religious development (see next chapter), the state often seems to turn a blind eye to the popular temple cults that now flourish in many parts of the countryside (see chapter 2). Even today, there are many ways in which the state responds to and interacts with religious believers in the different polities with a Chinese cultural heritage. In Hong Kong and Singapore, the legacy of colonialism has shaped approaches to religion that are derivative of the liberal political culture of the United Kingdom. In Taiwan, a society that is culturally Chinese, a sui generis liberal approach to relations between state and religion has been adopted. In other words, there are many ways in which a Chinese government can assert its authority over religion, beyond the use of coercion but also many ways in which Chinese religious believers relate to the state, besides dissent. This is clear when we look at China's long history, when we pay attention to the varieties of approaches adopted by the Communist Party since its creation when it deals with different religions, and when we consider the different policies of states that rule over populations with a Chinese cultural heritage. This is also clear when we look at the many ways in which Chinese people have practiced their religions with or without state permission, and still do today.

State Control of Religion in China: The Historical Context

The state has always sought to control religion in China, and rebels that opposed the state often claimed a religious authority. If separation between religion and the state represents a major characteristic of modern Western civilization, it is more appropriate to talk about the integration of religion and state in China. Not only did religious elites and personnel often provide legitimacy to the existing political structure in exchange for recognition from the state, but the state itself, on the basis of its "Mandate of Heaven," claimed supreme authority in religious matters. This symbiotic relationship between religion and state, however, had its downside: opposition to the government was often couched in a religious language, and when rulers faced challenges to their authority, they often struck hard at religion. Viewed in this perspective, the control of religion by the Party should not be seen as an anomaly, but as a continuation of an historical pattern, as described in the previous two chapters. In this chapter, we will examine state/religion relationships in contemporary Chinese political regimes: starting with the People's Republic of China, but then looking at other models in Taiwan, Hong Kong, and Singapore.

The Evolution of the Religious Policy of the Chinese Communist Party (CCP)

According to its own historiography, the Communist Party's religious policy went through four phases: from the beginning of the Party's history in 1921 until 1949; the United Front period (1949 to 1957); the "leftist" excesses (1957–1978); and the reform era (1978–).

COMMUNIST POLICIES BEFORE 1949

Before the CCP took power, its views on religion were informed by three different sources: the May Fourth Movement, Marxism-Leninism, and the views of Mao Zedong himself. The May Fourth Movement resulted from the climate of political instability that followed the collapse of the Qing dynasty in 1911, and from the inability of any Chinese government to oppose the punitive conditions imposed by Western powers after World War I. The humiliation felt by students and intellectuals led to a questioning of traditional Confucian values and inspired a strong criticism of what they considered as the root cause of China's inability to stand up against foreign powers. In addition, as we have seen in the previous chapter, when the CCP was founded in 1921, the dominant ideological trend of the times was the secularization of republican regimes.

Marxism-Leninism represented the confluence of two trends in the West. The German intellectual Karl Marx affirmed that religious beliefs were merely the expression of unequal social relations, offering succor to people who felt helpless to change their own social circumstances. In a communist society in which scientific progress would end scarcity and social justice would be achieved, people would no longer need to rely on the "opiate of the masses" provided by religion. For Marx, there was thus no need to persecute religious believers: if the conditions for the existence of religion were removed, it would simply wither away.

As leader of the Union of Soviet Socialist Republics (USSR), which replaced the old tsarist empire after the Russian revolution of 1917, Lenin looked at these issues from a different perspective because he was concerned with the issue of using Marxist theory to establish a socialist state. He agreed with Marx that the state should not impose its views on religious believers and that it was useless to try to force people to change their religious conviction. Lenin forcefully argued that religion should be a private matter, but he also added that for the Communist Party, which claims to understand the social origins of religious beliefs, atheism was the only appropriate understanding of religion.

Mao Zedong agreed with Marx and Lenin on the origins of religion in unequal social relations but he initially disagreed with their proposition that there was no need to forcibly eliminate religious belief. After Mao realized that China could not succeed in achieving a socialist revolution through the urban working class, which represented only a tiny fraction of society, and had to rely on the peasantry to achieve his goal of social transformation, he also saw that his intolerant policy toward religion had succeeded only in alienating peasants from the Party, and therefore he had to change his views. He accordingly subscribed to a United Front strategy, whereby the Party forged alliances with different classes and groups of people, including religious believers, as long as they supported the anti-imperialist goals of the Party. In the end, however, Mao agreed with Lenin and other communist leaders and supported the view that Party members themselves had to profess atheism.

THE UNITED FRONT POLICY, 1949–1957

After the People's Republic of China was established in 1949, the Party and the new government set up institutions to deal with religious belief in general, and with religious communities in particular. The basic policy was as follows: (1) constitutional guarantees for "freedom of religion" limited to the freedom of *private belief*, with restrictions on the *social expression and organization* of religion; (2) co-optation of religious leaders through the United Front policy; (3) establishment of state-sponsored national associations to manage the affairs of the five recognized religions; and (4) eradication of popular religion branded as "feudal superstition" and of redemptive societies branded as "reactionary secret societies." This policy basically continued, in a more radical fashion, the model already tested in the Republican period (1911–1949) and discussed in the previous chapter, in which the state tries to distinguish between *religion*, which is subject to state monitoring, and *superstition*, which ought to be eradicated. As a result of this structure of control, worshippers and practitioners are forced to align themselves within or against political orthodoxy, and as a result the lines between the boundaries of acceptable and illegal religiosity remain contested.

The Communist Party upheld the view that religion should be respected and integrated in a patriotic alliance to fight imperialism and help the Party advance the cause of socialism, an approach known as the United Front policy. To ensure that the United Front policy could be properly implemented, the Party issued in 1950 a policy of religious freedom that was meant to provide guidelines to Party cadres.[1] The policy guaranteed that religious adherents are free to believe, as long as they respect the law and do not harm social stability. It also allowed believers to change religion, to become nonbelievers, and to adhere to different sects within any of the five recognized religions. The policy, however, did not protect the right to proselytize, and it forbade the involvement of religious institutions in health care and education, on the grounds that these activities undermined the authority of the state and were therefore seen as subversive. In sum, the policy protected the right for individuals to believe, but it did not offer guarantees for religious associations to develop. This policy, along with the United Front policy and its theoretical justification, continues to be the foundation of the religious policy in the early twenty-first century.

Ostensibly to show that religious believers' interests could be represented, but in reality to ensure that Party directives could be carried out, the Party encouraged religious believers to set up their own "patriotic" religious associations. Associations were thus established to represent the Buddhists, Muslims, Protestants, Catholics, and Daoists. People in leadership positions in the religious associations, in theory, are religious believers, that is, clerics or laypeople.

The founding of the China Buddhist Association (CBA) in 1953 was relatively easy: monks had already tried to create a national association to promote their own interests during the Republican period. Because of the Land Reform Act of 1950, monastic property was seized by the state, and only a small portion was redistributed to monasteries. Some monks had views that were supportive of the Communist Party, and for its part, the Party realized that Buddhism could serve the interests of the state: many neighboring states in Asia counted a significant number of Buddhists, and good treatment of Buddhists within China could serve to illustrate that the PRC respected religion in general, and also that it was a major center of Buddhism itself.

The creation of a Three-Self Patriotic Movement (TSPM) for the Protestant Church of China in 1954 was also facilitated by the existence in Republican China of a National Christian Council that, since the 1920s, had promoted a theology of the missionary idea of "three-self": self-governance, self-support, and self-propagation. This TSPM faced a daunting task because of the wide divergence in theology, tradition, and history among the various denominations that had developed in China. In the late 1950s, the TSPM claimed that the Protestant churches of China had arrived at a postdenominational stage and that all the denominational traditions that were of foreign origin had no place in the PRC. Already during the period of the Korean War, all Protestant and Catholic missionaries had been forced out of the mainland.

The Islamic Association of China (IAC) was also established in 1954, and it, too, built on attempts by Muslims to build national associations in the early twentieth century. PRC policy has long been lenient toward, if not supportive of, Muslim institutions in China, since the Chinese government valued good relations with Islamic countries. This diplomatic approach was justified during the first three decades after 1949, in the name of solidarity with the Third World.

For Chinese Catholics, the situation was more problematic: the pope was viscerally anticommunist and forbade Catholics from cooperating with the new regime. In addition, the Vatican was a state that refused to recognize the PRC, recognizing instead the Republic of China in Taiwan. The faithful were thus torn between loyalty to Beijing and allegiance to the pope. It was only in 1957 that a number of lay Catholics agreed to set up a Chinese Catholic Patriotic Association (CCPA), whose head would have authority over them instead of the Holy See. Many Roman Catholics thus consider this association schismatic. Patriotic Association leaders forbid priests and bishops to speak out on government policies that go against Roman Catholic doctrine, such as the official directives on contraception and abortion.

Because Daoism is more polymorphic and decentralized than the other four religions recognized by the state, it was harder to organize the Daoists into a national association, which was established only in 1957: this suggests that it was more difficult to find a leadership that could generate support for a unified version of the religion. As an indigenous religion with little influence in other countries, Daoism does not have the international importance of Buddhism or Islam (seen by the government as diplomatic bridges to potential Third World allies) or of Protestant or Catholic Christianity (seen by the Party as instruments of Western imperialism). As a result, dealing with Daoism was never a priority in PRC religious policy.

As explained in the previous chapter, only a fraction of the Chinese people identified with any of the five officially recognized religions; this did not mean, however, that the "nonreligious" majority were secularized atheists. The vast majority of the people participated in the worship and rituals to their ancestors and in village and neighborhood temples to local saints, heroes, and deities. Many were members of religious charitable associations, pilgrimage groups, redemptive societies, and other types of networks. But because none of these groups or practices fit neatly under the modern category of *religion* as it had been imported in the early twentieth century, they were simply stigmatized as "feudal superstition." Even when these practices were not directly targeted by political campaigns, their social foundation was destroyed by other policies and social changes: most local temples and lineage halls were turned into schools, government buildings, or storehouses; priests were required to change professions in order to engage in "productive labor"; lay associations were disbanded or secularized into performing arts troupes. In the case of redemptive societies such as Yiguandao (see previous chapter), whose leadership had often consisted of local elites now demonized as feudal landlords, members of the Nationalist Party, and collaborators with the Japanese, a harsh persecution was launched in the early 1950s to exterminate them as "reactionary secret societies."

THE LEFTIST PERIOD AND THE CULTURAL REVOLUTION, 1957–1978

During the Great Leap Forward (1958–1960), the CCP policy on religion became much more radical. The mobilization of the population for the sake of accelerated development required considerable demands on the workforce, as well as requisition of tools from peasants for a disastrous campaign of rural industrialization. In that context, most property and land still owned by religious institutions was confiscated. By the time of the Cultural Revolution, not much was left of the previous wealth to destroy. Most of the monks and nuns, priest, pastors, and imams had to return to lay life.

In addition, the international context, which was marred by tension with the United States over Taiwan and with the Soviet Union over ideological disagreement, led to campaigns against foreign interference. Chinese Christians were often suspected of spying on behalf of their foreign coreligionists. With an estimated thirty million deaths due to famine, the Great Leap represented one of the greatest tragedies of the twentieth century, and one of the deadliest calamities of all Chinese history. Between 1962 and 1965, when the leadership of the Party repudiated the excesses of that policy and its chief architect, Mao Zedong, China experienced a brief revival of religious practice. This trend alarmed the radical wing of the Communist Party.

Mao decided to react and recover his authority and power. He launched a directive at the start of the Cultural Revolution (1966–1976) to denounce "capitalist roaders" that had "wormed their way" into the Party, and criticized feudal and bourgeois ideology, including the religious beliefs that were seen as supporting

BOX 11.1 The Worship of Mao

The British professor of religious studies Ninian Smart noted in 1974 in a short essay that "Maoism does function analogically as a religion for China" (*Mao*, London: Fontana Press, 1974, p. 88). Mao was indeed the object of intense veneration from the Chinese people during his lifetime. His ideas were studied as dogma, and the episodes of his life and of the party, such as the Long March, were elevated to the status of myths. Mao was an object of adulation for millions, and he never opposed the cult of personality his supporters had developed. This cult lives on today for many. Millions of peasants worship him, just as their ancestors in imperial times venerated heroic persons, virtuous leaders, or good magistrates. In those times, a few generations after their death, exceptional people were revered as superior spirits, and some of them were even "promoted" to the rank of deities. Many people look at him today as an exceptional personality deserving of worship. His birthplace of Shaoshan, visited annually by millions of people, has become a center of pilgrimage. Along with posters, pens, calendars, lighters, and other souvenirs bearing his picture, people can also find golden amulets traditionally used to bring good fortune and health, with the picture of Chairman Mao in the center where a representation of the Buddha or Laozi was traditionally placed.

them. Because he could not count on the support of the Party apparatus, Mao appealed to the enthusiasm of young people to "smash the old world and establish the new." One focus of this campaign was the destruction of the "four olds": old customs, old culture, old habits, and old ideas. The United Front Policy toward religion was repudiated, and religious institutions became prime targets of the attacks against the "four olds." The Red Guards sponsored by Mao ransacked, looted, and closed down temples, churches, mosques, monasteries, and cemeteries. Clergy had to return to lay life, and lay believers were ridiculed, persecuted, or physically attacked. Although the most tumultuous phase of the Cultural Revolution came to a halt after 1969, attacks against religion continued, culminating in 1975, when, under the instructions of the Gang of Four, the State Council issued a directive abolishing the Religious Affairs Bureau (RAB).[2]

REFORM AND OPENING, 1978–PRESENT

The first stirrings of the revival of religions were already noticeable by the time Mao died in 1976. The revival of religions in the 1980s demonstrated that his campaigns against tradition had failed. After Deng Xiaoping took power in 1978, the Communist Party admitted that under Mao, there had been "excesses" that needed to be corrected. In 1979, the State Council overturned the verdicts of the Cultural Revolution, and reinstituted the Religious Affairs Bureau (RAB), later renamed as the State Administration of Religious Affairs (SARA). In 1981, Deng could claim that a return to the United Front policy was in line with orthodox Party policy, and he could reassure religious associations that they could safely resume their activities under the CCP guidance.

According to the 1982 Constitution, people have the right to believe in "normal religion," but a definition of what is *normal* remains unclear and depends on decisions made at the discretion of local authorities. Moreover, the Constitution "prohibits religious activities that impair public order, health, or education and proscribes 'foreign domination' of religious bodies and religious affairs." In other words, Chinese are free, as individuals, to adhere to any religious beliefs, but their religious practice remains limited by a series of regulations. People can worship in temples, churches, and mosques that are registered with the government, but if they worship in settings other than the ones officially designated for religious practice, they place themselves in a situation of potential illegality. Monks, priests, pastors, imams, and other clergy are free to perform religious rituals, administer their religious institutions, train religious personnel, preach, and lecture to laypeople, but they must engage in these activities within locations government officials deem appropriate.

Article 36 of the Constitution also states the following: "No state organ, public organization, or individual may compel citizens to believe in, or not to believe in, nor may they discriminate against citizens who believe in, or do not believe in, any religion." The rules and the functioning of the Communist Party, however, often violate this stipulation. Although the Party has abandoned political campaigns promoting atheism, its regulations forbid citizens who are religious believers to join the Communist Party because the latter upholds the ideology of dialectical materialism and forbids cadres to be religious believers.

The regulations imposed on Party membership leave religious believers who do not want to recant but want to participate in political affairs the option of joining one of the eight satellite parties. In that capacity, or as individuals, they can run for positions in the government, in the national and local People's Congresses, or they can join one of the People's Political Consultative Conference Committees (PPCCC). Religious leaders, indeed, are usually nominated by the United Front Department for election to these bodies. The satellite parties, however, have no influence in the political process. Moreover, the overwhelming majority of the members of the People's Congresses and consultative bodies are members of the Communist Party.

There is an important exception to this practice limiting the political participation of religious believers. Party members who belong to one of the national minorities (see chapter 3) can participate in the religious life of their respective autonomous regions, prefectures, or counties. This dispensation results from the policy on national minorities, which gives special regard to the customs of ethnic minorities in order to avoid alienating them from Party rule.

In 1982, the Party also issued a directive, known as Document No. 19, that reiterated the basic foundations of the Party policy: respect for the freedom of religious belief, recognition that religion is a private matter and that coercion to undermine religion is ineffective, but also support for atheist education, therefore marginalizing the influence of religion over society. Provisions of that policy, which still remains in place, are a de facto constraint on the practice of religion. The document does not extend recognition to any other religion besides the five religions mentioned earlier, and therefore it does not change the state's attitude with respect to popular religion. Religious associations can train religious personnel and administer their own affairs, but they cannot do fund-raising or proselytize outside the bounds of churches, temples, and mosques. Finally, the Communist Party forbids its members from believing in religion and participating at religious events.[3]

In 1990, following the 1989 Tiananmen massacre and the riots in Tibet, the Party asked the State Council to convene a national work conference on religion to respond to these challenges to its authority. The conference issued Document No. 6, which emphasized the Party's need for control and regulation over religious affairs but also recognized the importance of religion in Chinese society. The document expressed the Party's concern over the potential negative effects of unregulated religion, and security forces were instructed to closely monitor religious activity. Beginning in the early 1990s, laws were enacted requiring the registration of religious venues by local government authorities. At the same time, religious associations were invited to contribute to society's progress. Jiang Zemin emphasized the need to reconcile tolerance of religious belief for the five recognized religions, along with strict control of religious orthodoxy. In doing so, he gave a greater degree of power over their own affairs to religious leaders.[4]

Throughout the 1990s, the Communist Party sought more openly to channel the resources of religion to its own ends: ensuring the prosperity of world religions such as Buddhism, Islam, and Christianity was seen as useful in refuting foreigners' claim that China not respect religious freedom. The enthusiasm of lay Buddhists in China and among overseas Chinese for the development of their religion also increased the value of Buddhist institutions in the eyes of the local governments, who saw in this renaissance of Buddhism an incentive to attract investments from "compatriots" in Taiwan, Hong Kong, and Macau, as well as abroad. Similarly, Daoist temples in Hong Kong, Taiwan, and Southeast Asia have enthusiastically renewed ties with their coreligionists on the mainland, with the blessings of the authorities. The role of Islam also became increasingly important, because China wants to secure for its growing industry safe supply of energy from major oil exporters in the Middle East, and because China wants to reinforce its relations with important regional powers such as Iran.

Hu Jintao, who became paramount leader in 2002, did not present any new approach with respect to religion and seemed bent to continue the policies of his predecessors. However, his advocacy of the principle of "harmonious society" gave more room for religions to claim that they could contribute their experience and teachings to the building of social harmony. Under Hu's tenure, various levels of the Chinese government have undertaken initiatives in the realm of religious affairs that appear to show more significant state support for religious institutions. In April 2006, with the support of the Religious Affairs Bureau, the First World Buddhist Forum was held in the city of Hangzhou, and a year later, an International Forum on the *Daodejing* was convened with the state's blessing in the cities of Xi'an and Hong Kong. These events served to underline the importance the Party sees in the positive influence of recognized religion on social stability and interethnic harmony. At the same time, the authorities began to open up to groups other than the five officially recognized religions, as described further below.

Geopolitical Issues and Chinese Religious Policy

The religious policy of the People's Republic has always been shaped by geopolitical concerns. During the 1950s, the main objectives had been (1) to cut the Christian churches off from the moral, financial, and administrative influence of the anti-communist and pro-Christian Western powers, the Holy See, and the enemy regime in Taiwan; (2) to avoid alienating the deeply religious Buddhist and Muslim borderland minority peoples, and reinforce their loyalty to China; and (3) to use Buddhism and Islam as diplomatic tools in relations with Third World countries. Beginning with the reforms of the 1980s, the same set of concerns remained, although the evolution of the Chinese economy and politics, coupled with world geopolitical events and trends, greatly complicated the issues. The promotion of "opening up to the world" and international trade provided many opportunities for believers of all faiths and organizations to expand and deepen transnational networks connecting China to other parts of the world, often with the encouragement of the authorities. The growing importance of relations between China and the United States and other Western economies significantly lowered the tension concerning Christians and their overseas connections, even if invoking religious freedoms for Chinese Christians and others became a ritualized component of meetings between Chinese and American leaders.

The overriding concern in dealing with the geopolitical implications of religion is maintaining and establishing the territorial integrity of the PRC as the sole government of China. This exacerbated the problem with the Vatican, which is one of the last states to persist in giving diplomatic recognition to Taiwan. Switching diplomatic recognition to Beijing remains a precondition for solving the problem of China's underground Catholic Church, discussed shortly. In addition, following the fall of the Berlin Wall and the dismemberment of the former Soviet Union into independent republics, the Party leadership became acutely concerned with preventing a similar occurrence in China: indeed, over 50% of the PRC's territory consists of borderland territories whose populations are largely non-Han, have strong cultural and religious ties to the populations of neighboring states, and have questionable loyalty to the central government. This is especially the case for the Tibetans, and for the Turkic-speaking Muslim Uyghurs in the far western territory of Xinjiang.

TIBET

The Chinese government claims that China is a "multinational" state and therefore wants to show to the rest of the world that all the different cultures and religious traditions of the country are protected. Party and government leaders are especially anxious to convey to the outside world that it seeks to promote that goal with respect to Tibet. To support their claim that Tibet was always part of China, they stress the fact that during imperial times, the Yuan and the Qing dynasties sponsored Tibetan Buddhism as an overarching faith common to Tibetans, Mongols, and Manchus. This legacy matters very much to the Communist Party, which had hoped that the religion could foster unity among nationalities after 1949. However, the new government had great difficulty in achieving this goal. When the Communists won the civil war and established a new government in October 1949, Tibet had enjoyed de facto independence for a few decades, even though the international community did not formally recognize it as a state. Tibet was still governed as a medieval theocracy, with the Dalai Lama as its most powerful religious and political leader—a system highly incompatible with communism. In order to pressure Tibet to submit to its rule, Mao sent the People's Liberation Army to its borders, while promising to respect Tibet's religious and political system. The Fourteenth Dalai Lama signed a "ten-point agreement" in 1950, in which he recognized Chinese sovereignty over Tibet, and stated that the Tibetan religio-political system was to remain untouched. But tensions rose throughout the 1950s, as the increasing Maoist radicalism that emanated from Beijing, and was being carried out among the Tibetan populations of neighboring provinces, led Tibetans to fear that their political system and religion would not be respected for long. These fears reached a boiling point in 1959, when a failed uprising, and the subsequent military occupation, forced the Dalai Lama and his government to flee to India, where they established a government-in-exile in the city of Dharamsala. This event, followed by the destruction that accompanied the Great Leap Forward and the Cultural Revolution, restrictions on the growth of Tibetan Buddhist monasteries, and systematic campaigns of "imposed modernization" increasingly alienated Tibetans from the Chinese government.[5]

By the 1990s, the Dalai Lama, while he was still worshipped as a living deity by Tibetans, had become an internationally respected, Nobel Prize–winning religious figure. Following the Marxist theory that poverty breeds religion, the CCP hoped to overcome that legacy though massive investment in economic development—enjoying a higher standard of living, the Tibetans would no longer be so devoutly religious, and they would even be grateful for the CCP's help. But these efforts did not succeed in changing Tibetans' view, and have even increased their alienation, because much of the economic activity and profits remain in the hands of Han Chinese.

CHINA'S MUSLIMS

The harmony in relations between the Han Chinese and Muslims, and therefore the relations between Muslims and the state, varies according to their ethnicity (see chapter 3). The Hui, who live scattered across the Chinese mainland, enjoy good relations and have few grievances against the government. The situation is different for many of the Turkic-speaking national minorities of China's western regions, in particular the Uyghurs living in Xinjiang. Many of them deeply resent the immigration of Han into their region. Before 1949, Uyghurs were a majority in Xinjiang, but in the last decade of the twentieth century, they were reduced to the status of largest minority. Although discontent among them is important, very few have organized politically, let along militarily, to oppose Chinese control over what they consider their ancestral territory. One of these groups, the East Turkestan Islamic Movement (ETIM), was declared a terrorist organization by the government in 2002. Links with al-Qaeda were alleged but never demonstrated. The aim of that organization, which is the creation of an independent state for the Uyghurs, however, is more political than religious. Therefore, repression against the organization is not so much a case of repression against religion as a conflict over territory and national identity. However, the Chinese regime is highly concerned that Islam could be used to reinforce Uyghur identity and strengthen separatist movements. In order to reduce the influence of Islam, since the mid-1990s the government has imposed strict controls on the religious practice of Uyghurs, going so far as to prevent schoolchildren from fasting during the month of Ramadan. These policies are likely to further alienate and radicalize Uyghur Muslims.

GRAY AREAS AND UNSANCTIONED RELIGIOUS ACTIVITIES

Sociologists of religion Rodney Stark and William Sims Bainbridge have argued that when relations between state and institutional religion are too intimate, such proximity may be detrimental in the long run to the religious organizations that are close to the government.[6] This proximity to the state for the religions recognized by the government opens up the issue of their credibility and their authenticity for the faithful. As a result, people who seek a more truthful expression of their religious belief may be tempted to join underground associations or organizations that are not recognized by the state. Many worshippers do not trust the leaders of the official religious associations, because they are too closely related to the government, and in particular to the Communist Party. This too close relationship between the government and official religious associations explains why many people may not want to participate in the events the government sponsors and would prefer to join activities organized outside official monitoring. Gatherings for religious celebration outside of locations designated for that purpose, however, are technically prohibited. Depending on the place, the time, the political climate, and the relationships with local officials, such gatherings may be shut down by the authorities, or they may be tolerated.

Fenggang Yang (see chapter 12) has called such activities the "gray market" of religion in China, in contrast to the formal activities of the official associations (the "red market") and those activities that are formally illegal and face the wrath of government repression—the "black market." Gray-market activities can be connected to both the officially recognized religions and to other beliefs and practices that do not fall under the five recognized religions, but are still tolerated.

The case of Buddhism illustrates this phenomenon. As the economic reforms transformed China into a more mercantile economy and accelerated the rural exodus, Buddhist institutions became a source of wealth, as laypeople donated funds to the reconstruction of temples and monasteries. Today, Buddhist institutions are involved in commercial, social, and cultural activities ranging from organizing summer retreats to supporting orphanages, selling amulets in temples and building gigantic Buddha statues as tourist attractions, that straddle the boundaries of what is considered an acceptable and legal form of religion in the eyes of the government.

Christian churches also thrive in the "gray market" of religion. In the more than three decades that have followed the end of the Cultural Revolution, Christianity—and, in particular, the growth of the Protestant churches—is the fastest of all religions in China. This growth benefited from the support offered by coreligionists abroad, including many overseas Chinese Christians, and the relatively open attitude of the authorities in the first decades of the reform and opening policy. However, many of these Protestants do not recognize the TSPM or the China Christian Council (CCC) and have joined "house churches," where worshipping is by definition clandestine. These churches are tolerated in some places but banned in others. A similar cleavage splits Chinese Catholics. Many Chinese Catholics who disagree with the Patriotic Association leadership worship in underground churches. For years the clergy has been divided between a persecuted church loyal to the Holy See and a clergy appointed by Beijing. In the late 1990s, however, many bishops ordained according to the rules of the Patriotic Association have requested and gained recognition of their ordination from the Vatican. A resolution of the conflict over the authority of the Catholic Church in China, however, remains unlikely as long as the Holy See recognizes the government of the Republic of China in Taipei instead of the People's Republic in Beijing. An even more divisive issue is that of the appointment of bishops, the authority for which in the Catholic Church has always resided with the pope. In 2007, Pope Benedict XVI pointed to a possible reconciliation by admitting that, for their spiritual good, Chinese Catholics can turn to bishops and priests who are not in communion with Rome if they have no other choice.

Another type of "gray-market" religious activity takes place under the guise of *qigong* gymnastics, breathing, meditation, and healing exercises (see chapter 5). *Qigong* became extremely popular in the 1980s and 1990s, under the institutional protection of the State Sports Commission as a form of physical fitness, of the State Administration of Chinese Medicine as a form of traditional therapy, of the All-China Committee for

Science and Technology as a pioneering mind-body science, and of the Commission for Science, Technology and Industry for National Defense as a form of parapsychology that could be used for military purposes. Under that legal framework, *qigong* groups could recruit adherents and finance and advertise their activities openly. Although *qigong* was not designated as a form of religion, many practitioners became deeply interested in Chinese cosmology and were drawn into the study and practice of Daoism, Buddhism, and popular religion.

One of the *qigong* groups, Falun Gong, claimed 100 million practitioners and became increasingly assertive in pressing its demands to the state. Because Falun Gong was not classified as a religion, thousands of CCP cadres could adhere to this movement without violating the Party stipulation forbidding them to be religious. After 10,000 practitioners staged a sit-in surrounding the headquarters of the Party leadership at Zhongnanhai in April 1999, Falun Gong was designated as an illegal "evil cult"—moving it from the "gray market" into the "black market"—and became the target of the harshest campaign against any social organization since the end of the Cultural Revolution. Groups that mobilize large numbers of followers and display an ability to assertively pressure or challenge the state are likely to be persecuted by authorities that fear the groups could organize popular resistance to the government. Other banned "evil cults" include certain Christian groups such as the Eastern Lightning Church, deemed heretical by the state-recognized Christian associations.

For other groups that do not fit within one of the five official associations, the government's attitude is ambiguous, evolving, and varies vis-à-vis different types of group. The Bahá'í Faith, the Church of Jesus Christ of Latter-Day Saints (Mormons), and the Russian Orthodox Church, as well as popular religion, enjoy increasing degrees of tolerance and tacit approval from the authorities. In the latter case, popular religious practices remain stigmatized as superstitions, but are also tolerated, if not encouraged, by local authorities as expressions of the national folklore or as "intangible cultural heritage." For example, the government has promoted ceremonies paying homage to the Yellow Emperor (*Huangdi*), the mythical ancestor of the Han people, since 1990. The governments of Shanxi and Henan, which both claim to be the ancestral land of the Yellow Emperor, have competed to build the most expensive shrine dedicated to his worship. The promotion of that cult was enhanced in 2008 with the decision to introduce a new public holiday, Tomb Sweeping Day, a traditional practice associated with ancestor veneration.

Other Chinese Polities

There are alternative frameworks for state-religion relations in Chinese states besides the Communist Party's approach. In spite of the continuities between imperial China, the Republican period, and the approach of the PRC authorities to religion, other configurations do exist that more closely resemble Western patterns of separation between religion and state and freedom of religion. The cases of Taiwan, Hong Kong, and Singapore illustrate the diversity of configurations that can exist in societies in which a majority of the population can claim a Chinese heritage.

TAIWAN

For decades the Republic of China in Taiwan pursued the policies that had been applied in mainland China during the Republican era, but this time, because of the military assistance and the economic cooperation offered by the United States, the Nationalist Party was able to effectively implement a wide range of policies. During the first three decades after 1949, the ruling party imposed a policy of control over religion that bore some striking similarities with that which was enforced in the People's Republic, down to the recognition of a limited number of religions, and the requirement that only one national association should be responsible for the interests of all adherents to a single tradition. A Buddhist Association of the Republic of China was created, ostensibly to rival the mainland's China Buddhist Association in the international arena, but also to ensure conformity with Chinese norms by the Taiwanese associations, which had developed their own local characteristics over centuries and which had been influenced by Japanese colonialism. But besides these similarities, some significant differences were noticeable. Some redemptive societies that were banned in mainland China, such as Lijiao (the "Teachings of the Principle"), and the Xuanyuanjiao (the "Teachings of the Yellow Emperor"), could be practiced freely, sometimes with the complicity of members of the government, and received official recognition by the state. As in the mainland, however, Yiguandao was banned as a "heretical sect."

While China was attacking Chinese religious traditions during the Cultural Revolution, Chiang Kai-shek proclaimed the launch of the Chinese Cultural Renaissance Movement in 1967. Although bureaucrats targeted the local variants of Chinese popular religion in the name of preventing waste and modernizing the country, the government of Taiwan adopted a policy that was far more lenient toward organized religions. It gradually relaxed control over civil society and showed toleration toward religions' development in ways that were unimaginable on the mainland. Hence, when the authorities realized that religions such as Yiguandao were conservative and pietistic, the government simply stopped surveillance of its members and quietly lifted the ban on its activities. In addition, Christian and Buddhist institutions were welcomed to provide services in education and health care.

The Presbyterian Church in Taiwan (PCT) played an especially important role on the island, despite its small number of adherents. Brought to the island as a missionary religion in the nineteenth century, it grew thanks to proselytizing by the local clergy and the use of the vernacular language. During the martial law period, the PCT developed a theology that stood for human rights, the right of self-determination for the inhabitants of the island, and the promotion of the aboriginal people's welfare. Many government opponents during the period of martial law found support from PCT clergy. Peng Ming-min, one of the founders of the movement for Taiwanese independence, was a member of that church, and Lee Teng-hui, although a member of the Nationalist Party while he was president, also belonged.

As a result of the policies of tolerance, religious institutions did not confront the regime during the crucial years that led toward democratization. Although their attitude can be construed as complacent toward the authoritarian regime, the approach of Taiwanese religious groups probably encouraged reformist politicians in government and moderate opposition activists. Today, twenty-six religions are recognized in Taiwan and religious groups are major forces for the promotion of civil society and social cohesion.

HONG KONG

The Hong Kong Basic Law protects religious freedom and prohibits religious discrimination, and the government has not changed its policy since the handover of the former British colony to the People's Republic in 1997. Although the Hong Kong Special Administrative Region (HKSAR) is under the jurisdiction of the People's Republic of China, religious believers in Hong Kong can, and do, get involved in local politics. There is a wide variety of religious beliefs in the HKSAR, and this is reflected in the government, which includes people of all faiths, as well as nonbelievers. Moreover, there is no officially recognized religion and no religious institution has to register with the authorities. The Chinese government's respect for this attitude of laissez-faire in the HKSAR gives some substance to the concept of "One Country, Two Systems" that is meant to guide relations between the PRC and the ex-colony. Because of these freedoms, adherents of religions that fear persecution seek asylum in the HKSAR. Falun Gong members, Catholics who refuse to recognize the authority of the mainland's "Patriotic" Association, and other members of unregistered religions have found there a climate to express their views without fear of being harassed. Moreover, Protestant churches and Buddhist charities use Hong Kong as a "rear base" from which they can proselytize or provide relief to the poor in the mainland. Relationships among religious groups in Hong Kong and the mainland are governed by the policy of "three mutualities" as laid down in the basic law: mutual respect, mutual noninterference, and mutual nonsubordination.

SINGAPORE

In contrast with Hong Kong, Macau, and, up to a point, Taiwan, the government of Singapore does not have to worry about the influence of the People's Republic of China in the management of its religious affairs. Like their counterparts in Taiwan, the authorities of the tiny island city-state promote the development of religion as

BOX 11.2 The Chinese States' Celebration of Confucius

Every year, Taiwan celebrates National Teachers' Day on September 28, which happens to be the birthday of Confucius according to the Western solar calendar. Others prefer to mark the birthday of Confucius according to the Chinese lunar calendar. In that case, it falls on the 27th day of the eighth lunar month, between the end of September and the beginning of November. The celebration of a holiday for teachers on Confucius's Birthday in Taiwan underlines the importance he accorded to scholarship and learning. The celebration follows a very elaborate ritual at a temple dedicated to him in Yuanshan, Taipei. In Hong Kong, the authorities have discussed a proposal to celebrate Confucius's birthday, but, concerned about the addition of yet one more public holiday, negotiations had to be conducted with the Christian community over which religious holiday, such as Easter, could be replaced by the birthday of Confucius. In the PRC itself, Confucius is not a target of criticism anymore, and in his native city of Qufu, very elaborate ceremonies are now performed to mark his birthday. In 2002, the Chinese government launched the development of the Confucius Institute, the equivalent to the British Council and the Alliance Française, to promote the teaching of the Chinese language and culture in foreign countries.

a source of social stability, as a cultural resource for the development of national identity, and as a provider of social services. The value of religious harmony is actively promoted by the Singapore government and supported by religious leaders of all faiths, and in that respect, the approach of the Singapore government to religion compares to that of Taiwan, Hong Kong, and Macau in its positive appreciation of the role of religion. However, the authoritarian and paternalistic nature of the government may invite comparison with China: the authorities of Singapore do not hesitate to use the Internal Security Act when they believe religious believers can threaten social stability. The act was used twice in 2001 and 2002, against members of the Jemaah Islamiyah. The revival of Islam in neighboring Malaysia and Indonesia and the presence of an important Muslim minority in the city-state have to be taken into account by the government in its effort to instill citizenship education in ways that are respectful of the island society's multiplicity of religions.

Conclusion

One striking characteristic of the relations between state and religion in China is the wide variety of approaches implemented across the country and over time. There exist important discrepancies between the formal laws and regulations promulgated by higher levels of governments and the ways in which local authorities implement or ignore policies determined above them. There are also remarkable differences in the level of trust by authorities toward different religions, depending on their contacts with foreigners, their influence on minority nationalities, their ability to generate material support, and their history of cooperation or conflict with the government. The state alternates between deregulation of religion and the maintenance of strict control; intellectuals close to the Party discuss openly the importance of religion in Chinese society, and many religious people try to cooperate with the authorities for the sake of the common good.

In sum, there exists a wide diversity in the modes of relations between state and religion across Chinese societies. The spectrum of relations range from what can be described as symbiotic, when the state sponsors religious activities and religious actors offer their support to the state via public rituals, to what can be termed adversarial, when police forces harass religious associations they fear, or when religious movements express dissent. Very often, relations between religion and state can also develop in a "zone of indifference," in which the state gives up the pretense of regulating religion and religious institutions desist from involvement in politics. This variety of relationship patterns obviously relates to the multiplicity of religious beliefs and practices in Chinese societies, which has changed over centuries as China has increased its exchanges with the world community and as it continues to amplify its exposure to different views of the world.

Notes

1. Beatrice Leung, "China's Religious Freedom Policy: The Art of Managing Religious Activity," *China Quarterly* (2005): 898.

2. Donald MacInnis, ed., *Religion in China: Policy and Practice* (Maryknoll, N.Y.: Orbis Books, 1989).

3. Pitman Potter, "Belief in Control: Regulation of Religion in China," *China Quarterly* 174 (June 2003): 320.

4. MacInnis, *Religion in China*, 19–26.

5. Wang Lixiong and Tsering Shakya, *The Fate of Tibet* (London: Verso, 2009).

6. Rodney Stark and William Sims Bainbridge, *The Future of Religion: Secularization, Revival and Cult Formation* (Berkeley: University of California Press, 1985).

12

Market Economy and the Revival of Religions
Fenggang Yang

At a spacious McDonald's restaurant in a skyscraper in a southern city of China, several dozens of young people gather around tables in a well-lit corner. With drinks and hamburgers in hand, they are engaging in serious discussion. Indeed, they are in Bible study. At each table, a leader, surrounded by five to ten people, raises questions and responds to inquiries according to a manual. As a matter of fact, there is a table for each of the twelve progressive lessons of the "Timothy Training Course," beginning with the introduction of basic Christian beliefs and ending with the lesson of instruction on sharing the "Good News." Progressing through the tables at weekly gatherings and graduating from the course within three months, one would become not only a new person, a Christian, but also an evangelist equipped to recruit and convert others. The standardized efficiency is just like that of McDonald's.[1]

This kind of group activity is illegal in China today. Government regulations require all religious activities to take place only within designated religious premises approved by the State Administration of Religious Affairs. Eventually, the weekly gatherings of up to 100 people at this McDonald's caught the attention of the police, who then raided the restaurant one night and took all the participants to the police station. The leaders were sifted out through interrogation and ordered to sign a pledge form to be released on bail or face extended detention and additional penalties. After midnight, the leaders finally complied and wrote down on the form, "We promise not to meet for Bible study at this McDonald's again." This satisfied the police, and the evangelists kept the pledge without stopping their Bible study gatherings. "We indeed stopped gathering at *this* McDonald's," a young man told me when I conducted interviews in summer of 2000, "but there are dozens of them in this city." A big grin glowed on his face.

The "Golden Arches" of the McDonald's restaurants have become commonplace in Chinese cities, often conspicuously dotting the rapidly changing skyline. McDonald's is a symbol of the increasing presence of the globalized market economy throughout China. Only three decades ago, China maintained one of the most stifling centrally planned economies under Communist rule, with a total ban on market exchanges.

During the decade of the Cultural Revolution (1966–1976), the Constitution of the People's Republic of China retained the article of freedom of religious belief, but in reality the constitution was shelved under the party-state dictatorship. Revolutionary authorities carried out the harshest suppression ever seen in the Communist bloc, banning practically all religions throughout the country. In the Soviet Union, a small number of Orthodox Christian churches remained open throughout the Soviet period. In China, however, all churches, temples, and mosques were closed down at the onset of the so-called Cultural Revolution in 1966.

In 1978, under the new leadership of Deng Xiaoping, the Chinese Communist Party launched economic reforms, gradually moving toward a market economy integrated into the world. The ban on religion was lifted in 1979, and a carefully selected number of Christian churches, Muslim mosques, and Buddhist and Daoist temples were given permission to reopen. Since then, all kinds of religions have revived, and many are thriving despite the restrictive regulations on religion. The economic reforms toward a market economy have been accompanied by a growing interest in religious practices.

How much of the revival of religions in the last few decades is fueled by the economic transition? In turn, what roles do religions play in the market economy or in the transition toward a market economy? In this chapter, I will describe the economic and religious changes in the last few decades and analyze the interactions between religion and economy. It appears that the transition toward a market economy has generated greater spiritual needs and desires among individuals. The globalizing market has created greater social space for religious practices, and, as the opening vignette indicates, religious organizations and individuals have creatively provided religious services in spite of various constraints. In the final part of this chapter, through a discussion of the Weberian theme of religious ethics and the spirit of capitalism, I will consider the debates on the degree to which China's Confucian heritage or religious culture positively or negatively affects the development of capitalism in Chinese societies.

The Centrally Planned Economy and Religious Repression

Before the establishment of the People's Republic of China in 1949, there were all kinds of religions, ranging from the world religions of Buddhism, Christianity, and Islam to myriads of sects and folk religious communities, to innumerable spiritual practices of individuals and families, as described elsewhere in this book. After 1949, the economy was gradually centralized and religion was increasingly suppressed. In the first decade of Communist rule, China went through a process of economic collectivization, violently suppressing resistance from the so-called exploiting classes of landlords and capitalists. The means of production, in

Marxist terms, which includes everything from farms to factories, tools, machines, transportation, communications, and so on, all became either state owned or collectively owned. Factory and service workers were organized into work units. Farmers were organized into People's Communes and production brigades. The state made annual and five-year economic plans regarding what to produce, how much to produce, and who would produce what and where. Any residual economic activities outside the state and collectives were treated as "capitalist tails" to be chopped off.

Along with the collectivization process, the five officially recognized religions (Protestantism, Buddhism, Islam, Daoism, and Catholicism) were coerced into forming "patriotic" associations under the close control of the Communist Party. Religious activities outside the premises of the five "patriotic" associations were suppressed, just like the "capitalist tails" in the economy. Other forms of traditional spiritualities were suppressed as "feudal superstitions" and other forms of organized religion were banned as "reactionary secret societies."

In the second and third decades of Communist rule, China continued to promote a centrally planned economy. During those years, under so-called socialist principles, everyone supposedly received comprehensive welfare from cradle to grave. In the cities, a job was guaranteed for everyone, and the job was assigned or reassigned by officials with or without the individual's consent. Housing was guaranteed, so to speak, and assigned by the work units. Education and health care were provided, and controlled, by the state through the work units and residential districts under the Communist Party. The rural areas had far fewer state welfare benefits, and these were left to the management of the collectives—the People's Communes and production brigades. Although there were periods of rapid economic growth and improvement of material life, the Chinese centrally planned economy was a "shortage economy" typical of Communist-ruled countries,[2] characterized by chronic shortages of consumer goods, long queues in shops, long delays in services, and shortages throughout the production process. Most of the essential consumer goods, ranging from food and meat to clothing and bicycles, were rationed. Rations were gradually phased out during the reform era.

The centrally planned economy claimed a high level of social equality and of certainty, which was believed to render religious beliefs unnecessary. Improvement of the individual's material life supposedly depended upon the planning and management of the collectives and the state, instead of on individual fate or supernatural forces. Meanwhile, once the collectivization process was completed in the cities in 1956 and in rural areas in 1958, atheist propaganda and ideological struggles against religious beliefs were intensified. Atheist propaganda was implemented throughout the school system, from kindergarten to college, and through the mass media. Consequently, people who grew up between the 1950s and the 1970s commonly had little experience or knowledge of religion except antireligious notions learned from atheist propaganda. The centrally planned economy provided the material basis for the effectiveness of ideological propagation.

Economic Reforms and the Reinstatement of Religions

After the death of Chairman Mao in 1976, the new leadership of the Communist Party began to acknowledge some of the failures of central planning. Toward the end of 1978, the new leadership under Deng Xiaoping ventured to launch economic reforms. Starting in the rural areas, farms were leased to families, who then made their own decisions regarding what to grow and what to do when. Except for a set amount of grain handed over to the state, farmers could sell their remaining products at the market. Subsequently, individuals in urban areas were allowed to engage in certain kinds of commerce, family-based workshops, and small-scale private businesses, which quickly filled the needs that the state-owned enterprises had failed to meet in the shortage economy. Ultimately, in 1992, at its Fourteenth Congress, the Chinese Communist Party officially pronounced that the goal of the economic reforms was to establish "a socialist market economic system." While the meaning of *socialist* remains debatable, the transition toward a market economy has advanced rapidly since then. Market competition has been introduced in various industries and social sectors. Privately owned businesses and joint ventures of transnational capital have increased.

The transition from central planning to a market economy, in spite of numerous challenges and missteps along the way, has been quite successful, with continual rapid growth of gross domestic product (GDP). By the end of the 1990s, China's economy successfully entered the "post-shortage period."[3] In 2001, China joined the World Trade Organization (WTO), marking the official integration of the Chinese economy into the globalized market. Since 2004, the Chinese government has repeatedly appealed to American and European countries in the WTO to recognize China's economy as "a full market economy." By 2005, about 65% of China's GDP came from the private sector of the economy, while state-owned enterprises continued to monopolize the communication and energy industries and to dominate in transportation. The Chinese Communist Party itself has also undergone far-reaching changes, including opening its doors to admit capitalists into the Party, even though the proletarian rhetoric remains in CCP official documents. By 2008, the rising entrepreneurial class had grown large enough to be recognized as a "new social class" in official discourse, and admitted as a new political force in the National People's Congress and the Chinese People's Political Consultative Conference.

As the country embarked on the economic reforms, the CCP adopted a policy of limited tolerance toward religion in 1979 in order to rally all social forces for the central task of economic development, as described in the previous chapter. Once religion was reinstated, however, it charted its own course of development and has grown continuously in the last three decades. The revival of religions has been widespread throughout the country. Evidently, the economic and social changes have rendered the restrictive regulations ineffective.

The Revival of Religions despite Restrictive Regulations

Document No. 19 (1982) acknowledged the failure of Cultural Revolution efforts to eradicate religion. Chinese government sources state that in 1956 there were about 3 million Catholics, 0.8 million Protestants, and tens of millions of Buddhists and Daoists.[4] These are the only available national estimates of the numbers of religious believers prior to the Cultural Revolution, when all religions were banned. Religious believers were again counted after the Cultural Revolution, however, and by the time of Document No. 19, the number of Catholics remained the same—about 3 million, the number of Protestants had multiplied to 3 million, and there were many Buddhists and Daoists (it is difficult to find specific numbers of Buddhists and Daoists due to the lack of formal membership in these religions).

A decade after Document No. 19, the Chinese government's 1991 *White Paper on the Status of Human Rights in China* reported that Catholics had increased to 3.5 million and Protestants to 4.5 million. Only a few years later, the new estimates were about 4 million Catholics and more than 10 million Protestants.[5] Moreover, nongovernmental or non-Chinese sources gave even higher estimates: about 12 million Catholics and as many as 50 to 70 million Protestants by the end of the twentieth century. Meanwhile, Buddhism, Daoism, and folk or popular religious beliefs and practices have also revived, even though it is difficult to estimate the numbers of believers (see chapter 10).

The Market Economy Fuels the Revival of Religions

Rapid industrialization, urbanization, and globalization have accompanied the market transition over the last three decades. Products made in China—ranging from toys, shoes, and clothes to televisions, computers, and automobiles—have become more common in many parts of the world. While farmers have become factory workers, many rural towns have become cities. Meanwhile, the existing metropolises have constantly expanded. According to published Chinese government statistics, the urban population increased from 17.9% in 1978 to 30.1% in 1998, and to 44.9% by 2008.[6] In other words, there are 594 million urban residents in China today, which is almost double the total United States population. In addition, there is the "floating population" of about 150 million—migrant workers who move en masse to the south, the east, or the north in search of jobs in coastal regions or metropolises. Most of the migrant workers come from economically disadvantaged villages and are officially classified as rural residents. These "peasants-turned-workers" have been increasingly integrated into the globalized economy—working for foreign enterprises or producing for the markets in other parts of the world.

On the other hand, however, the market economy has also enlarged the gap in material wealth. The "iron rice bowl" of jobs at state-owned work units has been smashed for the majority of factory and service workers. Both the state-owned and collectively owned enterprises have entered market competition. Subsequently, many workers have been forced to retire in their fifties with very little in retirement benefits, while many others simply lost their jobs when factories or companies were closed down or sold out. Housing has been privatized, and market competition has been introduced into education, health care, and other social sectors. The market transition has forced many people to struggle to find their own way to survive.

There are many factors that have contributed to religious growth during the reform era. However, the transition toward a market economy is the major contextual factor. Both the achievements and challenges of the market transition may have fueled the revival of religions.

First, achieving wealth in an emerging market economy drives people to seek supernatural intervention. During the period of the centrally planned economy, frugality and equality were treasured values. At the onset of the economic reforms, the authorities tried to unleash people's drive for wealth with the slogan, "Getting rich is glorious." However, with myriads of sociopolitical and natural constraints, it was difficult to reach the goal of getting rich by relying solely on one's own mundane efforts. Besides laboring hard and working through stifling regulations and personal networks, some people naturally appealed to gods or tried to manipulate supernatural forces for better fortunes. Conveniently, they fell back on Chinese traditional forms of worship. Once absent from public view, the god of wealth and other divinities have become ubiquitous at restaurants and private businesses throughout cities, towns, and villages.

Praying to the supernatural is practiced not only by people pursuing wealth; poor people who have lost job security and life certainty in the market economy also turn to the spiritual for solace and fortune. Consequently, fortune-telling, physiognomy (divination through analysis of facial features), glyphomancy (analyzing the parts of written characters), fengshui, and the like have become widespread. Many cities have a de facto "fortune-telling street" with dozens of fortune-tellers. There are millions of practicing shaman-doctors or spirit mediums. In the past, the authorities adamantly deplored and suppressed such folk beliefs as superstitions. During the reform era, the orthodox ideology of Marxism still dictates opposition to such beliefs and practices. However, the market economy has created a thirst for spiritual imagination beyond ideological control. This has affected even Chinese Communist Party members, despite the fact that they are required to be atheist according to CCP membership rules. A recent study by a researcher at the State Administration College has revealed that a majority of Communist Party and government mid-rank officials believe in some form of the foregoing practices.[7]

The uncertainty in the emerging market causes even people who have had good fortune to seek religious answers, as described in chapter 1. I interviewed a salesman for a pharmaceutical company who became a Christian. After graduating from a medical school he was assigned a job, but soon he quit that job and became a salesman. He told me that he could not understand why he had succeeded in the perilous market while his former classmates or friends commonly failed. He would not believe that he was smarter or worked harder than others. "By chance or probability I should have failed too." On Christmas Day, 1995, he fortuitously stepped into a church.

> The hymns were beautiful. They sang and sang and sang, without stop. Very interesting. I thought, wouldn't it be fun to come on Sundays to practice singing? The sermon was very good too. I understood it, although it was in the local dialect. It was very moving, touching my heart. So I began attending church regularly. As a matter of fact, I loved going to church. For a while, I went to church at least twice a week, by riding a bicycle for forty minutes each way, sometimes in rain.

The Christian activities were interesting to him and compatible with his lifestyle. But he also emphasized that Christians were elected and blessed by God. For him, this was a powerful explanation for his good fortune. After conversion, he quit smoking. He said he had tried several times to quit, but each time he ended up smoking even more. This time, however, it was actually without much struggle. "The cigarette simply became nauseating." He viewed this as another sign of God's blessings on him.

Evidently, for those who have accumulated wealth, the desire for religion or spirituality does not abate. While some have converted to Christianity, other entrepreneurs have become patrons of Buddhist and Daoist temples and monks, donating large amounts of money to build temples and provide for the monks and priests. For some, the purpose of such religious practices is to seek continual blessings in this world. For others, the purpose is to accumulate religious merits for the afterlife. Of course, there are also religious philanthropists who, fearing divine retribution, wish to compensate for the sins they have committed through their business activities in the primitive, chaotic, emerging market.

More important, regardless of whether they are rich or poor, people seek meaning in addition to physical and psychological health. In the centrally planned economy, meaning was supposedly provided by the Communist Party. Individuals struggling in the market economy, however, have to make personal choices, including formulating their own meanings or choosing among existing meaning systems. Therefore, many meaning-seeking converts can be found among intellectuals as well as among farmers, workers, and others. Some celebrities first made their religious conversion public, accidentally serving as role models for many others. For example, Ms. Chen Xiaoxu was once a very popular actress who played the beloved romantic protagonist Lin Daiyu in the classic novel-turned-television series *Dream of the Red Chamber* in the 1980s. By the early 1990s, she had become a very successful advertisement entrepreneur. By the end of the 1990s, she converted to Buddhism, and eventually, in 2007, became a Buddhist nun (and soon after died of cancer). Ms. Chen was but one of the entrepreneurs and celebrities who have made their religious conversion public, which commonly stimulated much public interest and open discussion in all sorts of media.

Second, besides the loss of job security and life certainty, the social structure during the transition toward a market economy has also undergone dramatic changes. During the period of the centrally planned economy, almost everyone had a clear affiliation with a work unit or commune. People worked, lived, grew, aged, were cared for, and controlled in such a collective. However, in the market economy people change jobs more frequently. The identification with the company becomes more transitory and the sense of belonging transient. Individuals struggling in the market not only seek meaning and comfort in spirituality, but many also look for new kinds of social belonging. Some religions and spiritual movements provide such an alternative collective identity and a better sense of belonging. This is an important reason for the rapid growth of Christianity throughout the reform era. Many observers point out the breakdown of the state-supported health-care system as an important reason for the conversion to charismatic Christianity, for such Christian beliefs highlight spiritual healing. Although this may be an important reason, it cannot explain why Christianity has grown faster than other religions, such as Daoism, that also offer spiritual healing. The more important factor, I think, is that Christianity provides a new form of group belonging and identity, which is absent in most forms of traditional Chinese religion. Within the Christian community, people express love and care for one another and support one another in crisis. Love and support often keep people in the group even if the physical healing does not happen.

During the market transition throughout the 1980s and 1990s, *qigong* was probably the most visible form of spiritual practice. The word *qigong* means, literally, "the power of *qi*" (air or breathing). Simply put, *qigong* is a form of physical exercise, meditation, and healing. The *qigong* phenomenon is not merely an individualistic practice for physical health, but also a form of social interaction among fellow practitioners. Falun Gong was but one of the largest *qigong* groups, which placed a strong emphasis on mutual emotional support and collective practice. Its rapid growth after 1992 was due at least in part to its increasingly religious overtones in a more receptive culture, at a time when the system of cradle-to-grave social security was being dismantled, thousands of work unit employees were being laid off, and the revolutionary morality was being cast aside for a merciless and often corrupt market culture.[8] In 1999, the Chinese government banned Falun Gong and other *qigong* groups. After that, some followers "took refuge" at Buddhist temples or were baptized into Christian churches.

Third, in order to lure tourists and overseas Chinese for investment, some local governments have restored traditional temples and temple fairs. "Building a religious stage to sing an economic opera"—in other words, exploiting religion to develop the economy—was the plain intention of many local governments. In rural areas, many villages and towns have restored temples dedicated to historical heroes who have become accepted by the locals as tutelary gods. In Hong Kong, the Wong Tai Sin Temple was a flourishing folk religious temple built by refugees who fled the Communist mainland.[9] All previously existing Wong Tai Sin temples in the mainland had been destroyed before and during the Cultural Revolution. By 2001, how-ever, at least a dozen Wong Tai Sin temples had been rebuilt in Guangdong and Zhejiang provinces. Most important, six of the ten temples documented in a 2002 work "were founded with the support and sometimes at the initiative of agencies of the local government."[10]

The initial revival of religions during the reform era is largely the result of the central government's shift from political struggles to economic development. To rally people of all walks for economic development, the government has allowed the restoration of a limited number of temples, churches, and mosques. Also because of the focus on the economy, some local governments have even actively engaged in restoring traditional religious temples in order to attract investment and tourism by overseas Chinese. Evidently, the purpose is not so much to ensure religious freedom and the constitutional protection of religious practices but pragmatic considerations for the central political goal of economic development. When religious activities get in the way of economic development, governments have discouraged them. When certain religious organizations have grown large and effective, and are perceived as threats to Communist Party rule or the government's authority, they are unremittingly suppressed.

Creative Responses of Religious Believers to the Market Economy

Religious believers are not merely passive recipients of healing, meaning, and belonging. They are also active agents in the construction of belief systems, social networks, and religious organizations. Some believers rise to become leaders of reli-gious organizations or spiritual movements. The market economy has both provided financial resources and created opportunities for this type of religious expression and expansion.

First, religious leaders and organizations in the market economy have had more financial resources to produce religious materials and provide religious services. The most evident phenomenon is the restoration and expansion of many temples, churches, and mosques. Throughout the 1980s, when the economy was in transition from the shortage economy, the restoration of religious venues depended heavily upon government appropriations and overseas donations. In the 1990s, however, more and more temple, church, and mosque construction projects relied on fund-raising among believers in China. Meanwhile, Buddhists, Christians, and *qigong* groups have provided audiovisual materials as well as books to propagate their religion, often distributed free of charge, although donations are encouraged. Religious websites have rapidly proliferated in the twenty-first century.

Under current regulations, the construction of religious buildings and the pub-lication of religious materials are strictly restricted. The authorities have taken rou-tine actions and carried out periodic campaigns to curb unapproved religious expansion. For example, whereas China prints more Bibles than any other country in the world each year, the Amity Printing Company in Nanjing is one of few permitted to print the Bible. And Bibles can be distributed only through the churches under the state-recognized China Christian Council and Chinese Christian Three-Self Patriotic Movement. To build a church, a mosque, or a temple, the application for permission has to go through government agencies at the county, prefecture, and provincial levels and may not start without the official approval of the provincial government. The violators of printing and construction regulations have often been detained, jailed, and fined, the publication materials confiscated, and the buildings demolished.

However, financial resources have become sufficiently abundant for many religious groups to quickly refurbish and replace what has been lost to government crackdowns. In Guangzhou, a well-known Protestant house church was located at the house of Samuel Lamb (Lin Xiangao), which attracted hundreds of worshippers in the late 1990s. To accommodate the crowd, closed-circuit television and sound systems had to be set up on all three floors of his little townhouse. From time to time, the police and religious affairs officials raided the house church and took away all the equipment. However, in a matter of a couple of days or a week, new equipment would be brought in and the worship gathering would resume. Also, there have been many reports of Christian churches and Buddhist temples that were demolished during a crackdown and then rebuilt within months. This often happens in the economically better developed coastal provinces of Zhejiang, Shandong, Fujian, and Guangdong, but increasingly in inland provinces as well.

Second, religious leaders and organizations have seized opportunities created by the market economy to spread and expand. While local government officials have tried to "build a religious stage to sing the economic opera," religious believers have grasped such opportunities to legitimately revive their religious practices and restore temples. Similarly, while the government wants to expand tourism for economic benefits, religious leaders have captured such opportunities to revive and expand religious activities. During this process, however, religious goods and services have been commodified.

The most successful example in this regard is the Shaolin Buddhist Temple in Henan province. When the economic reforms began in the early 1980s, the temple had only a dozen old, feeble monks surviving as farmers cultivating the land surrounding a few dilapidated buildings. Following the 1982 release of the popular kung fu movie *Shaolin Temple*, starring Jet Li, tourists began to arrive at the site of the famous temple deep in the mountains. Local government agencies, including the Bureau of Tourism and the Bureau of Cultural Relics, came to reap the economic benefits. Responding to this, the monks negotiated and persuaded the authorities to allow the temple to be restored and expanded. Eventually, Shaolin Temple became a large compound of newly constructed magnificent buildings in traditional styles, with many modern facilities. The number of monks increased to over a hundred. Its land has increased to over 300,000 square meters (about 75 acres), whereas the residents of the surrounding villages were forcefully relocated by order of the local government. Shaolin Temple has expanded by relying on tourist income as well as sales of religious services and goods.[11]

To solicit donations and increase income, Shaolin and other Buddhist and Daoist temples have devised various mechanisms that meet the needs of individuals in the market economy. One such mechanism is tourist admission tickets to temples, which are common throughout the country. Another successful mechanism is auctioning off the privilege of lighting the first incense sticks at the temple on the Chinese New Year's Day. To seek blessings, good fortune, and merits in the next life, some entrepreneurs willingly pay thousands of yuan for such a privilege, which they sometimes hand over to government officials as a special gift or bribe. In the end, the temples benefit from such patronage. Ordinary religious goods such as incense sticks and statues of gods or Buddhas are commonly sold at the temple for a price several times higher than at secular shops. Overall, the commodification of religious goods has significantly benefited some Buddhist, Daoist, and folk religious temples but is less pronounced for Christian churches and Muslim mosques.

Third, the market economy has created and continued to enlarge the social space for practicing religion. In the past, the work unit was an all-inclusive community, through which the Communist Party enforced strong social and political control. During the market transition, however, companies, as economic entities in the market economy, have been losing some of their social functions, including those of political and ideological control. Profit-minded employers gain little benefit from interfering with the religious beliefs and practices of their employees, unless they need to avoid penalties by certain government agencies. Moreover, some businesspeople find that employees who are religious believers tend to be more honest and diligent workers, and subsequently may encourage their religious faith. Some companies even house religious activities, either unintentionally, like the McDonald's in the opening vignette, or intentionally, in the case of Christian chapels or Buddhist shrines being set up on the premises of factories and other companies.[12] Meanwhile, some privately owned or managed apartments and office buildings have rented out properties to religious groups for religious gatherings. This kind of Christian "house church" has become more and more common in Beijing, Shanghai, and other large cities. Unless pressured by the police, the State Administration of Religious Affairs, or other government agencies, the owners or managers have no problem with such usage as long as the religious tenants pay their rent just like anybody else.

Indeed, the globalized market economy has facilitated many religions' entry and spread within Chinese society, rendering some religious regulations unenforceable. According to existing regulations, China does not admit foreign missionaries of any religion, and gives no legal status to any but the five officially sanctioned religions of Buddhism, Daoism, Islam, Catholicism, and Protestantism. Adapting to these restrictions, some businesses, including both foreign and domestic ventures, have made the spreading of a religion their primary purpose, with economic activity serving only the goal of engaging in a legal occupation and perhaps also providing financial resources to support the religious activity. This kind of business-based religious teaching is practiced by Christians, Buddhists, traditional Chinese sects such as Yiguandao, and newly introduced religions and churches such as the Bahá'í Faith, the Church of Latter-Day Saints, and the Unification Church.

Protestantism, Confucianism, and Capitalism

Until now we have focused on how economic changes in contemporary China—the rapid expansion of the market economy—have contributed to the revival of religions. We can also turn the question around: does religious culture contribute to the development of Chinese capitalism? Max Weber's thesis on the association between the Protestant ethic and the spirit of capitalism has been an important sociological theme that has inspired many studies. Weber argues that there is an affinity between the Protestant ethic and the spirit of capitalism, so that the first emergence of modern rational capitalism in Western Europe was probably more than accidental.[13] This was because Protestantism promotes rationality and an inner-worldly asceticism that encourages frugality and hard work, which are conducive to the accumulation of capital. Modern rational capitalism did not first emerge in societies where there was a lack of the Protestant ethic, even if the technological, financial, legal, and other institutions were favorable to capitalism. In his subsequent studies of world religions focusing on their economic ethics, Weber argued that capitalism had not emerged in China because Confucianism, the dominant thought system in China's history, did not provide an ethic conducive to the emergence of modern rational capitalism.[14] Weber's studies have been challenged ever since the initial publication of his writings. Some have pointed out the mistaken evidence that Weber cites, whereas others have emphasized that Weber's basic arguments still hold in spite of the minor errors in his data.

Over and above the debates surrounding philosophical positions and historical facts, the rise of several Asian economies since the 1970s further complicates the discussion. Has a "Confucian ethic" contributed to the rapid economic development of South Korea, Taiwan, Hong Kong, and Singapore? Since these societies' economic growth clearly has surpassed that in other parts of the world, it is tempting to claim that Confucianism, which is the shared ethical system of these East Asian societies, played a key role in this process. Some historians, philosophers, and politicians make this case and assert that Weber is wrong about Confucianism's role in economic development. In my view, however, the verdict is still out. This question would benefit from systematic empirical studies with updated social scientific tools. Weber's assertion also begs the question of how to define Confucianism.

The reality of religious plurality in these Asian societies and the internal diversity of Confucianism are important features to acknowledge. Therefore, we should ask the following research questions: What are the kinds of Confucianism that have contributed to the economic development of these Asian societies? What are the social mechanisms through which Confucianism functions in these societies? What specific type of contribution might it bring to economic development? Meanwhile, what roles have other religions played in the economic transformation of these societies? Before these questions are answered with empirical data, Weber's thesis cannot be conclusively refuted or confirmed.

The work of economic anthropologist Hill Gates provides some possible hypotheses in relation to these questions. In her book *China's Motor: A Thousand Years of Petty Capitalism*,[15] she analyzes the two dominant modes of economic production for the past thousand years in imperial China; both modes used the Confucian ideology but in different ways. The first was the "tributary mode of production," which refers to state-managed extraction and distribution of resources, notably through state-controlled commodity production, taxation, tribute, and redistribution through hierarchical bureaucratic structures. This system was controlled by a class of Confucian-educated scholar-officials, who upheld ideals of statehood, virtuous governance, and education. They had little regard for commercial pursuits and enjoyed a leisurely lifestyle. The second mode was the "petty capitalist mode of production," which consisted of small-scale firms that produced commodities for the markets. These firms were organized along kinship lines and were incorporated as clans and lineages (see chapter 2), which owned large landholdings and small workshops. They depended on their own family members for labor and used the Confucian idiom of ethics, filial loyalty and ancestor worship, to control their labor force—Gates calls these family firms "patricorporations."

The state and the family firms both used the Confucian ideology, the former for the purpose of governance and the latter for the purpose of managing the family's labor force. Under this system, a market economy flourished in China from around the tenth century (see chapter 8). But under the state's Confucian ideology, there was little rule of law, and it was difficult for nonstate firms to grow. The highest power and prestige accrued to members of the scholar-official class. As a result, kin-based enterprises could not expand through reinvestment into truly capitalist firms. Instead, investment was oriented toward the education of children to prepare for the imperial examinations, so that they could enter the leisured life of the scholar class and use their influence to bring economic benefits to the family.

In modern times, the relationship between the tributary state and the petty-capitalist family firms has undergone tumultuous changes. Although the elitist and intellectualist Confucian ideology of the state was overturned in 1911, the entrepreneurial "Confucian" ethic of the petty-capitalist Chinese family firms of Hong Kong, Taiwan, and Southeast Asia has adapted to the modern market economy.

Much of Chinese popular religious culture reflects and reinforces the orientations of petty capitalists. Popular religious symbols celebrate the good things of life: prosperity, joy, luck, wealth, good health, long life, success, high social status, peace, and family harmony. A strong connection is made in traditional culture between wealth and morality. Material success is seen as the result of cosmic recompense: as a reward for meritorious deeds committed in past and present lives, and also as a consequence of being a moral and trustworthy individual. Furthermore, wealthy individuals can perform charitable deeds, which will accumulate their good karma and raise their moral standing in society. As described in chapter 9, commercial and financial symbols permeate popular religious culture, from the use of accounting methods to keep track of good and bad deeds (called "ledgers of merit and demerit") in late imperial China to the practice, still widespread today, of using paper money ("hell bank notes") as offerings to the gods.

The anthropologist Jean DeBernardi, a field researcher on the religious culture of the Chinese of Penang, Malaysia, argues that Chinese notions of fate and pre-destined affinities (see chapter 1) allow individuals to simultaneously accept their lot in life and deal with the unpredictable vagaries of life, while at the same time giving them a sense of moral agency through which, by doing good deeds, they invest in a future better fate:

> When individuals invoke fate, luck, spiritual collisions, and coincidence as explanations for events in their lives over which they have little control, this may serve to build confidence, allay anxiety, and exonerate the individual from a personal sense of guilt in the face of failure. At the same time, however, the popular religious theodicy teaches that good deeds result in a longer life and greater success, thereby mitigating a fatalistic determinism with the message that a person can make his or her own luck through moral deeds. The habitus of popular religious culture may well provide a useful life orientation for dealing with the risks and rewards of contemporary life in a capitalist society."[16]

The conclusions of scholars such as Gates and DeBernardi, which are based on Chinese history and ethnographic research in Taiwan and Malaysia, offer many insights on the connection between Chinese religious culture, petty-capitalist family enterprises, and moral orientations in a market economy. But it is still too early to know how these ideas may or may not apply to contemporary mainland China. In China, the transition toward a market economy was initiated by the Chinese Communist Party, which for decades tried to eradicate Confucian and popular religious values altogether. Following two decades of economic reforms and social change, Confucianism has begun to revive in China in the twenty-first century, evidenced by the renewed interest among the people in reading and studying Confucian classics and conducting rituals at Confucius temples throughout the country. However, it is not clear that such "Confucian" practices have much in common with the culture of imperial-era or overseas Chinese. Empirical studies lack answers to the research questions suggested earlier.

Meanwhile, it has become important to study the ethics of Chinese Protestants, whose numbers have increased a hundred times since the founding of the People's Republic of China, from about 700,000 in 1949 to possibly as many as 70,000,000 today. In the religiously plural Chinese society today, these Christians comprise a significant religious minority. In what ways are they Chinese, and in what ways are they Protestant? Do they form a hybrid Confucian-Protestant ethic, as some empirical studies seem to indicate?[17] What role does a Confucian-Protestant ethic, if it exists, play in the market economy? A century after Max Weber, the world has become even more complex and has to be studied with updated theoretical and methodological tools.

Conclusion

The rise of the market economy in China under Communist rule has come along with a significant growth of various religions. The market economy has created uncertainty and thus generated needs among people for healing, meaning, and belonging. It also has created a social structural space for religious organizations and religious movements, and has provided financial and material resources for religious growth. Meanwhile, religious individuals and organizations have responded to economic marketization in ways that have rendered the restrictive religious regulations unenforceable. However, the question of how different religions have contributed to the healthy development of a modern capitalism, or the so-called socialist market economy, remains to be studied. The development of the market economy in China has challenged many existing theories and also provided great opportunities for research on many aspects of religious change in society.

Notes

1. George Ritzer, *The McDonaldization of Society: New Century Edition* (Thousand Oaks, Calif.: Pine Forge Press, 2000), 12.

2. János Kornai, *Economics of Shortage* (Amsterdam: North-Holland, 1980), and *The Socialist System: The Political Economy of Communism* (Princeton, N.J.: Princeton University Press, 1992).

3. Lü Wei, "Jin ru 'hou duan quan shiqi' de zhongguo jingji" ("Chinese Economy Has Entered the 'Post-Shortage Period'"), *Cai jing wenti yanjiu* (Research on Financial and Economic Issues) (Beijing, 2001): 3.

4. Luo Guangwu, *1949–1999 Xin Zhongguo zongjiao gongzuo dashi gailan* (A Brief Overview of Major Events of Religious Affairs in New China, 1949–1999) (Beijing: Huawen Press, 2001).

5. Li Pingye, "90 niandai zhongguo zongjiao fazhan zhuangkuang baogao" ("A Report on the Status of Religious Development in China in the 1990s") *Journal of Christian Culture* 2 (1999): 201–222.

6. See Cunfu Chen and Tianhai Huang, "The Emergence of a New Type of Christians in China Today," *Review of Religious Research* 46, no. 2 (2004): 183–200; National Bureau of Statistics of the PRC, *Statistical Report of National Economic and Social Developments, 2007*, http://www.stats.gov.cn/tjgb/ndtjgb/qgndtjgb/t20080228_402464933.htm.

7. This finding was released in a report: "Yiban yishang xianchuji gongwuyuan nan ju 'mixin'" ("More than Half of Public Service Officials at the County or above Levels Have Difficulties to Resist 'Superstitions'"), *Kexue Shibao (Science Times)* May 11, 2007, http://www.sciencetimes.com.cn/htmlnews/20075111932416561791 51.html.

8. Beatrice Leung, "China and Falun Gong: Party and Society Relations in the Modern Era," *Journal of Contemporary China* 11, no. 3 (2002): 761–784; Yunfeng Lu, "Entrepreneurial Logics and the Evolution of Falun Gong," *Journal for the Scientific Study of Religion* 44, no. 2 (2005): 173–185; David A. Palmer, *Qigong Fever: Body, Science, and Utopia in China* (New York: Columbia University Press, 2007).

9. Graeme Lang and Lars Ragvald, *The Rise of a Refugee God: Hong Kong's Wong Tai Sin* (Hong Kong: Oxford University Press, 1993).

10. Graeme Lang, Selina Ching Chan, and Lars Ragvald, *The Return of the Refugee God: Wong Tai Sin in China* (Hong Kong: Chinese University of Hong Kong CSRCS Occasional Paper No. 8, 2002).

11. On the history of Shaolin temple, see Meir Shahar, *The Shaolin Monastery: History, Religion, and the Chinese Martial Arts* (Honolulu: University of Hawaii Press, 2008).

12. Carol Huang, "Christianity in a Chinese Workplace? For Some," *Christian Science Monitor,* March 9, 2008.

13. Max Weber, *The Protestant Ethic and the Spirit of Capitalism* (Mineola, N.Y.: Dover, 2003).

14. Max Weber, *The Religion of China: Confucianism and Taoism* (New York: Free Press, 1951).

15. Hill Gates, *China's Motor: A Thousand Years of Petty Capitalism* (Ithaca, N.Y.: Cornell University Press, 1996).

16. Jean DeBernardi, *The Way That Lives in the Heart: Chinese Popular Religion and Spirit Mediums in Penang, Malaysia* (Stanford, Calif.: Stanford University Press, 2006), 80.

17. Nicole Constable, *Christian Souls and Chinese Spirits: A Hakka Community in Hong Kong* (Berkeley: University of California Press, 1994); Fenggang Yang, *Chinese Christians in America: Conversion, Assimilation, and Adhesive Identities* (University Park, Pa.: Penn State University Press, 1999).

PART IV

Global Perspectives

13

The Globalization of Chinese Religions and Traditions

Richard Madsen and Elijah Siegler

Chinese religions are now practiced throughout the world. Carried by Chinese migrants, they have for centuries served to establish the ethnic identity of communities throughout the Chinese diaspora. In more recent years, however, Chinese religions have been disseminated through modern media far beyond the boundaries of Chinese ethnic communities. Thus, fengshui, *yin* and *yang*, and Tao (*dao*) have become common terms in lexicons around the world. In their global travels, Chinese religions enter into many different social contexts and are practiced and understood in many different ways. As global migration patterns shift and as new media speed up the global confluence of cultures, these different ways of practicing Chinese religions undergo constant change.[1]

Chinese Religions and Ethnicity

A memorable feature of Chinatowns around the world is the smell of burning incense. The incense comes from little shrines tucked away in the back of shops and restaurants, from ancestral altars located in community association buildings and from temples to such deities as Lord Guan and Mazu. These religious artifacts serve to mark boundaries between insiders and outsiders—and to link the insiders into chains of relationships extending all the way back to ancestral homes in China. They are a distinctive feature of old Chinese communities from Manila to San Francisco to Vancouver to Amsterdam—communities that originally were established in the face of discrimination and exclusion. For example, Chinese workers who were brought to the United States in the late nineteenth century to help build the transcontinental railroad became the object of widespread racial prejudice and, starting in 1882, were subjected to the Chinese Exclusion Act, which restricted further immigration and denied those already in the United States the right to become naturalized citizens. The Exclusion Act was repealed only in 1943.

Under these circumstances, Chinese communities in places such as San Francisco had to take care of themselves. They developed institutions to govern themselves and buffer themselves from the outside world. The most important of these were clan (extended family) associations, tying together people who shared the same surname and, supposedly, the same common ancestor. There were also regional associations, representing those who came from a certain district (in San Francisco, they were mostly from Guangdong) and from the same linguistic-ethnic groups, like the Hakka. Finally, there were secret brotherhoods, whose membership to some extent transcended these divisions. These associations owned much of the community property found in Chinatowns. They provided jobs and social services to their members and regulated the activities of the community, for example, by mediating disputes. Among their leaders, the associations would have people who spoke English and could act as go-betweens with the outside community.[2]

Religion was an important resource for constituting such groups. The clan association hall contained a shrine to the clan's ancestors. Regional associations built temples to patron deities of that region, like Tianhou (Mazu) or Tan Gong (a patron of seafaring Hakka people). Secret societies like the Hongmen association (sometimes called "Chinese Freemasons" in the late nineteenth century) had their own patron deities, like Lord Guan.[3] These various patron deities divided as well as united the Chinese community. Different gods symbolized different loyalties. Thus, clan associations bound their members to common loyalty in opposition to other clan associations. But the overall system of associations dedicated to different protector deities marked off the Chinatown community from the world of the dominant American culture organized according to Protestant denominations or Catholic parishes. Religiously infused festivals, like the Chinese New Year, also brought forth public celebrations that bolstered the solidarity of the community and marked its distinctiveness from outsiders. An important form of public activity was the funeral, which, if the deceased was wealthy and influential, could involve a large procession and much communal feasting. Interment would be in a Chinese cemetery, built with money raised from the clan associations. Eventually, the bones of the deceased would be dug up, according to south Chinese religious custom, and sent back to the ancestral home in China.[4]

BOX 13.1 Transnational Burials

In nineteenth-century America, the Chinese practice of exhuming bodies and shipping the bones to join their ancestors back in China was seen by many Anglo-Americans as a menace to public health. But these prejudices were gradually overcome. Now, the remains of deceased Chinese are likely to go in the other direction. Having become settled in the United States, many Chinese Americans are bringing the ashes of their parents to be interred in their new home in America.

Even as immigrant Chinese communities used their religious rituals and icons to regulate their internal solidarity in opposition to a hostile host society, the host societies sometimes undertook efforts to convert the Chinese to the dominant faiths. In North America, for example, both Protestants and Catholics established missions in their Chinatowns. Such churches often attracted Chinese immigrants through English language lessons and other social services. In some denominations, such outreach efforts were inhibited by resistance from nativist members who believed that Chinese were unfit to become Christians. Within the Chinese community, conversion was inhibited by fear of the consequences of alienation from the clan and community associations that were so important for survival in a hostile environment. In an extreme case, in Victoria, British Columbia, in 1898, a Hongmen member was marked for death because he had compromised the society's secrets by converting to Christianity.[5]

In Chinese communities around the world, one can still find the religious legacies of historical exclusion and discrimination. Shrines and temples with their assorted patron deities and associated rituals still serve to mark families and regional associations off from one another and to mark the community as a whole off from its social environment. This is especially the case when the community is being replenished by illegal immigrants, whose fate is completely in the hands of clan and regional associations and secret societies. The Fujianese section of New York's Chinatown is a good example of this.[6]

But especially since the 1960s, in response to professional and commercial opportunities, new kinds of immigration flows brought well-educated and affluent Chinese to cities around the world. In North America, such immigrants usually settled in suburbs rather than the old Chinatowns, and the old clan and regional associations were much less important to them than to earlier generations. Religion was nonetheless important, not least because it provided places and occasions for Chinese immigrants to gather together as a community.[7]

Such immigrants, though, practice religion in different ways than earlier generations. They typically interpret their traditions in ways that foster their integration with their host country even as they affirm distinctive aspects of their cultural heritage. A good example is the religious activities of Taiwanese immigrants to Los Angeles, as described by Carolyn Chen in her book *Getting Saved in America*. The immigrants depicted here seem to feel a need to conform to the religious structure of the United States, in which most citizens (about 60%) have a formal affiliation with some organized religious community. About a third of recent Taiwanese immigrants (mostly middle-class professionals and entrepreneurs) become Christian. The favored form of Christianity seems to be the nondenominational evangelical Christian congregation, composed almost exclusively of Taiwanese.

In this new situation, conversion to Christianity does not alienate Taiwanese from their ethnic community but provides a distinctively Taiwanese way (emphasizing strong "family values" in worship services carried out in the Taiwanese language) of belonging to the American Christian mainstream. Another third of recent Taiwanese immigrants in Los Angeles, however, formally join a humanistic Taiwanese Buddhist organization, like the Hsi Lai temple, affiliated with Buddha's Light Mountain, or the Tzu Chi (*Ciji*) Buddhist Compassion Relief Association.

Although many of the latter might have gone to Buddhist temples on special occasions in Taiwan, they would not necessarily have practiced Buddhism in a way that that most religiously inclined Americans would think religion should be practiced—that is, to make a formal declaration of faith in a particular religious organization and to commit oneself (and one's family) to regularly attending worship services and to carrying out good works through the organization. This is also a distinctive way of affirming one's Chinese heritage while integrating oneself with American culture. In Chen's account, the Taiwanese humanistic Buddhist associations are actually more ecumenical, more concerned about reaching out through charitable works to non-Chinese Americans, and more concerned with fostering interreligious dialogue than the Taiwanese evangelical Christian organizations.[8]

In many parts of Southeast Asia, such as Vietnam, Malaysia, and Indonesia, however, even professionally educated overseas Chinese face more restrictions on becoming integrated with the dominant culture. Although their social life thus continues to be confined to ethnic enclaves, the Chinese middle classes in these situations still look to humanist Buddhist associations to be vehicles for creating good relationships with the wider community. Buddhist lay associations like Tzu Chi and the Buddha's Light International Association, for example, contributed large amounts of time, money, and expertise to relieve the suffering of victims of the 2005 tsunami in Southeast Asia. Unlike many traditional Chinese religion-based philanthropic bodies, these organizations distribute aid not only to members of their own extended kinship and regional groups, but also to people of all ethnicities and creeds who need help.[9]

BOX 13.2 Chinese New Year Parades

As the old forms of discrimination die out in the United States, Chinatown community celebrations become less a marker of separation from the wider community and more an invitation to the wider community to enjoy the richness of the Chinese contribution to the American cultural mosaic. Thus, Anglo, Latino, and African Americans join the annual San Francisco Chinese New Year Parade. Nonetheless, such community celebrations cannot completely transcend divisions. For example, there are often conflicts between immigrants from the People's Republic of China and immigrants from Taiwan (especially those advocating Taiwanese independence) over rights to march in the parade.

For the first and second immigrant generations at least, religious practice provides a way of remaining engaged with one's country of origin. This is done in different ways, according to whether the religious practice is more socially embedded in family and local community or more transcendent. Thus, for devotees of Tianhou in American Chinatowns, the connection with the ancestral homeland is personal. Devotees of Tianhou periodically bring the statue of the goddess back to its place of origin in China to recharge it with sacred power. But for middle-class, suburban practitioners of humanistic Buddhism, the connection may more often be virtual. The diasporic temples of humanistic Buddhist associations are usually branches of a primary temple in Taiwan or China. Followers of humanistic Buddhist associations regularly study books and videos from their masters in China or Taiwan. However, many of them also make pilgrimages back to those home temples, and they send their children to summer camps sponsored by the home temples.

The passage of generations in a foreign land, however, tends to weaken understanding of the religious practices of the homeland. As young people leave home and find themselves caught up in the study and work needed to succeed in the new society, they often do not have the time (even if they have the interest) to carry out the regular intellectual and moral cultivation needed to appreciate the deeper meaning of the rituals practiced at family gatherings or community festivals. The Chinese religion then becomes for them a hodgepodge of disconnected customs. Asian American students at American universities often take courses on Chinese religion precisely to gain an understanding of the reasons behind their family customs.

Between Transnational Institutions and the State

As Chinese spread around the globe, they have to reconcile their allegiances to different political authorities. The resulting tensions shape their religious practices and sometimes their religious practices contribute to the tensions. As it did during the imperial era, the contemporary Chinese government claims to be the arbiter of religious orthodoxy and heterodoxy. (The democratic government on Taiwan is based on a liberal model that guarantees religious freedom from most government interference.) In China itself, this leads to conflicts with transnational religious communities like the Catholic Church, which claim allegiance to an outside authority. Such conflicts become exacerbated when Chinese travel into the diaspora.[10]

For example, Chinese Catholics living in North America and Europe (especially of the first and sometimes second generations) often remained keenly interested in the fate of the church in China. Thus, illegal Fujianese immigrants employed in New York sweatshops sent some of their hard-earned money to build churches in their home communities. Many of these immigrants belonged to the "underground" segment of the church in China, and the money they sent was for building unregistered (officially unapproved) churches in their home communities. In the recent past the

Chinese government has systematically torn down such churches. Even if such acts were aimed at intimidating underground Catholics in China, the destruction of churches only strengthens the resolve of outraged compatriots living in New York. This in turn deepened conflict between Chinese underground Catholics living in New York and other Chinese American Catholics who more willingly accommodated the officially registered church in China.[11] Sometimes, the underground Catholics and the officially oriented Catholics in New York will not attend Mass together. Other times they clash over who gets to represent the Chinese Catholic Church to the general American population. There is currently a controversy over the picture of Mary, Our Lady of China that hangs in the National Cathedral in Washington DC. The Catholics oriented to the official church like the picture that has the approval of the American Bishops to hang in the National Cathedral. The picture is of Mary dressed in flowing blue robes, very similar to the depictions of Guanyin. The underground Chinese American Catholics, on the other hand, want this image replaced with one painted by missionaries to China in the early twentieth century, of Mary dressed in the robes of a Western-style queen and sitting on a throne with her son on her lap. For them, for Mary to be authentic means she should not look like a Chinese bodhisattva, but like a powerful foreign queen ready to call a corrupt Chinese government to task.[12]

Analogous conflicts between state authority and transnational religious authority still occur with the Dalai Lama. Exiled from Tibet to India, this Nobel Prize–winning religious leader has gained great moral stature around the world. He has become an authoritative teacher not only for Tibetan Buddhists seeking autonomy, but for all kinds of Buddhists, and indeed for a great variety of spiritual seekers. He has been warmly welcomed in Taiwan, but the People's Republic of China bitterly denounces him as a "splittist." When he dies, there will inevitably be a great struggle between the Chinese government and the Tibetan exile community on how to identify his reincarnation.

The struggles over the religious authority of the global Catholic Church and transnational Tibetan Buddhism on the one hand and the Chinese government on the other are the most dramatic struggles afflicting the Chinese religious world, but they are by no means the only struggles. From bases abroad, Chinese evangelical Christians launch missionary projects in China. Unlike nineteenth- and early-twentieth-century missionaries, who were mostly white Europeans, most contemporary missionaries to China are actually overseas Chinese. Often they travel to China in the guise of English teachers or business investors but carry out surreptitious proselytization in defiance of Chinese laws. They claim to be accountable to God rather than to any earthly government. In their countries abroad, such Christians often organize lobbying groups to urge their governments to pressure China to grant the human right of religious freedom.

Finally, leaders of Falun Gong and other movements dubbed "evil cults" by the Chinese government have escaped into exile abroad and have become the inspirational center for transnational religious movements. Some of them—Falun

Gong especially—have developed extremely sophisticated global multimedia enterprises. Examples include Falun Gong's websites (http://www.minghui.org; http://clearwisdom.net), newspaper (*Epoch Times*), and TV stations (*New Tang Dynasty*). Members of such organizations carry out demonstrations in public places around the world and have even interfered in major political events, as when a Falun Gong practitioner disrupted a public appearance of the American president George W. Bush and the Chinese president Hu Jintao at a White House meeting.

Some Taiwan religious leaders have also achieved global stature. Sheng Yen, the Master of Dharma Drum Mountain, divides his time between his monasteries in Taipei and New York. He has been a spokesperson at international Buddhist congresses and has taken part in interreligious dialogues organized by the United Nations. Hsing Yun, the founder of Buddha's Light Mountain, also travels constantly and has met with world political and religious leaders, including the Roman Catholic Pope. Citing frail health, Cheng Yen, the founder of Tzu Chi, does not leave Taiwan, but she, too, is recognized and admired around the world. Even though their origins were in Taiwan, the Buddhist movements started by these masters transcend the boundaries of any nation-state, have received global recognition, and are a source of nationalistic pride. (And it is a matter of national shame to be dependent on out-

BOX 13.3 Buddhist Karaoke

Francesca Tarocco

In China, Taiwan, and Hong Kong, the karaoke boom of the 1990s gave birth to a deceptively incongruous by-product, namely, Buddhist-inspired karaoke recordings. In recent years, the availability of audiovisual recordings of both traditional Buddhist chants and newly composed songs of Buddhist inspiration and content has significantly increased. These recordings vary greatly in both content and appearance. Some appear to be directed at an audience of Buddhist practitioners, while others target a more generic and composite audience in search of spiritual solace or a connection with traditional values.

The video *Buddhist Liturgical Singing, Karaoke Singing Instructions* is just one of many possible examples of Chinese Buddhist karaoke videos for educational and proselytizing purposes. The visual element of the karaoke video consists mainly of images of lotus flowers, statues of the bodhisattva Guanyin, and incense holders of various shapes and forms. The objects appear to float in space and are not shown in any particular ritual context, while standard special effects including fades, split screens, and page-turners are deployed throughout the duration of the video. The recording is produced and distributed in China by the Buddha's Light International Association (BLIA), a society bringing together monastic and lay devotee members of the Taiwanese Buddhist association Foguangshan. The association's logo is repeatedly displayed throughout the duration of the video. The charismatic Buddhist monk Hsing Yun, founder and patriarch of Foguangshan, a Chinese Buddhist denomination with a vast international network, created BLIA in

continued

BOX 13.3 (continued)

1991. The main focus of the association is to give lay Buddhist devotees a formal means of playing a leadership role in promoting Buddhism. Foguangshan's sources claim that Master Hsing Yun has been consistently deploying audiovisual materials for educational and proselytizing purposes since the late 1950s and that he cut the first ever ten-inch Buddhist record in 1957. Hsing Yun is also quoted saying that "Buddhism must be directed to the masses, it must be popularized and made artistic." Both Foguangshan and BLIA have a very positive view of entertainment, and especially of music and singing, regarding them as a possible means to attract converts as well as creating a collective identity. For them, modern communications technologies, including karaoke machines, are perfectly legitimate means to actualize and popularize the Buddhist message. Today, Foguangshan, besides publishing books and magazines, produces vast numbers of cassettes, videos, and karaoke recordings in multiple media formats. It also owns satellite television channels and radio stations. Although neither Foguangshan nor BLIA are officially present in China, their audiovisual materials are available there as well as through the Internet. They can be found both in commercial retail outlets and in shops near or within monastic premises. It is now fairly common for karaoke-inspired videos of Buddhist chanting, such as the one described earlier, to be played within monastic premises and appear on screens in China's major monasteries and pilgrimage places.

The phenomenon of Buddhist karaoke is not confined to traditional chanting. In fact, there are countless examples of newly composed Buddhist music, often rather startling mixtures of traditional and electronic instruments and of different vocal styles. There also exist several websites that promote the work of performers and composers of new Buddhist music. The Singaporean composer Daniel Yeo's BuddhaNet Audio offers downloadable MP3 format files of "Buddhist songs," several of which have a karaoke version (http://www.buddhanet.net/audio-songs_chinese.htm). The songs bear titles like "Journey of Realization," "Mundane Attachment," and "Bond Free," and a 2003 collection of songs borrows its title from the Buddhist recommendation to "Come Forth."

siders for everything that is considered valuable in one's religion, art, and culture.) These transnational Buddhist movements help to bolster a sense of Taiwan's nationalism, even as they transcend the boundaries of the nation state.

For the sake of its own national pride, China, also would like to be a source of cultural ideas and moral-religious movements that are considered valuable transnationally. The dilemma is that the Chinese government cannot tolerate any movements (like Falun Gong) that are beyond its control. The government is cautious about producing religious leaders who may receive world aclaim and have the leverage to function independently of the government in global circles. Some Chinese academics and officials have responded to this dilemma by calling for a reinstitutionalized Confucian State that then can propagate Chinese moral-religious values around the world. Planning meetings have taken place and scholarly papers have been written in China about how to carry this out. It is still too early to tell how far this will go.

In an effort to extend its "soft power," the Chinese government also has tried to insert Confucian values into international agreements. At international meetings like the UN World Conference on Human Rights in Bangkok in 1993, the government of China was influential in drafting a Declaration on Human Rights with significant Confucian echoes. Although the Bangkok Declaration affirms the Universal Declaration of Human Rights, it stressed that human rights "must be considered in the context of a dynamic and evolving process of international norm-setting, bearing in mind the significance of national and regional particularities and various historical, cultural, and religious backgrounds." The document gave more emphasis to economic and social rights than most Western documents—a notion that resonates with Confucian-inspired traditions of government paternalism. The Chinese government's effort to promote this version of paternalistic and authoritarian "Asian values," supposedly based on Confucianism, has much in common with that of the Singapore government.[13]

An identity based on "Confucianism" is indeed seen by other governments in Asia as the best way of categorizing and co-opting their Chinese populations. The Malaysian government, for example, has developed a Confucian curriculum for religious instruction of Chinese citizens, to go along with Muslim and Christian curricula for the other parts of its population. The Indonesian government has recently added Confucianism to its list of officially sponsored religions, in an attempt to placate and protect an often-persecuted ethnic minority. The kind of Confucianism favored by most Asian governments tends to be conservative, emphasizing duties to obey authority.

At the same time, other intellectuals and activists within Asia, including Taiwan, are arguing for more liberal interpretations of Confucian traditions. Central to the Confucian tradition, for example, are the Five Relationships described by Mencius: father-son, husband-wife, older-younger sibling; ruler-subject, friend-friend. Proponents of a Confucian-justified authoritarian government (such as found in Singapore) emphasize the hierarchical nature of these relationships. But in Asian societies, such as Taiwan and South Korea, that have undergone democratization, there is more emphasis on the mutual responsibilities inherent in these relationships. There are also feminist interpretations rejecting the patriarchy that seems to be present in a literal reading of the Five Relationships. Such interpretations emphasize that anyone, male or female, could become a Confucian sage through proper self-cultivation. Finally, Yu Dan, a female scholar and media personality from Beijing, has written a book (based on television lectures) on Confucianism as a vehicle for harmonious personal growth. Her writings have now become immensely popular throughout Asia, although some established Confucian scholars complain that they are not faithful to the socially oriented intent of the original works. In the long run, therefore, it is unclear what degree of success the Chinese government, and other authoritarian Asian governments, will have in promoting conservative, authority-focused versions of Confucianism as a global ethic.

Chinese Religions and Personal Spirituality

The global popularity of Yu Dan's writings points to a quest—especially prevalent among modern, educated, mobile middle classes around the world—to adopt parts of Chinese religions into repertoires of personal "spirituality." Among such social strata there are often searches for personal wholeness—a reconciliation between warring impulses and a harmony between body and mind and reason and emotions—but a wariness of religiously based demands for sacrifice of the self to social needs or the subordination of the self to external authorities. Parts of Chinese religious traditions—especially when lifted out of their original contexts—seem to promise this. There is also a desire on the part of many non-Chinese in Europe and North America for alternatives to what some would see as the dogmatic, moralistic, guilt-provoking demands of the monotheistic, Abrahamic faiths. For some, Chinese religions may seem like such an alternative.

Thus, for the past 200 years, movements within the West have learned from and appropriated aspects of Chinese religions. In the nineteenth and early twentieth centuries, these movements were especially common among intellectuals and artists. To cite a few examples, Emerson and the other nineteenth-century American transcendentalists were influenced by translations of the Confucian classics. The avant-garde Dada artists of the early twentieth century were fond of Laozi and Zhuangzi because their Daoist works seemed to defy the categories of Western logic. The Beat writers and poets of the 1950s called themselves "dharma bums." But especially since the countercultural movements of the 1960s, a fascination with "Oriental religions" migrated from intellectual elites to the middle-class mainstreams of the West. An important carrier of these trends is popular media. The ideas of Chinese Daoism of course permeate martial arts movies such as Ang Lee's *Crouching Tiger, Hidden Dragon.* But they also appear in transfigured ways in American classics such as *Star Wars*—"May the Force [Dao] be with you." Video games are also full of these ideas.

Some of this fascination with Asian religious themes leads to a blend of motifs from Chinese religion with the routines of ordinary life. Home decorators consult books on fengshui to achieve a proper balance of energies in the layout of their living rooms. Cooks consider how to balance *yin* and *yang* nutritional elements. Athletes practice the Daoist-influenced exercises of Chinese martial arts.

Other Westerners, however, take up a more serious study of Chinese religions, but usually in ways that are deeply shaped by their own cultural expectations. Surrounded by the smell of incense, refreshed by herbal teas, and soothed by the soft melodies of Chinese lutes, they regulate their breath and center their bodies to achieve psychic tranquility, physical health, and more pleasurable sex.

The Westernization of Chinese Religions

Through these processes, some parts of Chinese religions have become assimilated into Western cultures. Daoism—to be more specific, Daoism as the perennial mystical philosophy of Laozi, with perhaps some longevity practices appended—has undergone the most complete indigenization. The first American edition of the *Daodejing* appeared in 1898, translated by Paul Carus and D. T. Suzuki, who would go on to become popularizers of Buddhism. But this version would not be the last: by 1950, there were ten translations in print, and in the last thirty years new English translations have appeared in bookstores with great regularity. The values the *Daodejing* seem to advocate include many that coincide with Western 1960s counterculture: spontaneity, naturalness, quietude, and concern for the environment.

The *Daodejing*'s fascination for Westerners, as well as its status as the second most translated text in the world (after the Bible), can be attributed to its brevity, its lack of proper names, and especially its multiplicity of possible meanings. These traits continue to make the *Daodejing* central to the globalization of Chinese religion. In fact, many Westerners who identify themselves as following a path based in Chinese spirituality first embarked on this path when they read the *Daodejing* in a college or high school class or were lent it by a friend or family member.

Also entering into global circulation are popularized renditions of Chinese meditation, visualization, and movement exercises designed to promote health, longevity, and transcendence. Whether called *qigong*, inner alchemy, or a more proprietary term, these techniques have appealed to the West's growing interest in body-centered spirituality. Thus, the language of transformation and cultivation has found its way into the popular discourse about Chinese religions.

By the early 1960s this discourse had found a home in the "human potential movement," a generic name for a gamut of therapeutic techniques based on self-transformation, and indeed the growing popularity of the *Daodejing*, the *Yijing*, and the practice of *taiji* can be historically and conceptually linked to the famed California retreat center Esalen, often seen as the birthplace of the human potential movement, where Gia-fu Feng (1919–1985) and Al Chungliang Huang resided.

These self-styled Chinese "masters" were part of the wave of Chinese migrants who entered the United States after passage of the liberal immigration reform act of 1965. They were experienced in various Chinese religio-physical techniques and eager to teach these skills to willing Westerners. Their arrival coincided with young Westerners' search for spirituality outside traditional institutions (a phenomenon sometimes called "the new religious consciousness") that led them to embrace teachers and practices from Asia.

The 1970s saw the birth and growth of popular Western religious organizations inspired by Chinese religions, often with the word "Dao" or "Daoist" in their name. These organizations are mostly made up of non-Chinese but are usually led by Chinese immigrants.

The first such organization officially recognized as a tax-exempt religious institution in the United States was the Taoist (Daoist) Sanctuary, founded in North Hollywood, California, in 1970. The founder of the Sanctuary was not Chinese—though he often played one on TV (most famously as the Red Chinese agent Wo Fat on *Hawaii 5-0*). Khigh Dhiegh (1910–1991) was of Anglo-Egyptian descent and was born Kenneth Dickerson in New Jersey. Nonetheless, his Sanctuary was the first comprehensive popular Chinese religious organization in North America, teaching *taiji*, martial arts, the *Daodejing*, and the *Yijing*, and conducting seasonal Daoist rituals (albeit invented by Dhiegh himself). Dhiegh brought to the Sanctuary teachers from China, including one who had been trained at a Daoist mountaintop monastery in Guangdong.

In 1976, three students of the Taoist Sanctuary who were studying Chinese medicine in Taiwan met a Chinese doctor whom they invited to the United States. Hua-Ching Ni settled in Malibu, California, opened a shrine called the Eternal Breath of Tao, and began teaching classes privately in a venue he named the College of Tao. Over the years, Ni-sponsored organizations have multiplied—including a private acupuncture clinic known as the Union of Tao and Man—and an accredited degree-granting college, the Yo San University of Traditional Chinese Medicine.

A Thai-born Chinese named Mantak Chia (1944–) moved to New York City in 1979 and opened the Taoist Esoteric Yoga Center, later renamed the Healing Tao Center. Today, Chia attracts an international clientele to his Tao Garden in Thailand, while the Healing Tao USA is headed by Chia's former student, Michael Winn (1951–), and based in Asheville, North Carolina. Chia's classes and books teach a popularized, streamlined system of Chinese internal alchemy, though his popularity first spread through books revealing "secret" Chinese sexual techniques.

Moy Lin-Shin (1931–1998) founded the Taoist Tai Chi Society (TTCS) in 1970 in Toronto. This is perhaps the largest Daoist group in the Western Hemisphere. The Taoist Tai Chi Society teaches "Taoist Tai Chi," a modified form of Yang-style *taijiquan*, and has taught thousands of classes in over 400 locations on four continents. It claims to have some 10,000 dues-paying members worldwide. The Taoist Tai Chi Society's religious arm is Fung Loy Kok Temple (FLK), dedicated in 1981. The original temple was located upstairs from the *taiji* studio. Although most Taoist Tai Chi studios around the world dedicate at least a corner of their space to a small shrine, in 2007 the Society dedicated the Cultivation Centre, the largest Taoist edifice outside Asia, in the town of Orangeville, north of Toronto.

These groups represent the major institutional forms of popular Chinese spirituality in North America today. Although each group has a different emphasis, they all teach practices through a combination of weekly classes and yearly, or seasonal, retreats or seminars. What all these practices have in common is that they can be performed individually, not collectively, as a modular part of a daily regimen. The practices have been separated from their Chinese traditional context and adapted to an urban lifestyle in which well-being and spirituality are consumable commodities. Daoist regimens of meditation and bodywork are treated as pathways of self-realization that fit well with the Western culture of individualism.

A Global Confluence of Cultures

Even as Chinese religions are imported to the West and transformed by individual-istic Americans and Europeans to meet their own spiritual purposes, the transformed Chinese religions are often imported back into China and begin to reshape the ways that Chinese understand their religious lives. Thus, growing numbers of groups of Daoist practitioners from Western countries visit China on tours of Daoist monas-teries and sacred mountains. Although they report powerful experiences of the spiritual energies of the mountains, their feelings about the monks living there are more ambiguous: they often feel that the monks have lost touch with the true Dao because of years of living under Communism. Many Chinese monks, on the other hand, are annoyed by Westerners who seek mystical experiences and body and sexual cultivation techniques but do not have a strong foundation in morality or the rigorous and lengthy process of monastic discipline within a recognized lineage of masters. But in the end, both the Chinese monks and the Western spiritual tourists are changed through their mutual encounters.[14]

Similarly, after being imported to China and transformed by Chinese culture, a Sinified form of Christianity may be exported back to the West. A prime example is the "Local Church," a form of Christianity indigenized in the 1930s by the char-ismatic preacher Watchman Nee. The Communists suppressed the Local Church in the 1950s and Watchman Nee died in prison. But his disciple, Witness Lee, took this fluid, nonhierarchical form of Christianity back to southern California, from whence it spread throughout North America—where most of the members of its 200 branches are not Chinese—as well as through Taiwan and Southeast Asia. Meanwhile, remnants of the Local Church have reconstituted themselves in China and drawn spiritual and material support from coreligionists in North America.

The confluence of Asian and Western religious cultures thus swirls in dynamic feedback loops. Chinese religions are both contributors to and recipients of a global search for transcendence.

Notes

1. There are many books on Chinese immigrant communities. Notable examples for North America are Victor Nee and Brett de Bary Nee, *Longtime Californ': A Documentary Study of an American Chinatown* (Boston: Houghton Mifflin, 1974); David Chuenyan Lai, *Chinatowns: Towns within Cities in Canada* (Vancouver: University of British Columbia

Press, 1988); Peter Kwong, *The New Chinatown* (New York: Hill and Wang, 1987); and Gwen Kinkead, *Chinatown: A Portrait of a Closed Society* (New York: HarperCollins, 1992). A good book on forms of community developed by recent immigrants to the United States is Timothy P. Fong, *The First Suburban Chinatown: The Making of Monterey Park, California* (Philadelphia: Temple University Press, 1994). Most of such books on Asian immigration, however, give rather short shrift to religious affiliations. Notable exceptions include Carolyn Chen, *Getting Saved in America: Taiwanese Immigrants Converting to Evangelical Christianity and Buddhism* (Princeton, N.J.: Princeton University Press, 2008), and Fenggang Yang, *Chinese Christians in America: Conversion, Assimilation, and Adhesive Identities* (University Park, Pa.: Penn State Press, 1999).

2. Nee and Nee, *Longtime Californ'*.

3. Lai, *Chinatowns*.

4. Nee and Nee, *Longtime Californ'*; Lai, *Chinatowns*; L. Eve Armentrout Ma, *Hometown Chinatown: The History of Oakland's Chinese Community* (New York: Garland, 2000).

5. Lai, *Chinatowns*, 205.

6. Gwen Kinkead, *Chinatown: A Portrait of a Closed Society* (New York: HarperCollins, 1992); Peter Kwong, *The New Chinatown* (New York: Hill and Wang, 1987); Ko-lin Chin, *Chinatown Gangs: Extortion, Enterprise, and Ethnicity* (New York: Oxford University Press, 1996).

7. Timothy P. Fong, *The First Suburban Chinatown: The Making of Monterey Park, California* (Philadelphia: Temple University Press, 1994).

8. Carolyn Chen, *Getting Saved in America: Taiwanese Immigrants Converting to Evangelical Christianity and Buddhism* (Princeton, N.J.: Princeton University Press, 2008).

9. Richard Madsen, *Democracy's Dharma: Religious Renaissance and Political Development in Taiwan* (Berkeley: University of California Press, 2007). Also see chapter 8.

10. Richard Madsen, *China's Catholics: Tragedy and Hope in an Emerging Civil Society* (Berkeley: University of California Press, 1998).

11. Richard Madsen, "Chinese Christianity: Indigenization and Conflict," in *Chinese Society: Change, Conflict, and Resistance*, 2nd ed., ed. Elizabeth J. Perry and Mark Selden (New York: Routledge/Curzon, 2003), 276–293.

12. Lizhu Fan and Richard Madsen, "The Catholic Pilgrimage to Sheshan," in *Making Religion, Making the State: The Politics of Religion in Modern China*, ed. Yoshiko Ashiwa and David L. Wank (Stanford, Calif.: Stanford University Press, 2008), 74–95.

13. United Nations High Commission for Human Rights, *Final Declaration of the Regional Meeting for Asia of the World Conference on Human Rights* ("Bangkok Declaration"), Bangkok, March 29–April 2, 1993.

14. Elijah Siegler and David A. Palmer, *Dream Trippers: Global Daoism and the Predicament of Modern Spirituality*, forthcoming.

Conclusion: The Future of Chinese Religious Life
Glenn Shive

Near the end of this book's journey through the religious life of China, we look for nuggets of the future lodged in the many layers of description of the present. Each chapter of our book has revealed important aspects of religious life in Chinese societies. Each author has implicitly pointed to the future of religion in China. Drawing on core insights from the foregoing chapters, this concluding essay will reflect on likely themes for the further development of religious life in Chinese societies. We mean this not as oracle or predictor of events and religious circumstances in China; rather, we will push our analysis by asking questions about how these aspects of religion might play out among the forces of fast-paced change that are underway in Chinese society today.

We began in a vegetarian restaurant in the southern city of Shenzhen. This booming metropolis of over twelve million, next to Hong Kong, represents China's reform and opening policies over the past thirty years. Some say that one can glimpse the future of China in the city of Shenzhen. This would be true in other megacities on the eastern seaboard that face outward to the rest of world. Shenzhen is a good place to consider how religious life for ordinary people may evolve to shape the future of China's culture, society, and political order.

The young people Lizhu Fan and James Whitehead introduced to us migrated to Shenzhen from rural regions of China in search of a better life. These people appear to be moving from an era of "spiritual vacuum" left in the wake of Mao's destructive Cultural Revolution to a growing sense that individuals have agency and choice within a fundamentally moral universe. New forms of religious practice, drawing on a mix of Buddhist, Daoist, Confucian, and/or Christian ideas, help to create and sustain many loose-knit urban communities. This is a low-key level of religious life that goes mainly "beneath the radar" of the state, without formal structures or full-time clergy. Realms of secular and sacred, or public and private, dimensions of religion seem to interweave without clear distinctions of time or place or formal expression. Not apart from the world, this spirituality is practical and pragmatic.

Informed by core Chinese beliefs, this spirituality arises in response to the new "personal space" open to young Chinese in an emerging middle class.

What are the future prospects for this kind of spirituality in Chinese society? Certainly, cities in China will continue to grow. (Over 500 cities in China have more than one million people). Might these patterns of religious practice among new migrants to cities be just a unique stage of development that will yield to other forms of religion as China grows even faster in the future? Is this spirituality sustainable with such small-scale, informal organizational supports? Might we see more large-scale, interurban organizations arise over time? How might this subtle, personal scale of spirituality transmit itself through the burgeoning online world of the Chinese Internet, now the largest in the world? How might connections between the local and the global occur through the web in China and thus further give expression to the syncretistic spirituality of the new urban middle classes?

The state in China has pulled back from a pervasive pattern of intrusiveness in people's personal lives over the past thirty years. Individual mobility and freedom of choice in jobs and consumer life have grown enormously in China of the reform era. Yet the Chinese state, wary of the potential social and political power of organized religion, continues to deter collective efforts to organize people around their common religious sentiments. This posture of the state may thus promote small-scale, socially inchoate forms of personal spirituality. These religious and ethical practices may make people more compliant as citizens for a state that highly prizes social harmony. They may give urban people a sense of being distinctively Chinese even as they leave family and village origins and adopt other aspects of Western commercial culture. The new personal spirituality of the urban middle classes described by Fan and Whitehead, recast from the common religious heritage of traditional rural China, may evolve into a broad, benign set of "personal lifestyle options" that offer a sense of belonging and of social meaning in the emerging, consumer-based, market-driven culture of new Chinese megacities.

Beyond the canyon streets and city lights of Shenzhen lie the rural communities of Guangdong province, also in South China. In chapter 2, Wai Lun Tam emphasizes the enormous variety of forms and practices of village-based religion in rural China, where vastly different ritual practices are found in places a few miles apart from one another. What accounts for such diversity and particularity in rural religion in China? This pattern contrasts with the powerful forces of standardization of culture in the world today. It also counters the Western stereotype in recent times that Chinese tend to be conformists and appear (from the outside) to be so much alike. Ironically, an earlier Western stereotype of the Chinese emphasized their "individualistic" nature. In any case, the folk religion that Tam describes is a rich "cultural DNA" that ought to be understood on its own terms, and preserved in buildings and texts, stories and rituals that articulate highly contextual human identities in rural village life over thousands of years. We need to ask, then, about the future of rural China. Are the religious ideas and practices that Tam so vividly describes fading into a gradual sunset?

The survivability of rural village culture, including religion, is a critical issue for all societies, whether developed or developing, East or West. The integrity of these customs, such as fengshui, lineage halls, temples to local gods, annual *jiao* processions, and ritual ceremonies to pay respects to ancestors of clan and village, are all important resources for maintaining positive and productive life in rural China. Folk religion is a growing subject of research among Chinese academics and reflected in popular literature and TV shows. After years of condescension toward village-based religion as essentially "superstition," county and provincial government offices are increasingly embracing folk religion under a safe, secular term called "intangible cultural heritage." They are also awaking to the potential value of local shrines and temples for the domestic tourist economy as city people gain more leisure time and money to travel within China. There may be no clear distinction between the tourist gaze and authentic religious appreciation. The tourist and the pilgrim may commingle in the lively social cacophony that rises around shrines and temples in rural China.

Religious practices among China's many minorities are similarly vibrant and various, as the case studies in chapter 3 demonstrate. Yet the ethnic minorities that sit astride China's borders with other nations find themselves in an awkward position. Philip L. Wickeri and Yik fai Tam rightly point out that the overriding priority for the PRC government is national unity and preventing separatist (or "splittist") movements among minority groups on its international borders. In sensitive regions such as Tibet and Xinjiang, the national government has helped many Han people to migrate to these poorer interior regions, assuring Han dominance in minority areas. A new rail line from Beijing to Lhasa, for example, has recently carried many Han for the first time into Tibet, perhaps tipping a former and fragile balance between the two ethnic groups. China's treatment of ethnic minorities in former remote places hit the global headlines during the 2008 Olympics, much to China's embarrassment, which led to increased worldwide support for Tibetan autonomy. Many young people around the world are drawn to the person and teachings of the exiled Dalai Lama, who has generated a new and charismatic global reach for a once obscure branch of Buddhism practiced only in sparse villages on the high Tibetan plateau.

While the Hui Muslims have mostly assimilated into Chinese culture, the mostly nomadic Uyghurs of the central Asian steppes within China still identify with the *ummah* of Sunni Islam. Urban riots in Urumchi in summer 2009 between Han and Uyghur communities prompted China to clamp down hard in the Xinjiang capital. Urban renewal programs had abruptly bulldozed Uyghur sections of the city, while some Han resented the preferential treatment given to Uyghurs. Each group feared the other. Meanwhile, what the central government fears most is a possible alignment between Muslims in China's northwest and the radical Islamic movements in central Asia reaching into Afghanistan, Iran, and the Turkic regions of the former Soviet Union.

What is the future for interethnic relations, including possible interreligious dialogue, within China, in this new international context of culture, politics, and global media coverage? How will responses by religious and other sympathetic groups outside China to minority groups within China affect the potential for resolving conflicts and reconciling religious and cultural differences? Some in China's leadership believe that other governments and international NGOs intentionally seek to make trouble for China in interethnic relations in what they consider to be their own internal affairs. What should be the responses of the governments located next to these regions and that share ethnic populations? How should concerned groups around the world who have historical and religious ties with these non-Han ethnic groups relate to them and to the Chinese government? Will the Chinese government learn to modulate its responses to international groups? Or do these potential conflicts rooted in religious and ethnic difference on China's border regions indicate that more discord is ahead for China's interactions with its neighbors and the rest of the world?

In China, religion has been less a matter of what one believes in an abstract sense, than in what one does as an intentional matter on a regular basis to deal with the practical issues of life and death in the world. This may relate to the impression that religions in China seem not to make claims for exclusive truth, as is often the case among religious groups in the West. This may also help to explain the relative absence of proselytizing among Chinese religions. What works for one person or community may not be right for another. Carl Jung, the Swiss psychiatrist who studied Chinese religions, concluded that "was wirkt ist wirklich," or what works is real. Chinese are said to be "pragmatic" about their religion, which made sense to the American philosophers of pragmatism, William James and John Dewey. This may be the foundational attitude that guides the revival of religions in China today.

Anthropologist Adam Chau describes five modalities of doing religion in chapter 4. The key here is to focus on forms of practice, not on the content of formally articulated beliefs. Chau's modalities offer many creative lines of analysis of religion in modern life in China today. For example, the discursive/scriptural mode may give a clue to understanding the religious devotion of millions to Mao's *Little Red Book* in the Cultural Revolution. The personal/cultivational mode found strong expression in the Falun Gong movement in the late 1990s, which became so pervasive that the Communist Party banned and repressed it. With their nearly obsolete ideology of Marxism, the leaders of the Communist state can feel easily threatened by successful indigenous religious movements that offer personal cultivation and aid to people in dealing with the mounting stresses of daily life.

The liturgical mode can help us understand Chinese' deep attraction to ceremony as defining moments in the public life of organizations. Liturgies define relationships within, and the purposes for, social organizations. Confucianism was the ritual apex of the Chinese state in the dynasties from Han to the Qing. Confucian rituals are retuning to mainland China (they continued in Taiwan from 1949 onward) in schools and private associations. Will the Chinese state readopt Confucian rituals in some form as they try to strengthen their legitimacy, less by Marxian ideology (itself a foreign import), and more by the rising tide of Chinese cultural nationalism?

All religions concern themselves with matters of the body and our concerns about mortality. David Palmer gives us an insightful tour in chapter 5 of the cosmology in which Chinese have understood illness, health, and the cultivation of wisdom relevant to wellness and prosperity. Palmer shows that although many modern-minded Chinese have rejected this heritage as superstition (as happened earlier in the West as well), many others in China seek to reclaim a core of traditional ideas centered on *yin-yang* and the five elements to interpret the physical world, especially related to body, health, and human prosperity.

Most Chinese have considered morality to be deeply embedded in nature, not just a human invention used to regulate social behavior. Are the Chinese just being sentimentally attached to their own prescientific ideas about nature and causality? Will their reclamation of these traditions develop into some form of "science with Chinese characteristics" that will truly reconcile traditional cosmology with modern science? This challenge will come to the fore as China builds a new national health-care system from the rubble of the current health services in China. Will traditional Chinese medicine (TCM) be an integral and cost-effective part, alongside Western medicine, of this new system? Meanwhile, will TCM expand its influence in the West among health practitioners (and perhaps even insurance companies), even if its explanatory system, rooted in Chinese cosmology, remains at fundamental variance with Western medical science?

TCM is a powerful medium for transmitting Chinese culture and religious ideas around the world. Palmer begins his chapter with the 2006 film *Fearless*, a morality tale about body, malady, virtue, and values of the nation. Blockbuster films such as *Crouching Tiger, Hidden Dragon* have presented Chinese ideas of body and transcendence to an interested wider world. The *gongfu* (kung fu) film genre has grown far beyond its origins in Hong Kong, appealing to a worldwide audience. The diffusion of Chinese martial arts and exercise regimens has been another important social channel by which these ideas have come to the attention of other societies. As China continues to expand its economic and political reach around the globe, will its traditional ideas of body, health, and the cultivation of virtue find welcome reception in communities that do not have a Chinese cultural framework to support them? How easily will Chinese ideas travel across cultures in the twenty-first century? How much will they be changed in the process? We will come again to these questions at the end of the book.

Discussions of the body and religion lead naturally to practices related to gender and sexuality. C. Julia Huang, Elena Valussi, and David A. Palmer reveal a pervasive ambiguity about the place of women in Chinese religion. Chinese religion has created powerful roles for the feminine principle manifested as female deities of compassion, protection, and wholeness. Yet there has not been much room in Chinese religion for the ideas of modern feminism. Will this change?

What will be the impact of advancing modernization and globalization on gender roles and human sexuality in Chinese religion? The Communist revolution advocated the idea of "women holding up half the sky." This so-called liberation of women from the old constraints of rural patriarchy justified the transition of women from domestic roles into factory workers and citizens of the socialist state. Though political and economic elites in China have continued to be overwhelmingly male, more recently, women have gained more than half the university places in China, and professional women increasingly fill the modern urban workplace and introduce new ideas about work-life balance. Women are active in the service-to-society dimension of religion through voluntary groups that try to fill the huge gaps in social services needed in China, especially among its aging population. As in many other societies, more women than men are active in grassroots religious activities and organizations. How will these powerful social and economic trends reflect themselves in the religious life of individuals and of the broader society?

The revival of popular religion in the countryside in the reform era has ironically strengthened the patriarchic social ideology that held women in subservient roles. Perhaps that is one reason why so many young women in villages leave for factories and wage labor jobs in cities like Shenzhen. A major concern in China is the impact of the one-child birth policy that was instituted in the early 1980s. Thirty years on, the gender imbalance is about 120 boys born for every 100 girls. Will the social position of women rise due to their fewer numbers, or will men fight over marriageable women in ways that jeopardize their social position? As these changes occur, how will gender roles for women and men change in China, and how will these changes express themselves in the revival of Chinese religions?

Robert Weller set out to find an alternate to Western concepts for the man-nature relationship in traditional Chinese cosmology that might benefit societies (especially China) that have exploited their natural resources to dangerous unsustainable limits.

Embracing a Western development paradigm, China's rapid industrialization has caused enormous, perhaps irreversible, environmental damage to its own land and waterways. China has become the world's largest emitter of greenhouse gases, recently surpassing the United States for that dubious distinction. Where is the Chinese alternative idea of a close man-nature relationship that might have prevented the destruction of the human habitat from happening, or is that one of the great romantic ideas that West has about China? Did it ever exist? If so, did it become lost in China's wrenching changes in the twentieth century? What would it be like to rediscover a harmonious man-nature relationship and give it new relevance and power?

Meanwhile, the global environmental movement would be keen to unveil an alternative set of ideas for social and economic development that would not trash the environment for the next generation. Weller points to a deep pool of diversity in ideas about how man and nature interact, perhaps not on the grand scale of abstraction, but in specific and practical contexts, such as the ecology of rice paddies in mountain valleys, where a respectful intimacy between man and nature has been sustained over centuries. Perhaps the revival of religion in China will include a new Chinese environmentalism with public support for turning the development paradigm from a rapacious to a sustainable path for man in nature. Let us hope this is so.

Human beings must care for nature; they must also care for each other. Philanthropy—as expressed compassion—has been integral to Confucian clans, Buddhist temples, and Daoist mendicant healers throughout Chinese history. Their universalist ideas of compassion and benevolence can cultivate strong motivations for charity toward others within certain social and economic contexts such as disaster relief or mutual aid to extended clan members. Christian missionaries in China created new forms of education and social services as expressions of the social gospel beyond the idea of saving individual pagan souls. Now Christian groups in China are growing rapidly and generating their own resources, some of which they give back to the broader society in the form of homegrown social services for vulnerable groups and disaster victims in society.

The growth of domestic philanthropy was highlighted by the broad, spontaneous responses to the massive earthquake in Sichuan in May 2008 from throughout the country. The central government highlighted the response by the army to the tragedy. But also significant were the many small voluntary groups and individuals that poured relief in many forms into Sichuan, often unreported in state media. Citizen reporters used the ubiquitous Internet to give personal reports of the tragedy, which evoked generous responses from the society at large. This is evidence of the emergence of a civil society in China in which millions of small, voluntary decisions by caring individuals can be even more powerful than the state in mobilizing its bureaucracies to respond to a disaster.

The Communist state is ambivalent about the growing capacity of religious and other civic organizations to raise funds and deliver assistance to vulnerable groups in society. Thus religious groups in China do philanthropy in small-scale, low-key ways. Sometimes they confer and cooperate with the state agencies concerned; sometimes they quietly do their own thing. In any case, philanthropic expressions of religion are helping to create a new culture of civil society in China, accommodating government and reaching out beyond traditional geographic boundaries of China to other countries, including the United States.

Tragedies like the 2008 Sichuan earthquake not only call forth a philanthropic response. They also tend to raise spiritual issues and a hunger for answers to the larger questions of identity and meaning in life. Many Chinese, living middle-class lives in modern cities, are looking for tangible, subtle ways of validating what it is be Chinese. Religion offers ways to tie oneself back to the past and to bring something from the past into one's present life through texts, artifacts, and ritual practice. The protean forms of Chinese religion, like burning incense in a small shrine in one's house, make that possible on a personal level.

Religion has been made secular and more officially acceptable by being redefined as culture. A favorite new term one hears in China is "intangible heritage." Many Chinese today want to restore and preserve intangible heritage. A revival of religion in China may spring from a desire in people to be connected in a meaningful way to their own past and to the collective Chinese past.

Chapter 9 allows us to appreciate how the core ideas of Chinese religion today are rooted in the sociopolitical system that grew up in China over 5000 years. In this rich chapter, Palmer explains the historical origins of the core ideas of Chinese religion: divination; ancestor worship; the ruler, divinity, and political legitimacy; the Mandate of Heaven; the holistic cosmological system; body, cultivation, longevity, and the search for immortality; millenarian movements and challenges to the state; morality and its relation to economic prosperity; and the state's relationship with religious organizations.

Religions tend to rest on something that is old. We sense this as we linger in a cathedral built centuries ago or participate in a ritual that has been repeated innumerable times by a vast body of the faithful over eons of time. In Latin, the term *religion* derives from *re-ligio*, or "to tie back upon something." Chinese religion is steeped in history and historicity, or the feeling of time embedded in its texts, rituals, and religious artifacts.

China today is remaking itself through industrialization at a speed and scale unknown in human history. When or where have hundreds of millions of people moved from rural poverty to cities in just a few decades? Through wars, revolutions, and destructive political campaigns, China has destroyed much of the physical remnants of its history in the twentieth century. What was not pulled down in political campaigns has later been bulldozed to make way for new high-rise buildings and car-choked highways. A few fragments of the past are quickly surrounded by walls and made into theme parks and tourist destinations. China's rich past is only dimly present in today's China. Perhaps China needed to wipe out much of the heavy hand of the past to make room for modernization, conducted largely by the state under the banner of socialism. But perhaps they cut down too much, leaving China with mere fragments of historical consciousness among its people today. All Chinese know with pride that they have over 5000 years of history. A resurgence of pride in China's cultural heritage, including manifold expressions of religion past and present, is an important part of the cultural nationalism that grows in physical and virtual spaces in contemporary China. Religion and nationalism live uneasily together. How will they fare in China's future?

Although religion has a strong personal dimension of making meaning, it is also a matter of belonging to, and being defined by, communities and social organizations. This is the thrust of Vincent Goossaert's chapter on religious communities, traditions, and organizations in twentieth-century China. For centuries, Chinese recognized the Three Teachings: Confucianism, Buddhism, and Daoism. These Three Teachings did not function as separate institutions, each servicing their own believers. Rather, each served the whole society in its own way. Chinese authorities did not promote syncretism or the mixing of religions at the formal level, or interreligious dialogue, but recognized that people would draw upon elements of the Three Teachings in their lives in a variety of ways. Goossaert says the Chinese accepted "plurality" at a personal level but were averse to pluralism at an institutional level. This appears so today.

People who belong to a clan or village are automatically in the territory of a local god and are expected to contribute and placate the god accordingly. Later, Christian missionaries, especially Protestants, introduced a new idea that individuals, based on a personal faith orientation, should participate in a congregation of a specific religion, and eschew all other teachings or religious practices as false. The greatest impact of Christianity in China, Goossaert contends, was to create a new institutional model of what a religion should be. Gradually, the indigenous Three Teachings adopted this model and tried to reconfigure themselves as congregations of self-choosing adherents. The Nationalists and Communists, meanwhile, regardless of their opposing ideologies, did not differ much in their basic approach to regulating religion through national associations of clergy formally recognized by a state bureau of religious affairs.

Even the word *zongjiao,* now used in Chinese to mean religion, was imported from the West via Japan in the nineteenth century. Atheism, another new term, entered China in the twentieth century. Marxists put science and atheism together as positives, opposed to the negatives of religion and superstition. The social organization and official recognition of religion has much changed in the past hundred years, and will likely keep changing in the decades ahead.

The Chinese state's long legacy of regulating religion is also the subject of André Laliberté's chapter. Religion has been a prime source of legitimacy for the state. This is reflected in imperial rituals of Confucian orthodoxy upheld by the civil service and its bureaucracies. Gentry culture in the countryside also upheld imperial power. But religion was also a potential source of challenge to the legitimacy of the state—such as with the passing of the Mandate of Heaven—and as a means of mobilizing popular discontent against onerous taxation, corruption, and oppressive social control. More recently, Chinese religious groups that have independent ties to cobelievers in other countries, in the West or the Middle East, evoke additional suspicion by the state about legitimacy.

Unlike the United States, China has never had a doctrine of separation of church and state. This is made more complex by a Marxist state that advocates atheism and officially prevents religious believers from joining the ruling Communist Party. The Chinese Constitution guarantees the right of religious belief, but it is less clear what expressions of religious belief may be allowed in public life. The Communist state has waxed and waned in its tolerance for religion. While acknowledging the value of religion in building cultural cohesion and the role of ethical teachings arising from religion in promoting social order, the Communist state is also deeply wary of religion and religious groups as sponsors of alternative worldviews and visions of a good life that are at odds with the Communist orthodoxy. Laliberté describes how the Chinese state has organized patriotic associations for each of the five major religions at national and local levels. The state religious affairs offices at different times and in different places in China may loosen or tighten their control over registered religious bodies. The regulators of religion have a complex relationship with regulated and nonregulated religious groups. While official and "underground" religious groups are growing throughout China, the Communist state bureaucracy appears largely to tolerate them as long as the public expression of their religious life does not cross an invisible line. Where is that line? Based on vague and general guidelines from the center, local religious affairs bureaus describe that line for their changing convenience and concerns. Religious groups are deemed to have crossed that line if the state perceives their behavior in some way as a challenge to their legitimacy. Any religious group in any locality in China could represent, consciously or unconsciously, a potential or latent threat to the state. This has as much to do with the perceiver as the perceived.

Is China gradually allowing for a wider range of religious expression in public life? Mao and his avid leftist followers repressed religion, hoping it would fade away like folk superstitions before the juggernaut of socialist modernization. Later, Deng Xiaoping's reform era released the state clamp on religion and let religious groups find their own place in a more market-based society open to the West. Jiang Zemin followed this pattern for the most part, until the Falun Gong arose in the late 1990s. Falun Gong's power to organize at a national scale frightened the state into repressing this "evil cult," a state of affairs that continues today.

Hu Jintao has deep ideological instincts from his ascent through the channels of the Communist Youth League to the apex of the Party. On the one hand, he seems to encourage religion as an important ingredient for creating a harmonious society in China. On the other, this former Party boss in Tibet can resort to overwhelming force to prevent religious groups from crossing the line to oppose the regime, or seek to split away from China on its periphery. It may be ironic that the more the Communist state in China succeeds in its core objectives, the more religious groups in China will be allowed a greater public space to express themselves. But one dares not predict a straight line of development on the issues of authority, power, and dissent in regard to religion in China in any one direction, in any region of the country, for any length of time. Although there is broad agreement that there is only one China, there are certainly very many ways to be China.

Religion has grown as the Chinese economy has grown. Fenggang Yang explores the relationship between religion and economic development in China during the era of market reforms since the 1980s. The rapid growth of the market economy has given some people new resources to invest in religious infrastructure. It has opened new social space and networking opportunities for disseminating religion through the market economy. This new economic system has also generated new spiritual needs in people who have left the certainties of the Soviet-style work unit system of cradle-to-grave security. This confluence of new resources, expanded opportunities and spiritual needs has stimulated a profound growth of religion in China in the past thirty years.

The market economy creates new human problems, and also empowers people to devise new solutions for those problems. For example, the weak and corrupt health-care system in China has prompted growth of interest in spiritual healing. Fortune telling grows apace with new financial information to guide investors and day traders on the stock exchanges. Millions of migrants have left their villages for factory work in cities, creating new needs for a sense of community and belonging, which religious affiliation can often provide. So many new choices in the consumer economy; so many new anxieties about rising into the middle class! Religion can enable people to make meaning out of the new dilemmas of ordinary life that a generation before did not know.

Yang quotes the adage "building a religious stage to sing an economic opera" in reference to temples that have been rebuilt by and for the tourism economy in many villages. The God of Wealth has reappeared in China after decades of ostracism by the Communists. The Shaolin Temple has rebuilt itself in the image of the block-buster film. Religious organizations make money, and money helps to proselytize the religion. The local offices of the Religious Affairs Bureau often cannot enforce their restrictions. If they demolish a church or temple, the faithful may rebuild it in a few months in a nearby venue. Most religious groups spread their word on the Internet; many have publishing houses and can afford to give away books and video discs with spiritual content. Private education options are growing, giving religious groups new chances to communicate their message to young people while also making money on tuition from parents who want alternatives to poor quality public schooling. Yang ends his essay with a reflection on the famous Max Weber thesis about the Protestant ethic and the rise of capitalism in early modern northern Europe. He says the jury is out about what role Confucianism (or Confucian Protestantism) may be playing in China's economic surge. China may be creating a new reciprocal linkage between religious beliefs about the relationships between spiritual and material life, and economic performance by the individual and his or her religious group. Many Chinese may attest to the economic benefits of adherence to their religious faith.

Most sections of our book have focused on religion in mainland China, with some comparative mentions of Taiwan, Hong Kong, and Singapore. In the final chapter, Richard Madsen and Elijah Siegler reach wider to consider the globalization of Chinese religions in the twenty-first century. They first go to Chinatowns in the cities of North America and Southeast Asia, where religion has been an important resource in constituting and maintaining social cohesion and identity among Chinese overseas. More recent Chinese immigrants, often with advanced educations and cultural backgrounds, have settled in suburbs and joined churches, whether Christian or Buddhist, that are structured along American norms. These churches provide ways to affirm one's Chinese heritage while integrating with mainstream American culture. As subsequent generations assimilate deeper into American cultural life, they tend to see Chinese religion from the outside as a "hodgepodge of disconnected customs."

As Chinese religions "go global," they create new institutional arrangements to traverse national, cultural, and theological boundaries. Beyond local temple communities and congregations, Chinese religious groups have to reconcile their allegiances to conflicting political authorities. The unsettled church-state relationship in China seems to follow them as they settle and live as groups of Chinese abroad. Chinese Catholics remain keenly interested in the Catholic Church in their homeland, and often send funds to Catholic villages. Chinese evangelical Christians launch missionary projects among house churches in their native provinces back in China. The Dalai Lama, exiled in India, has come to represent Buddhism to a global audience, while also as a cultural/national identity to the fragile Tibetan diaspora. As the Falun Gong was suppressed in China, their leaders abroad developed sophisticated media enterprises to propagate their faith and attack the Chinese government for its treatment of followers inside China. To counteract such images of China abroad, the Chinese government has ratcheted up its public diplomacy through new uses of the sage Confucius. This has included a network of over 200 Confucius Institutes at universities around the world. Ostensibly to teach Chinese language as demand for instruction has flourished, these institutes fly the banner of Confucius as the preferred global icon of the cultural face of the PRC. A Communist state promotes Confucius abroad.

How well will Chinese religions ideas and practices travel beyond China? If they are closely linked to enacting customs of Chinese identity, will it be possible for non-Chinese to appropriate Chinese religion in their lives? Or will Chinese religion always be something exotic, albeit interesting, from outside Chinese ethnic identity? Will Chinese religion be "globalized" the way fengshui has become a decorating concept explained in stylish picture books sold in the airport kiosks of the world? To what extent is a religious idea, reframed in a different economic, social, and cultural context, still the same idea?

Madsen and Siegler complete their essay by describing how aspects of Chinese religious ideas have been grafted into the personal repertoires of spirituality in the West. This includes fascination with the oft-translated *Daodejing* text, *qigong* exercise and fengshui salons, and the self-styled masters of religio-physical techniques in the amorphous human potential movement begun in America in the 1960s. While attenuated from their social and philosophical origins in China, these fragments of traditional Chinese religions now circulate in modern accessible forms through the mass media, social networking, and other means of globalization that disseminate religious ideas around the world today.

We are likely to see much more of China's cultural heritage suited up to travel the world beyond traditional boundaries of China in the years to come. Chinese religions have evolved over millennia. They express some of the oldest ideas and intimations about man, nature, and transcendence that exist in our world today. Their expressions in contemporary China represent an important part of the "cultural

DNA" of the human condition in the twenty-first century. China's domestic political and cultural pressures will continue to mold these ideas in new ways as Chinese people find them compelling expressions for religious sentiments of modern life. The authors in our book have opened windows into the manifold world of Chinese religions today. They direct our gaze toward the paths along which expressions of Chinese religious life may move beyond its borders. We see the possibility of Chinese religious life interacting more deeply with other cultures and societies, and contributing in new ways to religious consciousness around our whirling globe.

{ GLOSSARY }

Ancestor veneration Belief and rituals that link the deceased ancestors and the living together and form a single clan or lineage. The relationship between the ancestors and the living members of a lineage is reciprocal.

Baoying Cosmic recompense, an important concept in Chinese philosophy and popular religion.

Cishan Chinese term philanthropy, based on Buddhist concept of compassion.

Dao (Tao) "The Way" in Chinese philosophy. It means the ultimate universal order, or the path to appropriate the Ultimate.

Dharma Refers to the teachings of the Buddha in a Buddhist context. Depending on the contexts in which it is used, this term can also mean the cosmic, social duty, and proper behavior in Hinduism.

Divination Religious procedure with the purpose of seeking advice and answers from the supernatural.

Falun Gong A new quasi-religious movement, founded by Li Hongzhi in 1992. Also known as Falun Dafa, it combines elements of *qigong*, Daoism, and Buddhism.

Fangsheng A Buddhist practice of liberating animals to gain merit.

Fengshui Chinese belief that *qi* (cosmic energy) can be captured and utilized by choosing certain geographical and temporal arrangements. A successful capture of *qi* can consequentially benefit the individual or the members of the community involved.

"Five Major Religions" According to the current policy of the People's Republic of China, there are five major religions whose institutions are registered with the government: Daoism, Buddhism, Roman Catholicism, Protestantism, and Islam.

Five Phases (also known as Five Elements or Five Agents) Chinese theory about the fundamental components of the universe. These elements are Wood, Fire, Earth, Metal, and Water.

Geomancy A kind of divination that involves reading and interpreting markings on the ground. This method exists in many different cultures. Some people translate it as *fengshui* in Chinese.

Guanyin (Kuanyin) The Chinese name of the Mahayana bodhisattva Avalokitesvara. This deity was originally depicted in masculine form but has been transformed into a feminine figure in Chinese Buddhism and folk religious traditions.

Huangdi The Yellow Emperor, a legendary figure considered to be the founding ancestor of the Han Chinese people.

Imam Islamic leader. The imam leads prayers in the mosque and, in certain contexts, can also act as a community leader among Sunni Muslims. For Shia Muslims, however, *imam* refers specifically to a line of spiritual leaders who were chosen by Allah as exemplars for the faithful.

Incense Spices molded in the shape of a stick or coil that produce a sweet fragrant aroma when burned and are used for various kinds of religious rites.

Jiao A grand Daoist communal ritual to ensure spiritual purification and prosperity in a community.

Li Rites, ritual, or proper behavior. An important term in traditional Confucian philosophy.

Lineage In the anthropology of Chinese traditional society, refers to a patrilineal descent group claiming genealogical ties to a common ancestor.

Mahayana "The Great Vehicle" tradition of Buddhism that originated in early Indian Buddhism. It spread to East Asia, where it became the dominant form of Buddhism.

Mandala A visual device, such as a colorful and graphic representation of the cosmos, used by Vajrayana Buddhists for religious and meditative practices.

Mandate of Heaven The traditional belief and political philosophy that the legitimacy of rulers comes from the approval of Heaven. Rulers enjoyed Heaven's blessings as long as they complied with the moral demands of Heaven and fulfilled their ritual duties.

Mantra A ritual formula chanted in specific circumstances to produce magical consequences.

May Fourth Movement A nationalist movement initiated by students, and then widely supported by intellectuals and people from all walks of life, against the unequal settlements made at the Paris Peace Conference after the First World War, which were considered especially unfair to China. This nationalist reaction fueled an intellectual movement that saw Chinese tradition as the cause of China's weakness and called for replacing tradition with science and modern thinking.

Mazu A popular goddess worshipped as the Protector of Seafarers, whose cult flourishes in the southeast coastal regions of China. Also known as *Tianhou*.

Mosque Islamic worship site. Muslims gather in the mosque for public prayers.

Mudra Ritual gestures, consisting mainly of various hand and finger signs, which are believed to have the power to bring about supernatural consequences.

Qi Literally, "air" or "breath," but commonly used to refer to the cosmic energy that sustains and regenerates the universal order.

Qigong Physical and mental exercises done to cultivate the internal *qi* of the human body for physical and spiritual enhancement.

Sadaqah Islamic voluntary gesture of goodwill and alms-giving. It is understood as complementary to *Zakah*, which is obligatory.

Shamanism A wide range of traditional practices and beliefs whose goal is to communicate with spirits.

Taijiquan (**Tai Chi**) A form of slow-motion Chinese martial arts and exercise practice.

Tantrism A widespread ritual and belief in Asian religious cultures. It holds that the universe, including human beings, is created and sustained by a spiritual energy. Therefore, the rituals of this form of religious tradition focus on channeling energy for liberation from ignorance and to achieve final liberation.

Theravada A Pali term that literally means "the Way of the Elders." One of the three surviving Buddhist traditions of the present day. One of the eighteen early Indian Buddhist schools/sects, it probably became a separate school of Buddhism around the first century BCE.

Tian (**Heaven**) The ultimate reality and moral authority in Confucianism and in folk religion.

Ummah It means "the Islamic world," but it can also be used to refer to any nation.

Yin-Yang The two primal forces in the universe. The Chinese believe that the balance of these two complementary forces will bring upon stability and prosperity, whereas their imbalance will have negative consequences.

Yuanfen Fateful coincidence, a common term in Buddhism and popular belief; sometimes translated as "destiny" or "fate."

Zakah One of the Five Pillars of Islam. It means "alms-giving." Muslims are required to donate a percentage of their wealth annually for the sake of helping those in need.

{ SUGGESTED FURTHER READINGS }

General Introductions to Chinese Religious Traditions, Teachings, and History

Adler, Joseph A. *Chinese Religious Traditions.* Upper Saddle River, N.J.: Prentice Hall, 2002.

Ching, Julia. *Chinese Religions.* Maryknoll, N.Y.: Orbis Books, 1993.

Fowler, Jeaneane, and Merv Fowler. *Chinese Religions: Beliefs and Practices.* Portland, Ore.: Sussex Academic Press, 2008.

Overmyer, Daniel. *Religions of China: The World as a Living System.* San Francisco: Harper & Row, 1986.

Thomson, Laurence G. *Chinese Religion: An Introduction.* Belmont, Calif.: Wadsworth, 1996.

General Works on Religion in Chinese Society, Politics, and Economics

Gates, Hill. *China's Motor: A Thousand Years of Petty Capitalism.* Ithaca, N.Y.: Cornell University Press, 1996.

Goossaert, Vincent and David A. Palmer. *The Religious Question in Modern China.* Chicago: University of Chicago Press, 2011.

Madsen, Richard. *Democracy's Dharma: Religious Renaissance and Political Development in Taiwan.* Berkeley: University of California Press, 2007.

Tsai, Li-lee. *Accountability without Democracy: Solidary Groups and Public Goods Provision in Rural China.* Cambridge, Mass.: Harvard University Press, 2007.

Weller, Robert P. *Alternate Civilities: Democracy and Culture in China and Taiwan.* Boulder, Colo.: Westview, 1999.

Yang, C. K. *Religion in Chinese Society: A Study of Contemporary Social Functions of Religion and some of Their Historical Factors.* Berkeley: University of California Press, 1961.

Yu, Anthony C. *State and Religion in China. Historical and Textual Perspectives.* Chicago: Open Court, 2007.

Case Studies on Religion in Modern and Contemporary Chinese Society and Politics

Ashiwa, Yoshiko, and David L. Wank, eds. *Making Religion, Making the State: The Politics of Religion in Modern China.* Stanford, Calif.: Stanford University Press, 2009.

Billioud, Sébastien, and David A. Palmer, eds. *Forms of Religious Reconfiguration in the PRC.* Special Issue, *China Perspectives* no. 4, 2009.

Chau, Adam, ed. *Religion in Contemporary China: Revitalization and Innovation.* London: Routledge, 2010.

MacInnis, Donald, ed. *Religion in China: Policy and Practice.* Maryknoll, N.Y.: Orbis Books, 1989.

Miller, James, ed. *Chinese Religions in Contemporary Societies*. Santa Barbara, Calif.: ABC-CLIO, 2006.

Overmyer, Daniel, ed. "Religion in China Today." Special issue, *China Quarterly*, no. 174, 2003.

Yang, Mayfair, ed. *Chinese Religiosities: Afflictions of Modernity and State Formation*. Berkeley: University of California Press, 2008.

Anthropological Studies of Chinese Popular Religion

Chau, Adam Yuet. *Miraculous Response: Doing Popular Religion in Contemporary China*. Stanford, Calif.: Stanford University Press, 2005.

DeBernardi, Jean E. *The Way That Lives in the Heart: Chinese Popular Religion and Spirit Mediums in Penang, Malaysia*. Stanford, Calif.: Stanford University Press, 2006.

———. *Rites of Belonging: Memory, Modernity, and Identity in a Malaysian Chinese Community*. Stanford, Calif.: Stanford University Press, 2004.

DuBois, Thomas D. *The Sacred Village: Social Change and Religious Life in Rural North China*. Honolulu: University of Hawaii Press, 2005.

Feuchtwang, Stephen. *Popular Religion in China: The Imperial Metaphor*. Richmond, England: Curzon Press, 2001.

Hsü, Francis L. K. *Under the Ancestors' Shadow: Kinship, Personality and Social Mobility in China*. Stanford, Calif.: Stanford University Press, 1948, 1967.

Jordan, David K., and Daniel L. Overmyer. *The Flying Phoenix: Aspects of Sectarianism in Taiwan*. Princeton, N.J.: Princeton University Press, 1986.

Wolf, Arthur P. "Gods, Ghosts, and Ancestors." In *Religion and Ritual in Chinese Society*, ed. Arthur P. Wolf, 131–182. Stanford, Calif.: Stanford University Press, 1974.

Daoism

Dean, Kenneth. *Taoist Ritual and Popular Cults in Southeast China*. Princeton, N.J.: Princeton University Press, 1993.

Goossaert, Vincent. *The Taoists of Peking, 1800–1949. A Social History of Urban Clerics*. Cambridge, Mass.: Harvard University Asia Center, 2007.

Kohn, Livia. *Daoism and Chinese Culture*. Dunedin, Fla.: Three Pines Press, 2004.

Lagerwey, John. *Taoist Ritual in Chinese Society and History*. New York: Macmillan, 1987.

Miller, James. *Daoism: A Short Introduction*. Oxford: Oneworld, 2003.

Palmer, David A., and Liu Xun, eds. *Daoism in the 20th Century: Between Eternity and Modernity*. Berkeley: University of California Press, 2011.

Schipper, Kristofer. *The Taoist Body*. Berkeley: University of California Press, 1990.

Wolf, Arthur P., ed. *Religion and Ritual in Chinese Society*. Stanford, Calif.: Stanford University Press, 1974.

Confucianism

Bell, Daniel A., ed. *Confucian Political Ethics*. Princeton, N.J.: Princeton University Press, 2007.

———. *China's New Confucianism: Politics and Everyday Life in a Changing Society*. Princeton, N.J.: Princeton University Press, 2008.

Berthrong, John H., and Evelyn Berthrong. *Confucianism: A Short Introduction*. Oxford: Oneworld, 2000.

Jensen, Lionel. *Manufacturing Confucianism: Chinese Traditions and Universal Civilization*. Durham, N.C.: Duke University Press, 1997.

Makeham, John. *Lost Soul: "Confucianism" in Contemporary Chinese Academic Discourse*. Cambridge, Mass.: Harvard University Asia Center, 2008.

Buddhism

Ch'en, Kenneth. *Buddhism in China: A Historical Survey*. Princeton, N.J.: Princeton University Press, 1964.

Gernet, Jacques. *Buddhism in Chinese Society: An Economic History from the Fifth to the Tenth Centuries,* trans. Franciscus Verellen. New York: Columbia University Press, 1995.

Huang, Julia. *Charisma and Compassion: Cheng Yen and the Buddhist Tzu Chi Movement*. Cambridge, Mass.: Harvard University Press, 2009.

Laliberté, André. *The Politics of Buddhist Organizations in Taiwan: 1989–2003*. London and New York: RoutledgeCurzon, 2004.

Pittman, Don A. *Toward a Modern Chinese Buddhism: Taixu's Reforms*. Honolulu: University of Hawaii Press, 2001.

Welch, Holmes. *Buddhism under Mao*. Cambridge, Mass.: Harvard University Press, 1972.

———. *The Practice of Chinese Buddhism*. Cambridge, Mass.: Harvard University Press, 1967.

———. *The Buddhist Revival in China*. Cambridge, Mass.: Harvard University Press, 1968.

Christianity

Bays, Daniel H., ed. *Christianity in China: from the Eighteenth Century to the Present*. Stanford, Calif.: Stanford University Press, 1996.

Brockey, Liam Matthew. *Journey to the East: The Jesuit Mission to China, 1579–1724*. Cambridge, Mass.: Harvard University Press, 2007.

Cao, Nanlai. *Constructing China's Jerusalem. Christians, Power, and Place in Contemporary Wenzhou*. Stanford, Calif.: Stanford University Press, 2011.

Charbonnier, Jean-Pierre. *Christians in China: A.D. 600–2000,* trans. M. N. L. Couve de Murville. San Francisco: Ignatius Press, 2007.

Hunter, Alan, and Kim-Kwong Chan. *Protestantism in Contemporary China*. Cambridge: Cambridge University Press, 1993.

Latourette, Kenneth S. *A History of Christian Missions in China*. New York: MacMillan, 1929.

Lian, Xi. *Redeemed by Fire: The Rise of Popular Christianity in Modern China*. New Haven: Yale University Press, 2010.

Madsen, Richard. *China's Catholics: Tragedy and Hope in an Emerging Civil Society*. Berkeley: University of California Press, 1998.

Wickeri, Philip L. *Seeking the Common Ground: Protestant Christianity, the Three- Self Movement and China's United Front*. Maryknoll, N.Y.: Orbis Books, 1988.

———. *Reconstructing Christianity in China: K. H. Ting and the Chinese Church*. Maryknoll, N.Y.: Orbis Books, 2007.

Islam

Gladney, Dru C. *Muslim Chinese: Ethnic Nationalism in the People's Republic*. Cambridge, Mass.: Harvard University Press, 1991.
———. *Dislocating China: Muslims, Minorities and Other Subaltern Subjects*. Chicago: University of Chicago Press, 2004.
Israeli, Raphael. *Islam in China: Religion, Ethnicity, Culture and Politics*. Lanham, Md.: Lexington Books, 2002.
Lipman, Jonathan N. *Familiar Strangers: A History of Muslims in Northwest China*. Seattle: University of Washington Press, 1997.

Tibetan Buddhism

Goldstein, Melvyn C., and Matthew T. Kapstein. *Buddhism in Contemporary Tibet: Religious Revival and Cultural Identity*. Berkeley: University of California Press, 1998.
Lopez, Donald. *Prisoners of Shangri-La: Tibetan Buddhism and the West*. Chicago: Chicago University Press, 1998.
Mitchell, Donald W. *Buddhism: Introducing the Buddhist Experience*. New York: Oxford University Press, 2007. Especially chapter 6, "The Tibetan Experience of Buddhism."
Shakya, Tsering. *The Dragon in the Land of Snows: A History of Modern Tibet since 1947*. London and New York: Penguin, 2000.
Tuttle, Gray. *Tibetan Buddhists in the Making of Modern China*. New York: Columbia University Press, 2005.

Chinese Medicine, Health Cultivation, and Sexual Disciplines

Croizier, Ralph. *Traditional Medicine in Modern China: Science, Nationalism, and the Tensions of Cultural Change*. Cambridge, Mass.: Harvard University Press, 1968.
Kaptchuk, Ted J. *Chinese Medicine: The Web That Has No Weaver*. London: Rider, 1983.
Kleinman, Arthur. *Patients and Healers in the Context of Culture: An Exploration of the Borderland between Anthropology, Medicine, and Psychiatry*. Berkeley: University of California Press, 1981.
Kohn, Livia (in cooperation with Stephen Jackowicz). *Health and Long Life: The Chinese Way*. Cambridge, Mass.: Three Pines Press, 2005.
Reid, Daniel. *The Tao of Health, Sex and Longevity: A Modern Practical Guide to the Ancient Way*. New York: Simon & Schuster, 1989.
Unschuld, Paul U. *Medicine in China: A History of Ideas*. Berkeley: University of California Press, 1985.
Van Gulik, Robert. *Sexual Life in Ancient China: A Preliminary Survey of Chinese Sex and Society from ca. 1500 B.C. till 1644 A.D.*, with introduction and bibliography by Paul R. Goldin. Leiden, The Netherlands: Brill, 2003. Originally published 1961.

Martial Arts and *Qigong*

Morris, Andrew D. *Marrow of the Nation: A History of Sport and Physical Culture in Republican China*. Berkeley: University of California Press, 2004.

Ownby, David. *Falun Gong and the Future of China*. New York: Oxford University Press, 2008.

Palmer, David A. *Qigong Fever: Body, Science, and Utopia in China*. New York: Columbia University Press, 2007.

Shahar, Meir. *The Shaolin Monastery: History, Religion, and the Chinese Martial Arts*. Honolulu: University of Hawaii Press, 2008.

The Religious Life of Ethnic Minority Communities

Covell, Ralph P. *The Liberating Gospel in China: The Christian Faith Among China's Minority Peoples*. Grand Rapids, Mich.: Baker Books, 1995.

MacKerras, Colin. *China's Minorities: Integration and Modernization in the Twentieth Century*. Hong Kong: Oxford University Press, 1994.

————. *China's Ethnic Minorities and Globalization*. London: Routledge/Curzon, 2003.

Safran, William, ed. *Nationalism and Ethnoregional Identities in China*. London and Portland: Frank Cross, 1998.

{INDEX}

CPSIA information can be obtained at www.ICGtesting.com
Printed in the USA
LVOW11s0100041214

416994LV00002B/62/P